SCANDALOUS LEADERSHIP

SCANDALOUS LEADERSHIP

PRIME MINISTERS' AND PRESIDENTS' SCANDALS AND THE PRESS

M. J. TROW

PEN & SWORD
HISTORY

AN IMPRINT OF PEN & SWORD BOOKS LTD.
YORKSHIRE – PHILADELPHIA

First published in Great Britain in 2023 by
Pen & Sword History
An imprint of
Pen & Sword Books Ltd
Yorkshire - Philadelphia

ISBN 978 1 39906 655 6

Typeset in INDIA by IMPEC eSolutions
Printed and bound in England by CPI Group (UK) Ltd, Croydon CR0 4YY.

Pen & Sword Books Ltd. incorporates the Imprints of Pen & Sword Archaeology,
Atlas, Aviation, Battleground, Discovery, Family History, History, Maritime,
Military, Naval, Politics, Railways, Select, Transport, True Crime, Fiction,
Frontline Books, Leo Cooper, Praetorian Press, Seaforth Publishing,
Wharncliffe, White Owl and After the Battle

For a complete list of Pen & Sword titles please contact

PEN & SWORD BOOKS LIMITED
47 Church Street, Barnsley, South Yorkshire, S70 2AS, England
E-mail: enquiries@pen-and-sword.co.uk
Website: www.pen-and-sword.co.uk

or

PEN AND SWORD BOOKS
1950 Lawrence Rd, Havertown, PA 19083, USA
E-mail: uspen-and-sword@casematepublishers.com
Website: www.penandswordbooks.com

Of the 101 politicians covered in this book, the most common phrase concerning them is

'UNFIT FOR OFFICE'

Depressing? Or expected?

Contents

Table of Prime Ministers and Presidents

American Presidents	Dates	Party	British Prime Ministers	Dates	Party
			Robert Walpole, Earl of Orford	1721–42	Whig
			Spencer Compton, Earl of Wilmington	1742–43	Whig
			Henry Pelham	1743–54	Whig
			Thomas Pelham-Holles, Duke of Newcastle	1754–56 1757–62	Whig
			William Cavendish, Duke of Devonshire	1756–57	Whig
			John Stuart, Earl of Bute	1762–63	Tory
			George Grenville	1763–65	Whig
			Charles Watson Wentworth, Marquis of Rockingham	1765–66; 1782	Whig
			William Pitt, Earl of Chatham	1766–68	Whig
			Augustus Henry Fitzroy, Duke of Grafton	1768–70	Whig
			Frederick, Lord North	1770–82	Tory
			William Petty Fitzmaurice, Earl of Shelburne	1782–83	Whig
			William Cavendish-Bentinck, Duke of Portland	1783	Whig
George Washington	1789–97	No Party	William Pitt, the Younger	1783–1801	Tory
John Adams	1797–1801	Federalist			

American Presidents	Dates	Party	British Prime Ministers	Dates	Party
Thomas Jefferson	1801–09	Democratic Republican	Henry Addington	1801–04	Tory
			William Pitt, the Younger	1804–06	Tory
			William Wyndham, Lord Grenville	1806–07	Whig
			William Cavendish-Bentinck, Duke of Portland	1807–09	Whig
James Madison Jnr	1809–17	Democratic Republican	Spencer Perceval	1809–12	Tory
James Monroe	1817–25	Democratic Republican	Robert Banks Jenkinson, Earl of Liverpool	1812–27	Tory
John Quincy Adams	1825–29	Democratic Republican/ National Republican	George Canning	1827	Tory
			Frederick Robinson, Viscount Goderich	1827–28	Tory
			Arthur Wellesley, Duke of Wellington	1828–30	Tory
Andrew Jackson	1829–37	Democrat	Charles, Earl Grey	1830–34	Whig
			William Lamb, Viscount Melbourne	1834; 1835–39; 1839–41	Whig
			Robert Peel	1834–35	Conservative
Martin van Buren	1837–41	Democrat	William Lamb, Viscount Melbourne	1835–39	Whig
			Robert Peel	1841–46	Conservative Whig
William Henry Harrison	1841	Whig			
John Tyler	1841–45	Whig			
James Knox Polk	1845–49	Democrat	Lord John Russell	1846–52	
Zachary Taylor	1849–50	Whig			

American Presidents	Dates	Party	British Prime Ministers	Dates	Party
Millard Fillmore	1850-53	Whig	Edward Stanley, Earl of Derby	1852	Conservative
			George Hamilton Gordon, Earl of Aberdeen	1852-55	Coalition
Franklin Pierce	1853-57	Democrat	Henry John Temple, Viscount Palmerston	1855-58	Liberal
James Buchanan Jnr	1857-61	Democrat	Edward Stanley, Earl of Derby	1858-59	Conservative
			Henry Temple, Viscount Palmerston	1859-65	Liberal
Abraham Lincoln	1861-65	Republican	Lord John Russell	1865-66	Liberal
Andrew Johnson	1865-69	Democrat	Edward Stanley, Earl of Derby	1866-68	Conservative
			Benjamin Disraeli, Earl of Beaconsfield	1868	Conservative
			William Ewart Gladstone	1868-74	Liberal
Ulysses S. Grant	1869-77	Republican	Benjamin Disraeli, Earl of Beaconsfield	1874-80	Conservative
Rutherford Birchard Hayes	1877-81	Republican	William Ewart Gladstone	1880-85	Liberal
James Abram Garfield	1881	Republican			
Chester Alan Arthur	1881-85	Republican	Robert Arthur Gascoyne-Cecil, Marquis of Salisbury	1885	Conservative
Stephen Grover Cleveland	1885-89	Democrat			
			William Ewart Gladstone	1886	Liberal
			Robert Arthur Gascoyne-Cecil, Marquis of Salisbury	1886-92	Conservative
Benjamin Harrison	1889-93	Republican	William Ewart Gladstone	1892-94	Liberal

American Presidents	Dates	Party	British Prime Ministers	Dates	Party
Stephen Grover Cleveland	1893-97	Democrat	Archibald Philip Primrose, Earl of Rosebery	1894-95	Liberal
			Robert Arthur Gascoyne-Cecil, Marquis of Salisbury	1895-1902	Conservative
William McKinley Jnr	1897-1901	Republican	Arthur James Balfour	1902-05	Conservative
Theodore 'Teddy' Roosevelt Jnr	1901-09	Republican	Henry Campbell-Bannerman	1905-08	Liberal
			Herbert Henry Asquith	1908-16	Liberal
William Howard Taft	1909-13	Republican			
Thomas Woodrow Wilson	1913-21	Democrat	David Lloyd George	1916-22	Liberal
Warren Gamadiel Harding	1921-23	Republican	Andrew Bonar Law	1922-23	Conservative
			Stanley Baldwin	1923-24	Conservative
Calvin Coolidge	1923-29	Republican	James Ramsay MacDonald	1924	Labour
			Stanley Baldwin	1924-29	Conservative
			James Ramsay MacDonald	1929-35	Labour
Herbert Clark Hoover	1929-33	Republican	Stanley Baldwin	1935-37	Conservative
Franklin Delano Roosevelt	1933-45	Democrat	Arthur Neville Chamberlain	1937-40	Conservative
			Winston Leonard Spencer Churchill	1940-45	Conservative
			Clement Richard Attlee	1945-51	Labour
Harry S. Truman	1945-53	Democrat	Winston Leonard Spencer Churchill	1951-55	Conservative
Dwight David Eisenhower	1953-61	Republican	Harold Macmillan	1957-63	Conservative

American Presidents	Dates	Party	British Prime Ministers	Dates	Party
John Fitzgerald Kennedy	1961-63	Democrat	Alec Douglas-Home	1963-64	Conservative
Lyndon Baines Johnson	1963-69	Democrat	James Harold Wilson	1964-70	Labour
Richard Milhous Nixon	1969-74	Republican	Edward Richard George Heath	1970-74	Conservative
			James Harold Wilson	1974-76	Labour
Gerald Randall Ford	1974-77	Republican	Leonard James 'Jim' Callaghan	1976-79	Labour
James 'Jimmy' Earl Carter Jnr	1977-81	Democrat	Margaret 'Maggie' Hilda Thatcher	1979-90	Conservative
Ronald Wilson Reagan	1981-89	Republican			
George Herbert Walker Bush	1989-93	Republican	John Major	1990-97	Conservative
William 'Bill' Jefferson Clinton	1993-2001	Democrat	Anthony 'Tony' Charles Lynton Blair	1997-2007	Labour
George Walker Bush	2001-09	Republican	James Gordon Brown	2007-10	Labour
Barack Hussein Obama II	2009-17	Democrat	David William Donald Cameron	2010-16	Conservative
Donald John Trump	2017-21	Republican	Theresa Mary May	2016-19	Conservative
			Alexander Boris de Pfeffel Johnson	2019-22	Conservative
Joseph 'Joe' Robinette Biden Jnr	2021 – present Not covered in this book	Democrat			
			Mary Elizabeth 'Liz' Truss	2022 (25 September -25 October)	Conservative
			Rishi Sunak	2022- present Not covered in this book	Conservative

Introduction

Scandal

The (1993) *Shorter Oxford Dictionary* defines scandal as 'cause for offence', from the Greek *skandalon*, meaning 'snare for an enemy, cause of moral stumbling'. Also 'moral perplexity caused by the conduct of a person looked up to as an example' and 'a dishonourable imputation', 'a disgraceful circumstance, event or situation, esp. one causing public offence or outrage'.

The emphasis is on three things. First, the idea of disgrace, a failing of morality. The problem with morals is that they are not absolute. In Oliver Cromwell's Interregnum (1649–60) if a man blasphemed, literally said 'Oh, Christ!' when he stubbed his toe, he was committing a scandal and an iron spike was driven through his tongue (the part of the body which had caused offence). In the 1890s, the author Thomas Hardy had to rewrite sections of his *Tess of the D'Urbervilles* because in the original, he had the hero, Angel Clare, carrying Tess in his arms! Scandal! Outrage! Horror! When I wrote, a few years ago, a book on swearing in the Second World War, I found that what has happened since 1945 is the creation of a topsy-turvy world, in which the 'f-word' is increasingly acceptable, whereas the 'n-word' is not. Anybody living through the war and at any time before it would have laughed this out of court. So, in terms of morality and what society finds acceptable, the Britain of Robert Walpole, the first prime minister and the America of George Washington, the first president, bears very little relation to today.

Secondly is the element of the sneaky, the Greek 'snare for an enemy', implying that scandal is invented to cause maximum embarrassment and lead to social ostracism and that this is 'malicious'. Sometimes, that is true, but very often it isn't. So in the so-called 'scandal sheets', the 'gutter press' of sections of the media, these are phrases invented by people who would rather you didn't know what they've been up to. The recent group of luvvies who called themselves Hacked Off is an example of that.

Thirdly comes the notion of example and respectability: 'a person looked up to as an example'. In Britain, in terms of politics, the prime minister is the highest in the land; in America, it's the president. And in both countries, America in particular, there was for years an aura about such people, a saintly 'untouchableness' that made them above suspicion and even above the law. We have had so many scandals involving prime ministers and presidents over time, thankfully, that this hagiographic nonsense has all but disappeared. Despite this, Boris Johnson's recent biography of Churchill is a giant step backwards.

Language devolves over time and I am using the word 'scandal' in its broadest sense. The recent QAnon organization in the United States believes that the American government is riddled with cannibalistic child-molesters who are bent on world domination (see Chapter 25) and were any of that to be remotely true, it would be a scandal on any level, by anybody's definition. Having read quite a lot of biographies of those in the top jobs in both countries, I can honestly say that QAnon is making it up! But the broader meaning of scandal does fit large numbers of office holders. Robert Walpole bribed his cronies to lie for him (it was the way of the world then). William Gladstone consorted with prostitutes (a criminal offence in the 1860s). Both David Lloyd George and James Ramsay MacDonald were up to their necks in insider trading. Andrew Jackson killed a man in a duel. Rutherford Hayes rigged his election result. Harry S. Truman authorized the use of a bomb which caused outrage at the time and still does today. John F. Kennedy was a skirt-chaser par excellence while passing himself off as a 'King Arthur in Camelot' with a loving Guinevere (Jackie) at his side. Richard Nixon ... don't even go there!

We have to be careful, of course, of using the 'Woke' tactic of judging the past by our own standards. Slavery was not just defended by every president up to (and including, for a while) Abraham Lincoln, it was defended by millions all over the world. In terms of basic morality, this was wrong, but we shouldn't condemn individuals for toeing the party line over this. In a hundred or a thousand years' time, historians will look back and dismiss today's generation for their views. We have to look at prime ministers and presidents through the eyes of their contemporaries (and that, all too often, makes scandalous and depressing viewing).

I am using scandal in its widest sense because it includes failure, not necessarily moral failure, but failure itself. It was a scandal that the Whig party in Britain should have held office for so long (an unbroken forty years in the eighteenth century). It was a scandal that Robert Peel should have been bought down because he put country before party in 1846. It was a scandal that Arthur Balfour allowed the building of concentration camps in South Africa during the Boer War. It was a scandal that Anthony Eden sent troops to Egypt in the Suez Crisis (1956) without consulting parliament. It was a scandal that Boris Johnson should hold garden parties having told the rest of the country not to. You get the general picture.

If you have the brass neck to climb (as Disraeli put it) the 'greasy pole' of politics to the very top, then, as prime minister or president, you must expect to take some flak.

I will, no doubt, be accused of bias in this book, of not providing balance and nuance as a good historian should. But, like you, I live in the 'Age of Hysteria', where the middle ground has all but disappeared and we are left with extremes. In the context of prime ministers and presidents, I hope I have been equally unfair to them all.

You have been warned. Now read on.

Chapter 1

The Prime Minister

Before anyone invented the term prime minister (it's French, by the way, as is cabinet, the group of leading politicians of the day), all power in Britain lay with the monarch. Medieval rulers like William I (the Conqueror) owned all the land in England and governed with the help of advisers and staff. Under the king were the tenants-in-chief, the barons whose estates dominated what were called the shires in Saxon times and were, after 1066, the counties. The Lords provided military back-up for the king wherever he asked for it (there was no standing army until 1660) and gave advice. They usually met three or four times a year at a place of the king's choosing.

The Middle Ages in Britain was characterized by ongoing feuds and clashes between kings and their nobles. The law gave rebels the right to challenge the king if he was deemed to be misgoverning them and one of these was Simon de Montfort, the Earl of Leicester, in the 1260s. De Montfort lost the battle (literally, at Evesham in 1265) but he did establish a second group of advisers – the Commons of England. These were not the democratic masses that we are used to, but men (no women at all) of property and standing within their communities – the knights of the shires. Edward I, who had defeated de Montfort, saw the wisdom of this. '*Quid omnes tangit, ab omnibus approbetur*' (that which affects everybody should be decided by everybody) he said in the legal Latin of his day.

Out of that, rather than the over-hyped Magna Carta of 1215, came the democracy that we know today.

But the king retained the power, at least until the 1640s. Then came the crunch. The English Civil War was essentially a power struggle between the king (Charles I) and parliament, the House of Lords and the House of Commons, that were the descendants of de Montfort's 'Commons of England'. In that parliament (the term just means a place to speak), the speaker chaired debates. He was a royal servant who spoke for the king and reported back to the palace what parliament was talking about. In spectacular clashes from 1640, it was clear that the Speaker was now *parliament's* servant, not the king's, and the whole thing got nasty.

The Civil War of 1642–48 was illegal according to the law of the land. So was the trial and execution of the king, which followed it, but parliament, who went on to make the laws, simply ignored that. In 1776, the American Congress did exactly the same thing, although they were unable to execute George III because they couldn't reach him.

When Oliver Cromwell's 'experiment in government' failed and the country realized that kingship was necessary, Charles II was brought back from exile in 1660. But things were never the same again. All kings from now on were 'constitutional monarchs', limited in what they could do. Parliament made the laws and controlled taxation and the armed forces. The king retained the right to call and dismiss parliament and to appoint ministers. He also called the shots on foreign policy but increasingly, the dynamics of politics meant that power slipped from the crown to parliament. It was impossible for the king to deal with nearly 600 members of Lords and Commons, so the need arose to create a single minister who acted as go-between and effectively ran parliament.

Alongside this development in the late seventeenth century, two political parties emerged. One was the Tories (a term of contempt originating in a gang of Irish thieves) and the other Whigs (a Scottish gang of outlaws). The Whigs disappeared in 1859 to become the Liberals and the Tories officially became the Conservatives in the 1840s (although the T-word, interestingly, has survived and is still a term of contempt). There was no third party until 1900 with the creation of Labour.

At first, the term 'prime minister', like Tory and Whig, was one of contempt. It was screamed across the chamber of the Commons and

Lords, much more unruly centres of appalling behaviour than today, as a criticism of a man who was seen as the king's crony and mouthpiece. The most obvious examples of these were to be found in the France of Louis XIV, the Sun King, who had an extraordinary psychological hold over his ministers. Since Britain and France had been at war – on and off – for eight centuries, *anything* French was regarded with a mix of suspicion and hatred.

The first man to be referred to in this way was Robert Walpole (see Chapter 4) although he didn't accept that. In 1741, he told the Commons, 'I unequivocally deny that I am sole and prime minister' and it was not until 1878, at the Congress of Berlin, that Benjamin Disraeli (see Chapter 15) referred to himself in writing as 'Her Britannic Majesty's Prime Minister'. The newspapers, however, had been using the term in its modern sense long before that.

Ever since Walpole, the prime minister has always been First Lord of the Treasury, stressing the importance of that branch of government. This is still the case, even now that the prime minister is not a Lord and the Treasury is run by the Chancellor of the Exchequer who lives next door to him at Number 11 Downing Street.

No British prime minister has ever had the powers of an absolutist monarch like Louis XIV or a modern dictator like Adolf Hitler or Xi Jinping. They don't even have the powers of an American president. So each of the individuals of Number 10 that you will read about in the pages ahead has to approach the top job in their own way, treading a path that has to take into account a huge variety of factors, many of them beyond their control.

Did they succeed? As one prime minister, John Major, never said, 'Oh, no.'

Chapter 2

The Fourth Estate

'When are you going to resign, Prime Minister?'[1]

Without the ladies and gentlemen of the press, we wouldn't know half the misdemeanours and shortcomings of our leaders. Virtually everything we *do* know about them, we see through the prism of the media, so we need to understand what we are dealing with.

It all started with the Civil War in England, with over 700 different news sheets in circulation. For the first time, this power struggle between king and parliament was fought for the hearts and minds of ordinary men. It was all about ideology, the cause, and that needed propaganda. In an age of slowly increasing literacy, pamphlets appeared, stuck on to walls and tree-trunks, distributed among the rank-and-file soldiery of both sides. Words were kept to a minimum, for the benefit of those who struggled with them and cartoons were the order of the day, lampooning Charles I or Cromwell or whoever the pamphleteer had taken a dislike to.

The absence of a Licensing Act meant that in London, pamphlets and 'journals' appeared everywhere in the 1640s, the hawkers themselves gathering information as well as spreading it. They caught gossip from journeymen from the provinces, listened to loudmouths in inns and some of this was duly reported as 'fact' the next day. A typical example was the point of view of Alice Jackson (who, as a woman, would have no say in politics for nearly 300 years) – she 'wished the King and Prince Rupert's heads were there instead of [two sheep's] heads … the King was an evil and an unlawfull King and better to be without a King than to have him King.'[2] Alice would fit right in on today's social media.

The parliament too was 'nothing but a Company of Robin Hoods and Little Jacks [Johns]'. Everybody was hungry for news and was perfectly happy to lap up broadsheets that told them that a pool in Lancashire had turned to blood, children had been born with horns. And of course, the whole of East Anglia was awash with witches – Matthew Hopkins, the Witchfinder General, told them so. Oliver Cromwell was knocking off the wife of one of his generals. Another military wife, Anne, spouse of 'Black Tom' Fairfax, wanted to be queen. All a journalist had to do was write the word 'true' and the public bought it. In our more guarded, litigious times, the journalists' favourite word is 'alleged'.

There was nothing admirable in this, but it was the built-in bias of the press which has never gone away and was carried over gleefully into more modern technical outlets – radio and television. As time went on and newspapers became available in greater numbers, the men who wrote them adopted a sanctimonious, holier-than-thou approach, criticizing every aspect of government that they did not like.

'Freedom of speech' journalists cry, 'the public's right to know'. But freedom of speech must, in a civilized society, be tempered by the laws of libel (*none* of the Civil War pamphlets would pass muster today) and the public rarely has a *right* to know because various matters do not concern them. They *want* to know, but that is a different thing.

In colonial America, various settlers inevitably brought their newspaper culture with them. Most impressive perhaps were the Germans who settled in Pennsylvania in the early nineteenth century. They spoke – and printed – what came to be known, confusingly, as Pennsylvania Dutch, but 'Dutch' was a mistranslation of *Deutsch* (German).

The larger towns in the colonies set up coffee-houses and taverns where events of the day were discussed and newspapers were hired out and sold, as in Britain. New York probably had the majority of these, but the first recorded was in Boston in 1676.

It was undoubtedly the rumblings of discontent over British rule that led to an increase in the number of newspapers. Editors and proprietors worked closely with dissidents complaining about 'no taxation without representation', billeting of troops and the various 'interminable Acts' the British government was passing at the time. It is possible to exaggerate all this – literacy in America has never equalled the situation in Britain and the claim made by a French visitor that 'from the landlord to the housemaid, they [the colonists] all read two newspapers a day' is clearly nonsense.

As in Britain, political issues dominated in the press. In the arguments that raged over ratification of the Constitution in the 1780s, the Federalists had their own newspapers and regular, brilliant contributors like John Jay, John Adams and Alexander Hamilton. These papers, like their party-rag equivalent in Britain, refused to print any articles by the opposition, keeping alive the bias and bigotry of earlier generations and paving the way for the 'cancel culture' of today. The Federalists used the now-familiar scare tactics – without a ratified Constitution, America would suffer economic collapse and fall prey to foreign invasion.

Occasionally, the American press, the freedom of which was enshrined in the First Amendment to the Bill of Rights, actually did the job of the state, although there was nothing resembling a government paper. When George Washington left office, he never actually delivered his farewell address – it was reported in the press instead, in September 1796.

Technology and increasing literacy have combined to make today's media intrusive. Political events (and scandals) that would eventually reach the papers after three or four days are now instant 'breaking news' and the public slavishly reads/watches it. The press of course, on both sides of the Atlantic, are in the business of making money and they are actually only reflecting the situation as it is – *everything* today is the responsibility of the government. In the past, very little was. The question, sometimes unspoken, sometimes written as banner headlines, is, 'What is the Prime Minister/President going to do about it?'

The development, which has led to today's situation, is the centralization of power in the hands of the government. No single prime minister or party was responsible for this, but the first head over the parapet by a long way is Benjamin Disraeli in the 1870s. Ironically, he was leader of a party (the Conservatives) who did not believe in such centralization.

As the Liberal prime minister William Gladstone warned in 1889, 'If government takes into its hands that which a man ought to do for himself, it will inflict greater mischiefs than all the benefits he will have received ...'

Compare Robert Walpole's job, for a moment, with Rishi Sunak's. Both men live(d) at Number 10. Both men 'kissed rings' (shook hands) with their respective kings (George I and Charles III). After that, their roles are chalk and cheese. Walpole's main concern was the economy (as, possibly, is Sunak's) but Walpole had the king behind him (irrelevant to Sunak) and a group of City financiers wholly committed to extending their own profits by going to war (there was no such thing as a global economy). Walpole's expenses were all about paying for backing in the House (which would be illegal for Sunak) and keeping the army and navy up to strength (although he did his level best not to use them). He had no concern for transport. There were no railways or even buses; no cyclists demanding more of the road than anyone else, for which they pay nothing. In the eighteenth century, the roads (and later waterways) were paid for by the travellers' tolls and business ventures.

Walpole had no involvement in education. Schools were private businesses and were few and far between. There were only two universities in the country (Oxford and Cambridge) and neither of them accepted females as students. People's health was their own problem. Doctors were rare and badly trained; they were also expensive. There was no National Health Service until 1948, and that was opposed by many of the medical fraternity who could see their incomes disappearing.

Rishi Sunak is expected to deal with it all – domestic policy, foreign policy, the economy, education, health, transport and a whole lot more. If any of this goes badly – as it does, because humans are not very efficient and most of their machinery is even worse – it is the government's fault. The education of the masses means that in the twenty-first century, *everybody* has demands to make. Yet the government is only so big (some would say *too* big) and there is only so much money to go round. Some years ago, women complaining about misogyny and sexual assault, especially in the media, set up the #MeToo movement to highlight how widespread the problem was. Nowadays, *everybody* is in the MeToo situation, not in terms of sexual harassment but in the sense of believing that their cause is the most important in the world and, naively, that it is only the government that is halting progress and stopping freedom. We may have a more literate population than ever, but we hardly have a more genuinely informed one.

In the days of Robert Walpole, the electorate was composed of *men* of property. That meant that the number of voters was tiny. At the hustings, where MPs argued their case and showed off their credentials as at a cattle market, the cluster of voters around the podium was so small that votes could be counted there and then by raised hands. And it was drinks all round on the winning candidate. In pocket boroughs, where the votes were in the pocket of a local landowning family, there was often no contest. Neither was there in rotten boroughs, which had been substantial settlements when parliament was first created in the 1270s but had dwindled or disappeared altogether by 1832. The Isle of Wight, for example, had only 1,000 voters, but returned five MPs to Westminster. Today, it has 110,000 voters and only one MP. Most appalling of all was Old Sarum, the Norman Salisbury, which came to be called 'the cursed hill' in 1832 because it had two MPs and no voters at all!

As more men got the vote in the widening of the franchise in 1832, 1867, 1884 and 1918 (the last date including women for the first time), voters were increasingly able to *read* what the election posters said, what their MPs' policies and allegiances were and what their parties stood for. Change came slowly to the franchise as it did to literacy on the grounds that if you teach a man to write his name, the first thing he will do is to write it on a petition demanding change.

Another development is the media revolution. By the time of Walpole's first year in office, England's first daily paper was printed. It was called *The Courant* and was only available in London. Not until 1896, with Alfred Harmsworth's *Daily Mail,* was there a national daily and the first prime minister to get it in the neck from them was Lord Salisbury, the grand old Conservative who believed in isolationism. Since the *Courant*, a whole street of newspapers has come and gone, siding with the Left or Right or claiming, with little justification, to be somewhere in between.

As journalist Ray Boston has pointed out,[3] the reason that Fleet Street became Britain's newspaper hub is that it was nearest to the centre of news, which is not Downing Street or the Houses of Parliament but the moneymaking activities of the City. There are exceptions, but the best prime ministers are usually those with a sound grasp of economics. By the late 1980s, the hordes of newspaper offices had left Fleet Street, largely because of the astronomic costs of renting.

In terms of freedom of the press, the beginnings were ominous. The Tudor state, which only came into being as a result of bad luck on the part of Richard III at Bosworth, was anxious to airbrush history and clamp down on anything it saw as seditious. All books and pamphlets had to be vetted by the Stationers' Company who worked for the Establishment. But there was a rabble outside this group – 'newsmongers' – who sold chapbooks and one-sided 'broadsheets' to a public hungry for news, the more salacious the better. While the Stationers' office's job was 'to instruct the nation in its duty and to scotch wild rumours' everybody else had other ideas.

The area around Fleet Street was Alsatia, a lawless cesspit of crime and gang warfare, where drunkenness and prostitution were the orders of the day and the death rate frighteningly high. Most of the copy being hawked in the area concerned royalty and the licentiousness of Charles II's court played into the hands of hacks who were prepared to print any whiff of gossip, however scandalous or unproven. There was 'little more than Billingsgate language' in any of them; (fish sellers were not known for polite conversation) and they were 'full of lies, forgeries, insolvencies and impieties'. The chief censor, soon after the Civil War, had been John Milton, the blind author of *Paradise Lost*, a rabid Puritan and misogynist.

When Roger L'Estrange was appointed as Surveyor of the Press, it was clear that government censorship had not vanished with Cromwell (who had died in 1658). L'Estrange believed that 'it makes the Multitudes too familiar with the actions of their counsels and of their superiors … and gives them not only an itch but a kind of colourable right to be meddling with the government.' This is the start of today's journalists' maxim 'the right to know'.

The almost total destruction of Fleet Street in the Great Fire of 1666 led to a rebuilding by Londoners for Londoners. Almost immediately, coffee-houses sprang up along it, where hacks and news-hawkers could buy thick Turkish coffee or tea while plotting their next assault on somebody famous. Nando's (which sounds very modern!), Groom's and the Rainbow were perhaps the best known. Charles II tried to abolish these places as centres of sedition, but such was the public outcry that he backed down.

From 1679 onwards, there was effectively a free press, the best-known broadsheet Benjamin Harris's *Domestick Intelligencer*, a firmly Protestant and Whig paper. His anti-Catholicism led to a huge fine (£500) and a day in the pillory outside his own office. Such was the support for him, however (including from some MPs), that nothing was thrown at him in twenty-four hours. Alternatively, nobody offered to pay his fine either!

With more changes to the law in 1696, there was something of a free-for-all among the press. They could still not print anything 'improper, mischievous or illegal', but these things were open to interpretation and various hacks continually pushed the boundaries. The government's Stamp Act of 1712, however, had the effect of increasing the cost of newspapers and many of them disappeared as a result.

New ones sprang up, however. By the time Robert Walpole was at Number 10, there were four dailies in London – Samuel Buckley's *The Courant* (1702); the *Post* (1719); the *Journal* (1721); and the *Post-Boy* (1728). Daniel Defoe, the satirical author of *Robinson Crusoe* warned newspapermen what the limits were in 1704: 'Governments will not be jested with, nor reflected upon.'

As if!

Newspapers have had considerable influence on political careers, not least those of prime ministers. One Number 10 wannabe, Lord Randolph Churchill, threw his career away by bleating to *The Times* about his boss, Lord Salisbury. Anyone who was anyone read *The Times*, with its letters from perpetually offended retired generals and admirals and Churchill had to resign. In the early twentieth century, Alfred Harmsworth owned half a dozen leading papers, was given a seat in the Lords as Lord Northcliffe and had a *huge* influence on the prime ministers of his day. In the Second World War, Max Aitken, another press tycoon, became Lord Beaverbrook and ran Winston Churchill's munitions ministry. More recently, the *Sun* had the brass neck to claim that they won the election of 1992 for Margaret Thatcher: 'It Was *The Sun* Wot Won It.' But since that paper also urged its readership to 'Nuke the Argies' during the Falklands War of 1982, nobody really took it seriously. Boris Johnson was a journalist before he went into politics, and, according to some, a flaky one at that.

In America, newspapers followed key events closely. The first publications in the colonies were Puritan tracts, as in *Keyes of the Kingdom of Heaven* (1644) by John Cotton. The first newspaper, the weekly *Boston News-letter* was based on the *London Gazette* and two-thirds of its content was British. In 1723, the 17-year-old Benjamin Franklin set up the *Boston Gazette*, followed by its Pennsylvania counterpart six years later. Bearing in mind the man's later revolutionary proclivities, the front page carried the headline 'God Save the King!' (no irony intended). The *New York Weekly* got into trouble in the 1730s for attacking the colony's governor. Its defence counsel spoke of 'the liberty of exposing and opposing arbitrary power ... by speaking and writing the truth'.

It was undoubtedly the tensions over the Stamp Act of 1765 that gave the American press its cutting political edge. Anti-British pamphlets appeared all over the place and Tom Paine, the pro-American English rabble-rouser edited the *Pennsylvania Magazine*.

After the War of Independence, when the United States had a voice of its own, President Thomas Jefferson wrote, 'Our liberty depends on the freedom of the press ... Were it left to me to decide whether we should have a government without newspapers or newspapers without government, I should not hesitate a moment to prefer the latter.' By 1813, 'Uncle Sam', scrawny, top-hatted, long-haired and wearing the Stars and Stripes had made his appearance in American propaganda. Fifteen years earlier, the *New York Tribune* had been founded, promising 'news of importance, not sensationalism'. How long was it, I wonder, before *that* idea disappeared?

When the issue of slavery became a burning one in the 1850s, most papers carried the verbatim texts of the Lincoln–Douglas debates. In the Civil War that followed, the North and South had their own papers, each pushing their cause, and foreign journalists sailed over to cover the war for their readers. The *Telegraph*'s George Sala was with the Yankee armies; W.H. Russell, of Crimean War fame, reported for the Rebs to *The Times*.

In Andrew Johnson's presidency, the *New York Daily Times* dropped the 'Daily' and over time, because of its dull front, came to be known as the 'grey lady', suddenly, in the Age of Hysteria (see Chapter 25) the most anti-British of all the American mainstream media.

In 1927, the first public demonstration of a television set was heralded by Herbert Hoover, the Secretary of State for Commerce, but it wasn't until 1939 that F.D. Roosevelt became the first president to address the nation on the new gadget to proclaim New York's World's Fair. From 1947 onwards, presidents routinely broadcast, despite the apposite warning from David Marsh of Boston University: 'If the television age continues with the present level of programming, we are destined to have a nation of morons.' But the morons weren't listening and an estimated 75 million watched Dwight Eisenhower's inaugural oath on television in 1953.

More recently, American papers were front and centre during the administration of Richard 'Tricky Dickie' Nixon. The *Washington Post* reached a kind of immortality by exposing the Watergate scandal (see Chapter 21) even if they did give rise to the irritating suffix 'gate' that now appears everywhere!

Along with the growth of newspapers came the satirical magazines, like *Punch* and its spin-off, *Judy*. The satire was guarded, handled for the most part with kid gloves and by no means as vicious as its seventeenth-century origins. Some things were off limits. For example, when Edward VIII abdicated in 1936, the entire British press was muted (muzzled?) whereas the Americans had a field day. In fact, as in other walks of life, the American pattern of no-holds-barred attacks on politicians (even, eventually, the president) has been adopted by the British media.

And so, to broadcasting. The British Broadcasting Corporation, set up with a noble charter in 1922 was, until recently, the envy of the world. It sought to educate, enlighten and entertain but today it struggles to do even the last of those three. During the Second World War, it was happy to trot out propaganda on behalf of the government because 'there was a war on', 'careless talk costs lives' and defeatism was a crime. Not until the arrival of 'hate crime' would the country see anything so childish again.

Television followed the same pattern. In times of crisis, prime ministers appeared looking gravely at the camera, echoing Neville Chamberlain's radio broadcast of the start of the Second World War. For years, there were the most boring little snippets, usually squeezed in somewhere near the nine o'clock news entitled 'A party political broadcast on behalf of the ... party' (there were only three at that point) and the entire nation went off to the kitchen to make a cup of tea.

Lastly (and I do not just mean that in terms of chronology), came social media, which is anything but. Since the 1990s and the advent of the personal computer, *anybody* can put forward their points of view, telling politicians and the world exactly where they (politicians and the world) are going wrong. What is extraordinary is the way in which politicians, along with actual media, schools and universities, cave in to this ill-informed, badly educated behemoth as if its views are worth hearing. There are now so many points of view, all of them conflicting, that no prime minister can win. As President Abraham Lincoln, who never had to worry about the Internet, famously said, 'You can please some of the people all of the time, you can please all of the people some of the time, but you can't please all of the people all of the time.'

Journalists, either professional writers and broadcasters or pub bores with keyboards, have taken on a mantle that no one asked them to and to which they have no intrinsic right. The fourth estate will tell you it is there as a watchdog to guard against the mistakes, excesses and self-centredness of the other three. In ancient Rome, the most powerful group were the Praetorians, the emperor's bodyguard. They had the power to make or break emperors, murdering Caligula when he made fun of one of them. Could the Praetorians be trusted if something as trivial as that was their motivation? The poet Juvenal summed it up perfectly: '*Quis custodes ipsos custodiet?*' (Who guards the guards?) So the fourth estate is a great idea as long as it behaves itself and lives up to the ideals it claims to uphold. All too often, however, that is not the case.

Chapter 3

Number 10

'My vast and awkward house'

(William Pitt *c*.1804)

The official residence of the prime minister has a long and chequered history. In common with many other London buildings, it has gone through many owners and tenants, several numbers and even different colours. Today, we see Downing Street through the prism of the lenses of media cameramen, where journalists of various persuasions pose idiotic questions to the comers and goers to Number 10, which they know will never be answered.

Outside the high-gloss black door with its white numbers have stood the world's great and good, hoping that their crossing of the threshold behind them will bring about the changes they want. The 'suffragettes' of the Women's Social and Political Union stood here, with their wide hats and long skirts, petitioning Herbert Asquith to give them the vote in 1913. He didn't. Mohandas K. Gandhi, the 'great soul' who wanted Indian independence, stood in his dhoti and was sneered at by Winston Churchill. But it was not Churchill the Indian nationalist had come to see. The prime minister in 1931 was Ramsay MacDonald, an altogether more sympathetic listener, Gandhi hoped, in his negotiations. Independence would take another sixteen years and would lead, ultimately, to Gandhi's assassination. It was outside this door that Neville Chamberlain waved his now infamous scrap of paper given to him by the Chancellor of Germany, Adolf Hitler, promising no further Nazi encroachments on somebody else's territory. It was 'peace with honour' and 'peace for our time' and within months, the Second World War had begun.

Whereas all the above were either invited to Number 10 or lived there, others were less welcome; because of that, permanent barricades were set up, manned by burly and increasingly heavily armed policemen. Anti-nuclear protesters wanted to ban the bomb there and anti-Vietnam protesters arrived in the 1960s, anti-Iraq and Afghanistan protestors in the early years of the twenty-first century. World problems, which often have nothing to do with Britain, are laid at the feet of the prime minister and he or she is obliged to deal with them for a salary that is little more than is given to a headteacher of one of the large comprehensive schools. Debris from V1 'doodlebugs' shattered Number 10's windows in 1944. After a sabotage attempt by mortar from the Irish Republican Army in February 1991, the famous door was reinforced with solid steel; it took eight men to lift it into position. And that door does not open from the outside. Inside, sitting patiently in an eighteenth-century Sheraton 'Charlies' shelter', once used by London's policemen, an attendant waits to open the door to visitors. They have all been checked and counter-checked already. In 2012, a particularly bumptious Member of Parliament was stopped by a policeman for riding his bike past the barriers. The MP allegedly called the officer a 'pleb' (a term which the Roman senate would have recognized, meaning riffraff) and the media had a field day. Whatever was or was not actually said, right and common sense lay with the policeman that day, but the MP in question was behaving exactly as most of his predecessors had done since the age of Walpole.

Before Downing Street even existed, somebody built a large house known as the House at the Back, probably about 1530. Henry VIII was king, the country (despite Protestant rumblings from 'Germany') was still Catholic and the 'back' in question was the rear of one of the king's palaces, fronting on to Whitehall around the corner. It was also next to a cock-fighting arena, where all-comers from noblemen to peasants jostled with each other in a frenzy of betting to see which birds would claw the others to death with their steel talons. Not for nothing were some cabinet meetings held in these premises – the free-for-all of the Commons and the men who worked there was forged on a common anvil. One of the earliest occupants of the House at the Back was Thomas Knevett who had surprised and captured the would-be assassin Guido (Guy) Fawkes in the vaults underneath St Stephen's Hall in November 1605. A series of royal children and their households lived there before it passed to George Monck, the Duke of Albemarle, in 1660. It was General Monck who, with his regiment of Coldstreamers at his back, returned Charles II to his throne in the Restoration of the monarchy. His secretary was Sir George Downing, a courtier who became an indispensable spy for both Oliver Cromwell and Charles II and it was he who, as a property developer, bought up the street that would later bear his name. That was not a smooth transition, however. The Hampden family had a claim to the land too and, having bought the property in 1654, Downing could not build on it for thirty years.

Between 1682 and 1684, Downing built a series of town houses along the cul-de-sac that ran towards St James's Park. Most of these had two storeys, complete with stables and outhouses. Despite being designed by Christopher Wren, the leading architect of his day who had produced a master-plan (never actioned for reasons of cost) for a new London after the Great Fire of 1666, the houses were built on sand, with foundations that were too shallow and materials that were inadequate. What a gift for lovers of metaphor.

Today, it is difficult to imagine Downing Street as the 'pretty, open place' referred to in an advertisement of 1720. Titled people flocked to it, however. Henry Nassau d'Auverquerque, Earl of Grantham[1] was second cousin to William III and his successor in the House at the Back was George Grenville, Baron Lansdowne. Men like this ruled England in the early eighteenth century.

In 1720, the properties devolved to the crown on Lansdowne's death and restoration and repairs ran to a staggering £2,522 (over £61 million today). Lead plumbing was introduced and 'a new Necessary House' (toilet) installed. In that year, the property was renamed Bothmer

House because its new occupant was Johann Casper von Bothmer, premier minister to the Elector of Hanover who would go on to advise both George I and George II.

There had been a succession crisis in 1714 with the death of Queen Anne, and despite the existence of a Stuart rival, James, the man's Catholicism made him ineligible to wear the crown, so the title shunted sideways to Anne's cousin, George of Hanover who duly became George I. Bothner was, therefore, the first leading minister to the king who lived in what would become Number 10 sixty years later. He complained, as many others had – and would in the future – about the 'ruinous condition of the place'.

In 1732, the king granted the property to Robert Walpole (see Chapter 4). Britain's first prime minister only agreed if the house could be given to all First Lords of the Treasury who followed him, in perpetuity; the king agreed. Walpole persuaded Mr Chicken, who lived at Number 11, to move further along the street and had both properties redesigned by William Kent who added a third floor and in effect made both houses a single property. On 23 September 1735, the *London Daily Post* wrote, 'Yesterday, the Right Hon. Sir Robert Walpole, with his lady and family, removed from their house in St James's Square to his New House, adjoining to the Treasury in St James's Park.' There were sixty rooms, with marble and hardwood floors, mantelpieces and mouldings. Despite his rough 'man of the people' exterior, Walpole was in fact a refined collector of the arts and he stocked his home accordingly. His study, which became the Cabinet Room, was 40 feet by 20 and overlooked the park.

Despite access to the Treasury building, Robert Peel had the connecting door locked in the 1840s, as a symbol that the prime minister does not control the state economy. 'Under [Tony] Blair,' wrote Andrew Blick in 2010, 'the locked door, symbolically and physically dividing No. 10 from the cabinet office, was passed through with such frequency that its meaning was lost.'

Walpole lived at Number 10 until his resignation in 1742, but the next five of his successors refused to live there. Apart from their country estates, they all had town houses far larger and grander than anything in Downing Street. Of thirty-one prime ministers between 1735 and 1902, only sixteen took up residence. The others leased the property to family or friends.

By the time Charles Townshend took office in the mid-1760s, the place was in a state of disrepair again. Parts of it were unsafe and it took eight years to complete the work. By 1783, the Duke of Portland had to move out because the stairs wobbled and there was dry rot everywhere. The *Morning Herald* was horrified that 'so much [£11,000] has this extraordinary edifice cost the country'. Lord North liked the place, but as he was 'the prime minister who lost America', we are entitled to call his judgement into question. Lord Goderich refurbished the house extensively in the late 1820s, but from then until 1877 it was largely vacant or just used for meetings.

The genteel St James's had become a cesspit by the 1840s, with rookeries of Irishmen not far away and centres of drunkenness and prostitution. The elegant 'swells' who worked at the Colonial Office at Number 14, the Foreign Office at Number 16, the West India Department at Number 18 and the Tithe Commission (responsible for the collection of church taxes) at Number 20, had to squeeze their way through a smelly throng, presumably keeping a close guard on their wallets. Such was the state of disrepair that by 1857 only three houses remained: – 10, 11 and the Whip's Office at Number 12.

It was not until 1902 that Arthur Balfour declared that Number 10 was the official residence of His Britannic Majesty's Prime Minister, with capital letters all over the place. In the 1940s, when all London was a target of the Luftwaffe's bombs, Churchill often slept in the underground bunker, (now the Cabinet War Rooms open to the public), but he had himself been photographed often going in and out of the famous black door to keep up morale among a depressed and sometimes terrified people. In more peaceful times, Harold Wilson didn't regard Number 10 as his house, because he wanted his wife, Mary, to have 'a proper home' in nearby North Street.

By the mid-twentieth century, the prime minister's official residence was again showing its cracks. Stairs were sinking and the dry rot was back. Under Harold Macmillan's premiership, there were serious discussions about demolition, but in the end it was decided to carry out extensive refurbishments, costing nearly £3 million, using as much original material as possible. Raymond Erith was the architect and the work was carried out by John Mowlem & Co. There were interminable delays because history kept getting in the way of this historic house – archaeologists had to investigate Roman, Saxon and Medieval remains in the Westminster sand. The black bricks of Number 10's façade were found originally to be a mellow yellow – the black was a result of two centuries of London's famous grime. Such was the iconic symbolism of the colour, however, that Mowlem's men painted the bricks black. Erith was disappointed with the end result – 'I am heart-broken,' he told the press.

This is the building which most of us know so well, thanks to the ever more intrusive media. But most of us never get to see the interior, especially if we missed historian Simon Schama's walking tour of the place in 2007 (it is still available on YouTube). Cameras are often allowed into 'My Lord's [Walpole's] study', now the Cabinet Room. The huge table was imported by William Gladstone, its top enlarged by Macmillan. The prime minister's chair, the only one with arms, stands halfway down one side, with its back to the fireplace. There is only one portrait here, that of the house's first true occupant, Robert Walpole.

There are three state rooms. It was in the 1796 Pillared Room that John Logie Baird gave a demonstration to Ramsay MacDonald in 1927. The inventor claimed that it would change the world; it was called the television. Harold Wilson hosted the American astronauts Armstrong, Aldrin and Collins here in 1970 and Tony Blair held a reception for the victorious England Rugby team after their success in the World Cup in 2003. The Terracotta Room is named for its coloured walls, but this changes from time to time. The White Dining Room was used until the 1940s for small, private functions and the prime minister's family. Edward Heath played his grand piano here.

Until 1877, all the fittings of Number 10 were provided by successive incumbents. This changed when Benjamin Disraeli, wholly in keeping with his chaotic grasp of finances, proposed that the country should cough up. Parliament agreed and so it has remained. The only *genuinely* poor prime minister, the crofter's son Ramsay MacDonald, instituted a system whereby cabinet ministers contributed to the purchase of books for the prime minister's library in 1931. That, too, has stayed. Various patriotic prime ministers, including Margaret Thatcher, insisted that only British paintings be displayed, contrasting with her arch-rival Edward Heath's Renoirs. John Major, a cricketing fan, had at least two artworks depicting the great game.

In 1985, to celebrate two and a half centuries of prime ministerial occupancy (albeit, as we have seen, not unbroken), Margaret Thatcher held a banquet in the State Dining Room, built at a cost of £2,000 by Lord Goderich in the 1820s. All living ex-prime ministers were there – Harold Macmillan, Alec Douglas-Home, Edward Heath and James Callaghan. The queen was there too, along with descendants of Herbert Asquith, David Lloyd George, Stanley Baldwin, Winston Churchill and Anthony Eden.

It is difficult to comprehend how a house can be so pivotal to affairs of state. Tony Blair and David Cameron caused raised eyebrows when they effectively swapped houses to Number 11 because their respective families were larger than those of their respective chancellors. Recent prime ministers have needed more space for their ever-growing staffs and when Boris Johnson put in a bid for new wallpaper for his and his wife Carrie's private apartments, the perpetually offended went on the warpath. An electoral commission was set up to investigate.

All that, of course, was before he had the temerity to sit in the garden with a glass of wine in front of him during the COVID panic. He would have to go ...

But Number 10 goes on. As Margaret Thatcher said in 1985, the house is 'one of the most precious jewels in the national heritage'.

Chequers – not so much. The sixteenth-century manor house in Buckinghamshire, 41 miles from Number 10, was perhaps originally the estate of Elias Ostiarus, an usher in the twelfth-century court of the exchequer. The modern title of Chancellor of the Exchequer has the same origin. According to accounting legend, at least, Medieval tax money was counted on a chequered cloth. Ostiarus' coat of arms had a chequered field (background) in memory of this.

The current house was built by William Hawtrey about 1565. It passed through various families until 1715 when it was purchased by John Russell, a grandson of Oliver Cromwell; Chequers still has the largest Cromwellian memorabilia collection in the country. The house was redesigned in the fashionable Victorian Gothic style but re-converted to its Tudor appearance in the 1890s. Like many grand country houses, Chequers became a convalescent hospital for officers during the First World War, after which its owners, Arthur Lee and his American wife, Ruth, made the momentous decision to grant the house for the use of future prime ministers. The philanthropic Lees realized that the twentieth century would throw up political leaders who were not to the manor born and had no country estates of their own. To that end, the Chequers Estate Act of 1917 granted use of the place for the good of the country. On a stained-glass window in the chapel are the words 'This house of peace and ancient memories was given to England as a thank-offering for her deliverance in the great war of 1914–18 as a place of rest and recreation for her Prime Ministers for ever.'

Breathing in pure air of the Chilterns, the Lees believed, would be an asset – 'the better the health of our rulers, the more sanely will they rule'. 'How's that working for ya?' as today's Americans ask. In Neville

Chamberlain's day, Chequers had one telephone, in the kitchen, but Churchill brought in a whole battery of them and for security reasons moved to nearby Ditchley during the Blitz (1940–43). More recently, Theresa May held her Brexit discussions here – the Chequers Plan – and Boris Johnson recovered from COVID 19 in its tranquillity.

Even though heads of state have been welcomed here and tough decisions no doubt have been made, Chequers remains out of sight. Whether by accident or design, the media have, by and large, left Chequers alone. The prime ministerial action happens in Number 10 and the Commons, so that is where the paparazzi flock. The peace of the Chilterns is still relatively undisturbed.

Chapter 4

The Whig Ascendancy

Sir Robert Walpole 1721–42

The problem lay, as so often in British history, with the king. George Louis was King of Great Britain and Ireland, but he was also duke and elector of Hanover. He was heir to a tiny German state (one of nearly 300) and had no concept of constitutional monarchy. Britain, by contrast, was on the verge of international greatness, trouncing the Dutch and the French to become the world's greatest superpower as the eighteenth century advanced.

George never learned English (unfortunate, you might say, for a king of England) although he spoke court French with the best of them. He appeared dour, without a sense of humour and, by 1714, the year of his accession, had become fashionably fat in the eighteenth-century style. He was rotten to his wife, Sophia Dorothea, and only had one mistress (quite abstemious by Hanoverian standards) – she was Ehrengard von Schulenberg, known as 'the maypole' in Britain.

Londoners never warmed to the new king. He had little idea that parliament, not king, was now in the ascendancy. The Scots loathed him – this wee German laddie had, after all, usurped the role of a good old Scots family, the Stuarts. England had already had a Dutch foreigner – William of Orange – on the throne. Here was another outsider. It was time for stability, the kind that could only be offered by an Englishman. Into the breech stepped Robert Walpole.

At the height of his fame, he once said that his intention was to join the church and become Archbishop of Canterbury. He was lying through his teeth. The Walpoles were a family of the gentry class, with estates in Houghton, Norfolk. Robert was one of nineteen children, remarkable even in an age of no efficient contraception. He attended Eton (the first of its subsequent twenty-one prime ministers) as a King's Scholar; then on to King's College, Cambridge. There is actually no academic skill in this; it was all about money. He inherited the family estates (wealth was the sole requirement for entry into politics) – ten manors in all, worth £2,169 (almost £62 million today).

He entered the Commons in 1701, as a Whig member for the pocket borough of Castle Rising. Pocket boroughs were 'in the pocket' of a particular family and it went with the position of squire; there was no election or rival. Whig and Tory were virtually interchangeable.

All statesmen of the eighteenth century were officially painted in powdered wigs, which got shorter and neater as time went on. Look at Walpole without his and he has the air of a prosperous butcher, his hair roughly cut, his girth huge. He played up to this physical roughness. In the Commons, on the front benches, he threw apples from his Norfolk estates to cronies, read his gamekeeper's letters before affairs of state and referred to his friendship with the Queen of England as having 'the right sow by the ear'. Well over half the MPs in Walpole's day were independent gentlemen, landowners like himself, and he played to their gallery for twenty years. Behind all that rusticity, however, was a razor-sharp mind and a sophisticated intellect.

Above all, the man had the ability to latch on to greatness. He knew perfectly well that politics (then as now, in Britain as in America) was about contacts – the old school tie, the club, the fraternity, who you knew. He smarmed around the Duchess of Marlborough and her war-hero husband the duke who had smashed Louis XIV's France by 1715. He became Secretary of War and Treasurer of the Navy. No government posts carried a salary – a man was supposed to be of private means and was doing what he did for the good of the country. Each post, however, carried perks of office and Walpole lined his pockets more successfully than most.

His most famous line – 'Every man has his price' – is a misquotation, but nevertheless sums him up. The Tory Bolingbroke hounded him on charges of corruption (which he was almost certainly guilty of) and Walpole ended up in the Tower of London, the end of many men's careers – and, indeed, lives.

As it happened, Walpole's time in prison was a piece of cake and he beat the case against him. His attack on the Tories – *A Short History of the Parliament* – was so libellous that no one would publish it. Walpole had a printing press set up in his house and ran off copies anyway, selling them on street corners throughout London. With his mastery of the Commons, the dirt he had on everyone and his connections, he had already become indispensable to George I before the South Sea Bubble burst.

This was the first economic crisis in the modern period and it, or something very like it, has come to bite umpteen prime ministers and presidents in the backside. The South Sea Company had over-invested and collapsed, leading to the crash of share values and the bursting of the bubble. Anyone who was anyone had invested in the scheme, including Walpole, but he had read the warning signs and bailed out just in time. Accordingly, when the crash hit, Walpole was squeaky clean and was appointed First Lord of the Treasury and Chancellor of the Exchequer (the equivalent of owning numbers 10 *and* 11 Downing Street) which gave him unassailable powers.

He and George I, his main source of power, spoke in dog-Latin because the Norfolk man spoke neither German nor French, which many rank-and-file members of both parties thought for years was right and proper. George spent half his reign back in Hanover and left the day-to-day business of government to Walpole.

The prime minister used government cash to buy people and did it carefully, like a business. The Secret Service Fund was dipped into to lure the talents of up-and-coming politicians and to silence opponents. He avoided European conflicts like the plague, even breaking treaties to do so. 'Forty thousand men dead on the battlefields of Europe,' he once boasted, 'and not one Englishman.' To the average Englishman of the 1740s, this smacked of treason. War cost more than anything else, and as a member of the country/independent 'party' in the Commons, saving money ran in his veins.

Then came 1727. If Walpole was George I's man, he was not his son's. A satirist wrote *Robin's Pathetick Tale*, a mock elegy, from the prime minister's perspective. The Hanoverians, generation after generation, all loathed their predecessors and the old king's death in June signalled a change of personnel. The king died in Hanover and Walpole drove two horses to death in the harness of the carriage taking him to Richmond to tell the Prince of Wales. The new king was unmoved and passed the reins of government to a pompous non-event, Spencer Compton, the Earl of Wilmington (see below).

George II had known he would inherit the throne of England since he was 17, so he had learned English and had a certain grasp of English ways. He was a British citizen from 1705 and his clutch of titles stretched from Cornwall (Duke of) to Cambridge (Duke and Marquess). The power behind the throne was Caroline of Anspach, tough, shrewd and a flirt. Her relationship with Walpole was typical of her. It was probably not sexual, although had it been, it is doubtful whether Mrs Walpole, Catherine Shorter, could have done much about it.

It was already traditional for the prime minister to write the king's speech at the state opening of parliament because George I's English had not been up to it in 1714. Spencer Compton's attempts were so awful that Walpole did it for him. He took the opportunity to increase the Civil List (the monarch's personal pocket money) by £100,000. Even the king had his price and Walpole was back. He was in Number 10 once more, but the death of Caroline ten years later lost Walpole a vital prop. Any prime minister in an age before modern party politics had to have 'the ear of the king' and without Caroline, as far as Walpole was concerned, he suddenly went deaf.

George II, like most of the Hanoverians, was a warmonger, defending Hanover and Britain against all comers. Walpole knew that wars cost money, no matter who won and the War of Spanish Succession (like other wars before and since) had virtually nothing to do with Britain.

To pay for this, Walpole set up the Sinking Fund and he reduced the interest on the national debt. To the delight of landowners, Whig and Tory, he slashed the hated Land Tax. His famous dictum 'let sleeping dogs lie', however, would bite future generations in the backside. In 1739 he said, 'I have old England against me; do you think I'll have New England likewise?' This came to be known as salutary neglect, giving the American colonies a freedom they had not earned. It did not stop the colonists whingeing, of course, in the 1760s, about 'no taxation without representation' (see Chapter 8).

'I am no saint,' Walpole said, 'no Spartan, no reformer.' He was, in fact, a sharp businessman who understood economics and parliamentary affairs like no one else. There was no idealism in Walpole, no great vision. His was a workaday government cashing in on the fact that, as an industrial and trading nation, Britain was fast developing into the powerhouse of the world.

During the season (May to September) he usually lived at Richmond. Whenever he could, he would hunt, ride and shoot on his Norfolk estates. In the Commons, he wore his Garter star (he was made Knight of the Garter (KG) in 1726) and interrupted proceedings with wit and elegance. The House of Commons, far more so than the Lords, was a wild, unruly place. There were originally barriers in front of the front benches – over the maximum reach of two drawn swords apart – so that deadly scuffles could not break out. One of the grimmest and most disturbing facts about British politics is that there is still no intelligence test for entry. In other words, any idiot can represent his/her constituents with a small amount of money that can be borrowed from any bank. Most of the intellectual debate in Walpole's day came from the party leaders like him; everybody else shouted loudly and made bleating noises.

Each November, the prime minister held the 'Norfolk Congress' where his cronies gathered for a knees-up at palatial Houghton Hall. One year, 540 empty bottles were returned to his London wine merchants. An eyewitness to all this wrote, 'Our company [sat down] to dinner a snug little party of about thirty-odd, up to the chin in beef, venison, geese, turkeys, etc; and generally over the chin in claret, strong beer and punch.'

Walpole ditched Catherine Shorter as soon as he could. His most famous son, the bitchy diarist Horace, was probably not actually his. His most famous mistress was Molly Skerrett, a Londoner from a landed Irish family. He got her settled in his son Robert's estate in Old Lodge, Richmond, and married her on Catherine's death, adding her £30,000 to his personal fortune.

What brought Walpole down was not his greed or his clear lack of scruple (today he would not last a month), it was the pushiness of the City of London in urging war so that their profits could increase. His Excise Bill was condemned by the press as 'that monster ... that plan of arbitrary power'. His Gin Act (1736) caused rioting in the streets – a nation of drunks saw this as a further abuse of power. A dodgy smuggler named Jenkins claimed that the Spaniards had cut his ear off and demanded justice. The ear in the glass jar was real enough but Jenkins' lifting of his wig to show where it had been was a *very* perfunctory affair and the whole thing was probably a scam. Several of Walpole's cabinet backed Jenkins, however, and Walpole snapped at his colleague the Duke of Newcastle, 'It is your war and I wish you well of it.'

In February 1742, the prime minister was defeated over a minor issue. They wheeled in the old and lame who had not attended parliament for years to vote against him and Walpole resigned. He was given the earldom of Orford. Elevation to the Lords (either the pinnacle of success or a cobwebbed retirement home depending on your point of view) became the usual pattern for ex-prime ministers over the years. Like nearly all of them, Walpole could not resist interfering in politics for the rest of his life. His style of government – the Robinocracy, or government of Robert – established a pattern of common sense, a yardstick of what would work in a naughty and imperfect world, which too many later prime ministers – and presidents – ignored at their peril.

Throughout his premiership, Walpole faced the wrath of the satirists – the paparazzi of their day. His opponents Bolingbroke and Pulteney published *The Craftsman*, the first anti-government rag and a sort of *Private Eye* of the 1720s. He was compared with the unprincipled blackguard and 'thief taker' Jonathan Wild. Jonathan Swift ridiculed him as Flimnap in *Gulliver's Travels* and in John Gray's *The Beggar's Opera* (1728) he was another rogue – Mr Peacham.

Spencer Compton, Earl of Wilmington 1742–43

'The favourite nonentity of George II' was elected to parliament while out of the country, as a Tory who had defected to the Whigs. Chosen as Speaker of the Commons, despite, on his own admission, having 'neither the memory to retain, judgement to correct, nor skill to guide the debates'.

The 'dull, important Lord' was put forward as a rival to Walpole and became prime minister (briefly) after the great man's fall, but he achieved nothing in the few months of life he had left. Drink, it was said, killed him. Undoubtedly, Horace Walpole had his own agenda when he wrote of Compton's 'private debauches, his only pleasure money and eating, his only knowledge forms and precedents; his only insinuations bows and smiles'.

But he was probably right.

Henry Pelham 1743–54

Henry Pelham was feisty, nearly coming to blows with William Pulteney in the Commons and once taking on a mob threatening Walpole on his way in. Holding a sword to the throat of the nearest oaf, he asked, 'Now, gentlemen, which of you will be the first to fall?' His ministry was a continuation of Walpole's – 'only the name over the shop-front was altered'.

John Carteret, the Earl of Granville, said, 'He was only chief clerk to Sir Robert Walpole and why he should expect to be more under me, I can't imagine.' The king, however, thought he was a better economist than Walpole. The 1740s did not go well. The British Army was defeated at Fontenoy and half of Scotland rose to put the deeply stupid dilletante 'bonnie prince' Charles Stuart on the British throne. The Jacobite rebellion known as 'the '45' failed but Pelham resigned. As Carteret could not form a ministry, the king recalled him.

Spare a thought, though, for William Pulteney, 1st Earl of Bath. In what, in one sense, is the shortest premiership ever, he was summoned by the king on 10 February 1746. He could not form a ministry, however, as nobody in the house would support him. One contemporary wrote:

And thus ended the second and last part of this astonishing Administration which lasted 48 hours and 3 quarters, seven minutes and eleven seconds; which may truly be called the most honest of all administrations; the minister, to the astonishment of all wise men never transacted one rash thing; and, what is more marvellous, left as much money in the Treasury as he found in it.

Luck was, however, on Pelham's side. Deeply opposed by Frederick, Prince of Wales (carrying on the tradition of the Hanoverians' hatred of fathers and their ministers), the death of the prince, hit by a cricket ball, removed that particular problem.

Socially, Pelham was a keen gardener and gambler (his favourite bolthole was White's in St James's). He ate too much, as most gentlemen did and caught a fatal cold in the park in January 1754. Far more honest than Walpole (not a difficult hurdle), someone wrote that Pelham 'would never have wet his finger with corruption if Sir Robert Walpole had not dipped in it up to the elbow'. His 'broad-bottomed' coalition ministry was lampooned in the press in obscene drawings that showed a giant defecating with a huge backside facing the reader.

Thomas Pelham-Holles, Duke of Newcastle 1754–56; 1757–62

Spencer Compton, not known for his wit, nevertheless said of Newcastle, 'He always lost half an hour in the morning, which he was running after for the rest of the day without being able to overtake him.'

In a political situation which would be impossible today, Newcastle had 60–70 MPs beholden to him for their places. This was because Newcastle was richer than God. He was also fussy and over-emotional. On one occasion, seeing the Duke of Grafton ill in bed, he hugged him, weeping, with Grafton shouting at him to 'get away'. Horace Walpole's verdict – 'He was a Secretary of State without intelligence, a duke without money and a minister hated and despised by his master.' (I told you he was bitchy!) 'Ambition, fear and jealousy are his prevailing passions' was Lord Waldegrave's opinion, but he had to concede that, with all that, he hung on in there, holding the top job twice. Newcastle's speeches were ugly, his casual conversation rambling and he used bribery as widely as Walpole had. He was such a snob that he took his expensive gold-plated crockery with him whenever he went out to dine.

Newcastle also caused uproar by modernizing. In 1752, the calendar was changed, from the Julian to the Gregorian. Bearing in mind that most of Europe had done this in 1582, it was ridiculous of Britain not to have done the same, but when the Pelhams did it, people were outraged. 'Give us back our eleven days!' screamed an election campaign slogan in 1754. The whole thing was a Catholic plot and Newcastle was behind it, people believed. As a wag wrote at the time, 'In seventeen hundred and fifty-three, the style it was changed to Popery.'

By the time Henry Pelham died in 1760, the dynamics of politics was changing. Walpole's tenure was so long that most MPs expected the king's minister to come from the Commons, not the Lords. The Seven Years War (1756–63) erupted despite Newcastle's Walpolean instincts and did not go well. Throughout, one of the future – and truly great – prime ministers, William Pitt, was sniping at Newcastle as a failure.

Newcastle resigned and another nonentity, William Cavendish, was appointed by the king. That was a flop and Newcastle was soon back, but it was Pitt who directed most of the policy, leading to the *annus mirabilis* of 1759 and victory over the French in Canada, India and the West Indies.

Then, in 1760, the curse of the Hanoverians struck again. George III kicked Pitt and the Whigs out and brought in Lord Bute. Newcastle desperately tried to hang on to office but he eventually resigned in May 1762. When he died of a stroke in London six years later, he had spent £300,000 buying power and, in the end, had little to show for it. As one biographer said, 'An amused posterity has granted [Newcastle] a unique fame as the most curiously ridiculous being who ever took a leading part in public affairs.'

William Cavendish, 4th Duke of Devonshire 1756–57

He didn't really want the job, but William Cavendish was head of one of the old Whig families at a time when the Whigs were in the ascendancy. He was modest, honourable, trustworthy – all the things that make a prime minister instantly forgettable! George II persuaded him to take the post in place of the Newcastle/Pitt alliance, and Devonshire, shamefully, allowed Admiral Byng to be executed on the deck of his own flagship for alleged cowardice. As the cynical Voltaire said, the English execute an admiral now and again 'pour encourager les autres' (to encourage the others).

Bitterly unhappy in a post he couldn't handle, he accepted the job of Lord Chamberlain with gratitude. As Lord Waldegrave said, 'He lost no reputation, for great things had never been expected of him.'

John Stuart, 3rd Earl of Bute 1762–63

Frederick, Prince of Wales, said of Bute, 'A fine, showy man who would make an excellent ambassador in a court where there is no business.'

Women found him attractive, however; he had 'a fine leg' at a time when dancing was considered a vital accomplishment for a gentleman (and a prime minister!).

Bute was a royal crony and it was purely that that got him the top job. He loved dressing up and took part in plays and pantos at country houses. When George became king, Bute was told to amend Newcastle's 'king's speech' but the only change he made was to drop 'Englishman' and put 'Briton' instead. If this was a *very* early example of political correctness (Scotland had been part of Britain since 1707) it didn't go down very well.

The Earl of Shelburne said that Bute 'panted for the Treasury, having a notion that he and the King understood it'. Nobody wanted a Scot at Number 10 (there would be echoes of this down the years with Ramsay MacDonald, Tony Blair, Gordon Brown and several more) and Buckingham Palace became known as 'Holyrood House'. An army jackboot (a pun on his name) was burnt near his London house, along with a petticoat, hinting at an affair between him and the king's mother.

It was Bute's misfortune that his time in office coincided with the career of the most deadly satirist in history – where is he today? – John Wilkes. George III was guaranteed to go into one of his legendary tantrums whenever he heard the man's name and Wilkes, MP and general pain in the backside of the Establishment, published a weekly journal, *The North Briton* (the polite name for a Scot). Famously, the French royal mistress, Madame de Pompadour, asked Wilkes, 'How far does the liberty of the press extend in England?' to which the rabble-rouser replied, 'That, Madame, is what I am determined to find out.' The first edition of *The North Briton* in 1762 said, 'a free press is the terror of all bad ministers'.

Interestingly, many years later, when Wilkes had become Lord Mayor of London and was out of the limelight, an old woman saw him in the street and shouted his old war cry 'Wilkes and Liberty!' Wilkes told her not to be so stupid.

Bute's hand in bringing about the Peace of Paris, which ended the Seven Years War, was obvious and criticized by Wilkes and most Englishmen. France had been trounced (again!) and had been let off far too leniently. In public, the prime minister needed a gang of heavies to protect him – 'the scoundrels and ruffians that attend the Bear Gardens'. He resigned, after only four months in office, abandoned by the new king, and spent his last years on the Isle of Bute and a villa by the sea at Christchurch, Hampshire. To the giggling press, he was always 'Sir Pertinax MacSycophant'.

George Grenville 1763–65

The Whig families, the Temples, Pitts, Grenvilles and Lytteltons, were a sort of Whig mafia, in which family comes first and political ideals a very distant second. George Grenville was one of the most stupid of his family, long-winded as a speaker and embarrassingly tactless. As a young politician, he was one of the 'Boy Patriots' who took exception to Walpole's treaty-breaking which sullied the country's reputation. Horace Walpole hated him. 'Scarce any man ever wore in his face such outward and visible marks of the hollow, cruel and rotten heart within.' He sat as MP for a pocket borough in Buckinghamshire and held it for thirty years. He was tight-fisted, which appealed greatly to a political class not keen to spend money on the needy. He was also a bore – parliamentary bills were said to be his favourite reading material. As Bute's number two – although officially there was no deputy prime minister at the time – he naturally got the job when the North Briton fell.

George III was unimpressed. 'When Mr Grenville has wearied me for two hours, he looks at his watch to see if he may not tire me for an hour more.' It did not help that George was still consulting the 'exiled' Bute, which made Grenville's role untenable. Eventually, George fumed, 'I would rather see the devil in my closet than Mr Grenville.' He had said the same thing about Wilkes!

With hindsight (historically dangerous but used by today's media all the time) he was the prime minister who introduced the Stamp Act, a belated and bungled attempt to make the American colonists behave. Outed by the king after a cack-handed Regency bill drafted by Grenville, he died in Piccadilly in November 1770.

Charles Watson Wentworth, 2nd Marquis of Rockingham 1765–66; 1782

Was he the most pointless prime minister of the eighteenth century? Charles Rockingham certainly had all the credentials. On the Grand Tour, which any respectable young nobleman went on at the time, soaking up the Classical culture he had learned at Westminster School and St John's College Cambridge, 'some imprudent gallantries damaged an already weak constitution'. Since the Grand Tour was actually a glorified pub and brothel crawl, with a side order of sightseeing, we get the picture.

He loved gambling and horse racing, the sport not only of kings but the Wentworths too. He asked for – and was given – a KG in 1760 and had enough bottle to oppose Bute and even the king over the fiasco of the Peace of Paris, for which he was dismissed from all royal offices. 'I thought,' said George, 'I had not two men in my Bedchamber of less parts than he.' Even so, the Whigs were still in the ascendancy and the king reluctantly called on Rockingham (as he was now) to form a government. Horace Walpole could not leave it alone. 'A weak, childish, ignorant man, by no means fit for the head of administration.'

Clinging to old Whig beliefs, Rockingham tried to appease the American colonists by repealing the Stamp Act (too little, too late perhaps) and by not silencing Wilkes when he had the chance. As the anonymous pamphleteer 'Junius' wrote, the ministry had 'dissolved in its own weakness'. He was a poor, nervous speaker in the House and his sympathies lay increasingly with the Americans, which effectively marked him out as a traitor manqué.

After sixteen years, he was back, as useless in 1782 as he had been earlier. The vengeful and long-living Horace Walpole was still around to say, 'No man ever attained twice the great object of his wishes and enjoyed it both times for so short a session.'

William Pitt, Earl of Chatham

William Pitt was most people's idea of a nightmare. 'He had the eye of a hawk, a little head and a long acquisitive nose,' said a colleague. In today's history books, he is often referred to as 'Pitt the Elder', to distinguish him from his son, also William Pitt – 'the Younger'.

The elder Pitt, who was made Earl of Chatham during his political career, was a maverick. Dogged and sure he was right, he pursued a ferocious 'blue water' war against France, obliterating their opposition in India, Canada, North America and the West Indies. At the time, this not only created the British Empire 'on which the sun would never set', it marked him out as one of the greatest prime ministers in history. By a quirk of the unwritten constitution, however, he was never actually a prime minister at all, merely leader of the government.

As an orator, he was a genius, enthralling the Commons and later the Lords with his fiery speeches. On the other hand, he was difficult, argumentative and, by the standards of the time, honest. Today seen as a strength, that virtue alone made parliament suspicious of him. His grandfather 'acquired' (the details are hazy) a diamond the size of an egg in India. Today's 'wokerati' would howl with outrage at such 'cultural appropriation' but it was standard in the late seventeenth century. The eldest Pitt bought the stone for £25,000 (£3.5 million today) and sold it to the Duc d'Orleans for £135,000 some years later.

Chatham (as he was known) went to Eton, cradle of so many prime ministers, and hated it. He was a sickly child and was plagued by physical – and, increasingly, mental – problems throughout his life. He bought a commission in the King's Dragoon Guards (the extortionate prices were laid down in Queen Anne's reign) but mixed with politicians from the Whig persuasion who nevertheless hated Walpole.

At 27 he 'won' the seat of Old Sarum, the rottenest of the rotten boroughs and became leader of the 'Boy Patriots', the forerunner of many such groups in British and foreign parliaments who represented the new, up-and-coming generation who are always critical of their elders. Walpole quashed Pitt's military appointment, calling him 'this terrible Cornet of Horse' but he was immediately grabbed by the Prince of Wales as Groom of the Bedchamber in token opposition to his father.

For most of 1744, Chatham was taking the waters at Bath (a useless cure to which virtually the whole of the landed classes was addicted) suffering physically from gout (said to be caused by too much red wine) and mentally from wild mood swings which would undoubtedly have him diagnosed as bipolar today. Some people called him mad; his sister, Elizabeth, certainly was.

The Seven Years War with France began badly for Britain – losses in the Mediterranean, Canada and the West Indies. Still crippled with gout, Pitt's speeches in the Commons made him indispensable to George II, who hated him, and he was made Secretary of State in November 1756. Newcastle was prime minister, but the waging of the war was in Chatham's hands. 'I am sure that I can save this country and that no one else can' was his humble summing up of the situation.

It seemed he was right because 1759 was the *annus mirabilis*, the year of miracles, with the war with France completely reversed in terms of British successes. And, at the height of it all, with the monumental stupidity for which he would become famous, the new king, George III, came to the throne, fired Chatham and substituted him with the ineffectual Bute.

When Chatham came back, in 1766, he was sicker than ever. He was not actually First Lord of the Treasury (that was the Duke of Grafton) but Lord Privy Seal. Nevertheless, he was regarded as prime minister and the title was now fully established. Chatham's health was deteriorating fast and he resigned in 1768, haranguing Grafton, Lord

North and the king, over the increasingly cack-handed dispute with the American colonies. There was hypocrisy in all this, that the infant press of the time, and historians since, have missed. He described merchants of the East India Company, spreading their power over the sub-continent, as 'lofty Asiatic plunderers', even though his own grandfather had been one. He demanded parliamentary reform, even though he had sat as MP for the 'accursed hill' of Old Sarum. And his position in the American context was extraordinary: 'If I were an American [actually, in the early 1770s, there was no such thing] as I am an Englishman, while a foreign troop landed in my country, I would never lay down my arms – never, never, never!' When the rabble-rouser Tom Paine was writing the same thing, a few months later, he was declared a traitor with a price on his head. When Chatham softened all this by saying that independence of the colonies was not the answer, his bipolarism (or madness in eighteenth-century speak) became obvious.

Chatham increasingly lived alone, despite an adoring and adored wife and three children, in a small house in Hampstead. His doctor dosed him with port and madeira and told him that exercise was bad for him. He made speeches in the Lords, each more rambling and incoherent than the last, which appalled those who remembered his greatness and merely confirmed to others that he had been mad all along. He collapsed in the chamber, but clung on to life for another month. Bizarrely, there are still House rules covering this – no member of parliament is allowed to die on the premises.

George III was unimpressed. When the Lords voted to attend Chatham's funeral en masse, he wrote, 'I am surprised at the vote of a public funeral and monument, an offensive measure to me personally.' The royals had not forgiven Chatham for his hatred of the house of Hanover.

Chapter 5

The Prime Ministers Who Lost America

Augustus Henry Fitzroy, 3rd Duke of Grafton 1768–70

Grafton had a dubious pedigree. The surname Fitzroy means illegitimate son of the king. This particular Fitzroy was the great-great-grandson of Charles II and his mistress Barbara Cleveland.

He was hit by the satirist 'Junius', probably Sir Philip Francis, in a series of anti-government letters. Junius cut to the chase: 'Charles the First lived and died a hypocrite. Charles the Second was a hypocrite of another sort and should have died on the same scaffold. At the distance of a century, we see their different characters happily revived and blended in Your Grace.'

The young Grafton attended Westminster School, was given a Cambridge degree (his right as a member of the nobility) and became MP for Bury St Edmunds and Lord of the Bedchamber to the Prince of Wales. In 1757, at the age of 22, he inherited his father's duchy. His hobbies, which took up most of his time, were hunting and racing. So far, so stereotypical.

By the age of 30, and for no discernible reason, he was appointed Secretary of State by Rockingham and resigned a few months later. The press had a field day. There is no doubt that the success of *The North Briton* unleashed a torrent of abuse from what would become in the next century Fleet Street, the hub of the newspaper business. The papers accused Grafton of 'a love of ease and indulgence to his private amusements', claiming that actual politics got in the way of all that.

When Chatham came to office, Grafton became First Lord of the Treasury, simply because George III could not bear to give Chatham the top job. Almost immediately, this eminently unsuitable and inexperienced young man got into trouble. Lord Townshend proposed a tax on tea for the American colonists and, while Grafton opposed it, he did not have the gravitas to overturn the situation.

The point about 'Junius' is that, unlike most of today's media, he was a man on the inside, who knew where 'the bodies were buried'. Grafton's first wife, Anne, was expecting a child by her lover, the Earl of Upper Ossary and all London knew about it. In the meantime, he was knocking off Nancy Parsons, a tailor's daughter, herself the ex-mistress of a slave trader called Horton. In the scurrilous, underground but nonetheless burgeoning press, she was 'The Duke of Grafton's Mrs Horton, the Duke of Dorset's Mrs Horton, everybody's Mrs Horton'.

Even his hunting was held against him. George III (who was often in the saddle himself) wrote, 'Pretty occupations for a man of quality, to be spending all his time tormenting a poor fox that is generally a much better beast than any of those that pursue him.' Horace Walpole, who would have been perfectly at home in a Fleet Street job, wrote that Grafton thought 'the world should be postponed to a whore and a horse race'. Chatham refused to talk to him face to face; Grafton, in his words, was 'unequal to the government of a great nation'.

Frederick, Lord North 1770–82

North is usually credited as the 'prime minister who lost America', just as George III is the king who lost it. In office, North was seriously overweight and he would loll on the Lords' front benches, pretending to be asleep during opposition speeches. His education was Eton, Oxford (where he was a noted linguist) followed by the de rigueur Grand Tour. After Grafton, his home life – one wife, seven children – was disappointingly dull for the scandalmongers. There were, however, rumours that the man was a royal bastard – in various portraits he could certainly pass for George III.

As a personal friend of the king, he felt duty bound to accept George's offer to make him prime minister. There were grumbles when he was

KG and the king paid off his debts (unthinkable today?). When North was apparently dozing complacently in the Commons, the MP on his feet shouted, 'Even now, in the midst of these perils [imminent war with the colonies] the noble lord is asleep!'

North opened one eye. 'I wish to God I was!'

Like Grafton, he knew he wasn't up to the job and repeatedly asked the king to let him go, but George was stubborn to the point of imbecility and would not cave in. He presided over a series of attempts to force the colonists to pay their way (something no predecessor had tried to do) and then to offer sweeteners when they complained. Once the 'shot heard round the world' was fired at Lexington, North consistently underestimated the colonists' determination and fighting abilities. Not a military man himself, he did not understand strategy and never sent enough men or spent enough money. The upshot was the eventual surrender of Cornwallis at Yorktown in 1781.

Most Britons saw the colonists as tax-dodgers, but some, from Chatham to Tom Paine, believed the highfalutin hokum of the Declaration of Independence that the king – and, by association, his prime minister – were tyrants, despots and agents of the devil. In the years ahead, Americans would forget that France, the Low Countries, Spain, Prussia, Russia and Scandinavia were all out for British blood. Cornwallis surrendered at Yorktown because he had let Washington outmanoeuvre him on land, but also because a French fleet had closed off the sea. Without that, he could have withdrawn to fight another day.

North was concerned to do the king's bidding and to save money at the same time. The only halfway competent general in America, 'Gentleman Johnny' Burgoyne, complained, quite rightly, that he had insufficient everything except powder and shot. The Earl of Sandwich, in charge of the navy, was not only cheese-paring in terms of shipbuilding, he was hardly ever there at the Admiralty, preferring to spend his time with naughty goings-on at the Hellfire Club, as, incidentally, did his enemy, the founding father Benjamin Franklin.

George III finally let North go in 1782. 'Remember,' he told the minister, 'it is you who desert me, not I you.' The American failure led to a constitutional crisis. North, claiming there was no room for the 'animal called a Prime Minister', got a golden handshake of £4,000 a year. He stayed in politics, attacking his successor, Shelburne, and being accused of treachery by George III, by now well on his way to a full-blown mental breakdown. North died of dropsy (oedema caused by various conditions) in 1792, aged 60.

William Petty Fitzmaurice, 2nd Earl of Shelburne 1782–83

Shelburne was an outsider. He was an Irishman, born in Dublin and was described by a courtier as 'facetious, a foreigner and a Jesuit'. All this counted against him in a country that was staunchly Protestant and thought of itself as the land of John Bull, the true-blue Englishman.

On the other hand, he was seriously rich, owning huge estates in Kerry and served with distinction at the Battle of Minden. He was handsome, a colonel and ADC to the king by the time he took his seat in the Lords. George III hated him (as he hated many people) calling him 'the Jesuit of Berkeley Square'. After years of the vicious Holy Inquisition, the Jesuits had been thoroughly discredited and were actively kicked out of several European courts and capitals.

One of several men (other than the king) whom Shelburne had upset by his Machiavellian skulduggery was Lieutenant Colonel William Fullerton, who accused the Irishman of consorting with the enemy (the American colonists). The pair fought a duel (technically illegal) and a ricochet hit Shelburne in the groin – 'I don't think Lady Shelburne will be any the worse for it.' The scandal raged for weeks, the press claiming that Fullerton was a government agent and should have been charged with attempted murder.

Shelburne was brought in after North's resignation, but he still hoped to prevent American independence by creating a voluntary association. If this sensible policy had been adopted, say in 1770, there might have been no War of Independence at all. Now, it was too late and many people regarded Shelburne as a potential traitor. Edmund Burke, a boring speaker in the Commons (he was known as 'the dinner gong' because as soon as he stood up, the gong sounded and everybody trooped out) called him 'a Borgia, a Catiline and a serpent with two heads'. Everybody had a Classical education in the House in those days and understood what he was talking about.

Shelburne's peace treaty with the colonies was rejected by the Commons as being too humiliating. The king did not back him either and he resigned. His liberal ideas and grasp of economics (he was a friend of Adam Smith, the 'father of economics') would have made him a good, perhaps even a great, nineteenth-century statesman, but the eighteenth only saw him as a snake-oil salesman.

William Cavendish-Bentinck, 3rd Duke of Portland 1783

Portland served twice as prime minister, first as a Whig, then as a Tory, which perhaps says it all about his integrity. Like most residents of Number 10 in the early days, he was obscenely rich, once spending £30,000 on an election in Carlisle (he carried the money, in coin and notes, in his coach). But a fairly clever marriage and his mother's inheritance made him solvent again and he bought the 'Portland' vase for £1,000. Most noblemen had large collections of antiquities in their town and country houses; Portland was no exception.

George III detested the Whigs and Portland in particular and his choice of minister either speaks volumes for the king's often incomprehensible behaviour or the lack of quality among the Lords and Commons. They clashed over the amount of the allowance to be given to George's eldest son, the Prince of Wales. The king could not stand him either and there were screaming rows between George and Portland until the prime minister agreed to half the amount he had suggested. He was defeated over a minor India Bill and George III breathed a sigh of relief.

Chapter 6

The President

They couldn't decide what to call him. Should it be George IV? Your Most Benign Highness? His Majesty the President? Clearly, for an executive leading a federal republic, it could be none of these. In the end, George Washington was just plain 'Mr President' and all his successors have followed suit.

'Across the pond', what the Americans call the Atlantic, of course, they did things differently. By the time the term Prime Minister was in use in Britain, the two European countries vying for control of North America were Britain and France (the Dutch dropped out earlier).

Until the 1770s, the thirteen British colonies in North America had the same king as the rest of the rapidly expanding empire. The problem was that the colonists themselves were a motley collection of runaways, fugitives, religious misfits and slaves. They were in it for what they could get and felt no allegiance to a king or country 3,000 miles and several weeks' sailing time away. The big mistake of the British government was to appoint a series of governors and effectively let the colonies run themselves (see Walpole).

Because the British were fighting the French during this period – and when weren't they? – colonists became used to 'Redcoats' marching all over their farms and hunkering down in their homes under the billeting system *and* they were expected to pay for it. One of the many rallying cries of the infant revolutionaries was 'No taxation without representation', conveniently ignoring the fact that 95 per cent of Britons were in exactly the same boat. Only a handful of Englishmen were wealthy enough to be represented (the Commons in the 1760s was 400 strong) yet everybody paid taxes.

Arrogance by George III and his ministers (several of whom we have met in the course of this book) and intransigence and greed on the part of the 'founding fathers' (we'll meet some of them too) led to open warfare at Concord and Lexington – 'the shot heard round the world'. Military incompetence on the part of the British, as well as an awful lot of help for the colonists, from France, Holland and other European powers, meant that the War of Independence (1775–83) was an American victory.

And amidst all the waving of the new flag, the Stars and Stripes, and the parties and euphoria, the ex-colonists had some hard decisions to make. The thirteen colonies had fused into one (*e pluribus unum* – out of the many, one, as the United States motto said) for long enough to defeat the British, but the old animosities and resentments remained. Out of this came the first bad decision. America would be a *federal* nation, united under God but with a separatism among its thirteen (now fifty) states that has never gone away. That might work tolerably well for a small country like Switzerland, with its semi-independent cantons, but as America grew, state rights versus federal would lead to the Civil War (1861–5).

Another problem was the law. Clearly, civilization cannot survive, and certainly cannot thrive, without a legal system. The founding fathers had a blank slate. They could create whatever system they liked, but they were inevitably men of their time. The Britain from which many of them had originated had a bicameral (two chamber) system, so the Americans followed suit. Because the Roman system of government and justice was so admired by the classically trained founding fathers, one of those houses was called the Senate. And the American constitution, unlike the hated British version, would be written down from day one. What nobody seems to have taken into account was the ever-changing nature of history. To quote today's T-shirt philosophers, 'shit happens', and the Constitution had to reflect that fact. The only solution was to add amendments to the Constitution, creating a clunky, unworkable document to which Americans still cling in desperation, arguing incessantly over what the founding fathers actually meant.

The biggest problem of all, however, was leadership. Just as the founding fathers had only experienced a bicameral system, so they had only experienced kingship, albeit a constitutional type. The problem was that mad, bad King George was their *bête noire*, directly responsible for all the ills that the colonies had faced. The obvious thing was to choose an American king and the obvious choice was their most successful general, George Washington. *That* of course would have meant another King George and the idea was too much for most people to stomach, Washington included. The solution was to emulate the Greeks and to elect their leader on a rotational basis. The susceptibilities of the time meant that this could never be a woman (females in the new country had no more rights than their British counterparts) but among men, the field was wide open. And this leader would not be a king or a prime minister in the British tradition, despite the fact that Gouvernour Morris, one of the framers of the American Constitution, wrote, 'Our President will be the British [prime] Minister.' The leader of the new nation would adopt a title that no one in Britain had ever used – 'Ladies and Gentlemen, the President of the United States' – to the accompaniment of dreadful music.

Leaders of democracies are hedged round with checks and balances within their own governmental structures – and if they fail, the ladies and gentlemen of the press (the Fourth Estate – see Chapter 2) keep an eagle eye on their behaviour. Constitutional irregularities will raise a mild 'tut tut' in the media; financial or sexual misconduct will unleash an avalanche of confected outrage and abuse. Today, prime minister wannabe, Keir Starmer, cannot define the word 'woman' (which is odd in a former Attorney General and party leader) but that is as nothing to Boris Johnson who once visited a garden party at the height of COVID. President Joe Biden seems confused over names, places, dates, and this is regarded in the same category as Donald Trump, who walked off with boxes of classified documents to which he had no right when he left the White House.

The world's press is notoriously selective and partisan in what it chooses to condemn in the behaviour of the leaders of the free world. We shall come across umpteen examples of this in the pages to follow.

Chapter 7

The White House

Abigail Adams didn't like it. The wife of the second president, John Adams, she wrote to her daughter about the problems with the house in Washington in 1800. She was the first FLOTUS to occupy it, found it too big, with no bells to ring for servants and it was still largely a building site. She wrote, 'You must keep this to yourself and when asked how I like it, say that I write you the situation is beautiful, which is true.'[1]

If the United States was to be taken seriously as a new country on the world stage, rather than a ragtag of ex-colonial misfits, it would need not only a leader but premises grand enough to command respect.

The leader was George Washington and unlike British prime ministers, he was at once the head of state and commander-in-chief of the armed forces. He was in fact a king without a crown and the role of president would morph over time into that of the 'leader of the free world'. Where could such a man live?

Washington had two houses in New York and at first, in the late 1780s, the founding fathers proposed that New York, part of which had been bought from the Indians for $24-worth of trinkets by the Puritans of New England over a century earlier, should be the new nation's capital. So Washington lived in Samuel Osgood House, Manhattan, between April 1789 and February 1790. That spring and summer he moved into the Alexander Macomb House nearby.

Then it was decided to move the government to Philadelphia with its Revolutionary associations, Liberty Bell etc., so Washington's final residence was the President's House in that town. When John Adams became president, he moved in here. The second move, to a flat, swampy, mosquito-infested piece of land in the former colony of Maryland, makes little sense, but it was Congress's wish under the Resident Act of 1791 and the elaborate plans drawn up by French architect Major Pierre L'Enfant looked impressive. The District of Columbia (named vaguely after Christopher Columbus, the fifteenth-century explorer) was 10 miles square and is still the alternative name for Washington (named after the first president). Confusingly, of course, the same name was used for the state in the north-west which was admitted to the union in 1889; hence 'DC' to avoid confusion.

When they got there, nobody liked it. L'Enfant himself called it 'a mere contemptible hamlet'. The Treasury Secretary Oliver Wolcott wrote, 'The people are poor and, as far as I can judge, they live like fishes by eating each other.' Even in the 1860s when DC was well established and its principal buildings either complete or under construction, the novelist Anthony Trollope called it 'the empire of King Mud'. The districts of the District of Columbia had unenviable names like Swampoodle and Foggy Bottom. It was a malaria deathtrap.

Nevertheless, Congress and George Washington persevered. American know-how (by definition imported from Europe) would conquer all. The design of the president's mansion at the end of Pennsylvania Avenue was thrown open to a national competition which was won by Irishman James Hobson, who later designed the Capitol building down the road. It was based on designs of grand houses in Dublin which were themselves an amalgam of the genius of the Roman architect Vetruvius and the Renaissance Venetian Andrea Palladio.

Construction began on 13 October 1792, much of the work carried out by immigrants not yet citizens and black labour, slave and free. The project took eight years to complete and cost $232,371.83 (almost $300 million today). Its sandstone walls were whitewashed with lime, casein, lead and rice glue which gave the place its iconic name. It had porticoes, bays and bows in the Neoclassical style and was called the president's palace or mansion. It was not until 1811 that the term White House was first used and only in 1901, under Teddy Roosevelt, did that become the official name under Executive Order. On 2 November 1800, John

Adams wrote to his wife Abigail, 'I pray Heaven to bestow the best of blessings on this House and all that shall hereafter inhabit it. May none but honest and wise men ever rule under this roof.' Rather like a similar sentiment expressed at the British prime minister's retreat at Chequers, this was rather a pious hope! Adams' words were carved into the lintel of the State Dining Room under Franklin Roosevelt in the 1930s.

When Thomas Jefferson moved in, he said that it was 'big enough for two emperors, one pope and the grand lama [presumably the Tibetan holy man the Dalai Lama] in the bargain.' Despite this implied criticism, Jefferson considerably extended the place, adding east and west wings to disguise stables and outbuildings.

That was almost the end of the White House because in 1814 most of it was burned down by a British Army under General Robert Ross. The American militia were caught napping in the war of 1812 and President James Madison ran, leaving his wife Dolly to save the original Declaration of Independence. The Marines under John Barney held fast, but British opposition was too strong and soon the whole town of 8,000 inhabitants was ablaze. The attack was in retaliation for American assaults on Toronto, then confusingly called York, weeks earlier.

Rebuilding of the White House took two years, but there were no structural changes. The photograph of 1846, during the Polk presidency, is the first one taken and shows the building as it would have been thirty years earlier.

The Civil War threw Washington into the public spotlight more than at any time in its history. Rather like London in the 1940s, the capital was virtually in the front line; the Confederate Army was camped in Virginia, just across the Potomac and sometimes within shelling range. In the Blitz of the Second World War, London had its nightly air raids, its anti-shatter tape over windows, sandbags, searchlights, barrage balloons and anti-aircraft guns. In the Civil War, Washington looked like an army camp, with tents and cavalry lines, cattle and sheep waiting to be slaughtered to feed the troops. The White House was in danger of subsiding into the swamp and there was talk of demolition.

Faint hearts held out, however, and in 1881, Chester Arthur began a series of refurbishments as soon as Lucretia Garfield moved out, still mourning her assassinated husband. More than twenty wagonloads of furniture and effects went with her, to be sold at public auction which, in effect, paid for Arthur's rebuilding. All that remained from earlier days were busts of John Adams and Martin van Buren. The Red Room's ceiling was gorgeously painted with the Stars and Stripes and a huge glass screen by Tiffany installed. Ten years later, William Harrison's First Lady, Caroline, tried to set up an art gallery but Congress objected and the project was shelved. Much of the 'Victorian' furniture was removed by the modernizing Teddy Roosevelt to give more space for his large family, but it was the even larger William Taft who had the famous Oval Office built by extending the West Wing. In 1925, Congress allowed gifts of furniture to be given to the White House for the first time.

After a fire on Christmas Eve 1929, adding to the disasters of that year, two months after the Wall Street Crash that plunged the West into a crippling recession, Herbert Hoover had to move out for repairs to be carried out. Under FDR and because of his polio, the White House became 'wheelchair friendly' for the first time and the Oval Office was moved to its current location alongside the Rose Garden.

By the late 1940s, poor maintenance had led to the building's increasingly decrepit condition. The house's original wooden frame was rotting and Harry Truman had the whole thing replaced with steel. For nearly three years he lived in Blair House elsewhere in the capital and added air-conditioning in a city notorious for its fierce summer heat. With a certain irony, as the president who unleashed atomic bombs on the world (against the Japanese in 1945), Truman had a bomb shelter added to a house that was far outside the range of any missile then in existence.

The most detailed refurbishment took place under Jacqueline (Jackie) Kennedy during her husband's brief incumbency. First Ladies had always worn the trousers in respect of household management, but Jackie was steeped in history and fine art. She bought back a number of items previously sold by presidents' families and staff and had all the state rooms redecorated in historical styles. The only period *not* covered, inevitably, was anything to do with the British Empire! Wallpaper was rescued from a grocery store in the City – it had been there since 1934. The first White House guide book came out in 1962 and American television broadcast a tour of the house. With the glamorous young president, his lovely wife and their children, this was the fairy-tale Camelot. What could possibly go wrong?

There were no structural changes after the $5.7 million outlay under Truman, and in September 1961 the White House was officially designated a museum by Congress. No objects from the complex could be sold and when not required were stored in the Smithsonian Institute down the road. Successive presidents could refurbish the private apartments to the First Ladies' hearts' content, but any change to the public rooms had to be ratified by Congress, who were, after all, picking up the bill.

In the early 1970s, Pat Nixon refurbished the Red, Green and Blue Rooms and added over 600 items to the house's décor. Nixon had a bowling alley set up in the basement and a state-of-the-art pressroom built over FDR's old swimming pool. There was a certain irony in this; it was, after all, the journalists of the *Washington Post* who exposed Nixon's Watergate shenanigans.

Jimmy Carter and Ronald Reagan set up and extended the computer and laser-printer capabilities of the place but Reagan did not like solar heating; that would have to wait until 2003 – and not until the Obama administration were roof panels installed.

Various scares in recent years, especially aircraft landing uninvited on the South Lawn, have led to greater security. A section of Pennsylvania Avenue that runs along the edge of the grounds, is now permanently closed to traffic, much to protestors' annoyance. As in London's Downing Street, there is a more or less permanent stream of such protestors wandering beyond the White House railings, ranting pointlessly.

The White House is the most photographed building in America, perhaps the world. And the man who lives there is the hope of millions, not just in the United States themselves. A difficult line has to be drawn, therefore, between the president's availability and his safety. 'Open house' was the norm in the early nineteenth century, with one notoriously drunken party at Andrew Jackson's inauguration in 1829. The 'open houses' did not come to an end until the 1930s, but Bill and Hillary Clinton threw the house open for New Year celebrations to see in the new millennium.

Today, with its elegant facades, sumptuous grounds, tennis courts, movie theatre, jogging track, putting green and five full-time chefs, it handles 30,000 visitors a week, all gawping at the home of the most powerful man in the world. Unlike Downing Street, the White House has had its own fictional television series, *The West Wing* (1999–2006)

It isn't quite like that at Camp David …

The president's country retreat lies in the Catoctin Mountains in Frederick County, Maryland, some 62 miles from Washington DC. Technically, it is a military installation and is run by a team composed of the Seabees, the US Navy and Marines and the Civil Engineering Corps. It was built between 1935 and 1938 but in 1942, perhaps to escape the pressures of war, FDR converted it into a presidential retreat called Shangri-la. It was renamed Camp David by Dwight Eisenhower in 1953, in honour of his father and grandfather.

When the president is not there, family and staff enjoy the chalet-style apartments or play golf and pony trek in the mountains. Lyndon Johnson hosted several state occasions there and Richard Nixon was a frequent visitor. It is Ronald Reagan who holds the record for the most attendances, riding in the woods whenever time allowed. George Bush's daughter was married at Camp David in 1992 and after the attack on the Twin Towers in New York on 9/11, George W. Bush used the place as a safe base for cabinet meetings.

Most of the presidents for the past half century have also had 'summer' and 'winter' White Houses which are used for formal government business from time to time. When he left office in January 1989, outgoing president Ronald Reagan cited the seventeenth-century pilgrim John Winthrop who saw his new colony of New England 'like a City upon a Hill'. Reagan saw the whole United States in the same way (albeit ignoring Winthrop's religious mania, bigotry and racism). 'And how stands the city on this winter night?' Reagan asked as he stood in the Oval Office with the flags furled behind him. 'After 200 years, two centuries, she still stands strong and true on the granite ridge and her glow has held steady no matter what storm.'

He might have been thinking, too, of the White House itself.

Chapter 8

The Fathers Who Founded

George Washington 1787–97

It is important to realize that George Washington and his immediate successors were, as far as the British were concerned, traitors. No international court, given the *realpolitik* of the time, would have supported what the Americans did. And the fact that there were, in Britain, a handful of voices who spoke for them, does not make 1776 any less illegal. All in all, it wasn't a very good start.

Washington has come down to us in a halo of sanctity. He was the iconic first president and in the eyes of many Americans over time, could do no wrong. He established a pattern of ceremony: a four-year term of office (eight if there appears to be a demand); an inaugural address delivered in the open air rather than in a chamber; universal observation of Thanksgiving; selection of the nation's capital site and so on. Even the famous 'Stars and Stripes' flag is based partly on the Washington family coat of arms. Most of the gush came from Mason Weems, a dewy-eyed cleric who wrote what accounts to hagiography a year after Washington's death in 1799. In that book, young George chops down a cherry tree and, consumed by guilt, has to confess his wrongdoing to his father. To Weems – and millions of Americans – Washington was the man who could not tell a lie. If that was true (which it wasn't) then the behaviour of later presidents has been downhill all the way.

In 1774, when Washington was a junior officer in what was still (just) the British Army, he wrote to a comrade, 'I think I can announce it as a fact, that it is not the wish or interest of that government [the Congress in Philadelphia] ... to set up for independency. I am as well satisfied as

I can be of my existence that no such thing is desired by any thinking man in all North America.'

Within months, colonial minutemen opened fire on British troops at Lexington and Concorde. The following year, the founding fathers drew up the Declaration of Independence and this was followed by the writing of the Constitution and the decision to inaugurate Washington as president. In fact, Washington changed tack several times, both before and during his presidency, which hardly justifies his sainthood. Early on, he had a positive attitude to American Indians (both sides employed them as scouts in the War of Independence) but by the 1790s, he called them 'animals of prey'.

Washington's attitude to slavery, though moderate by the standards of the time, topples him today from any pedestal. American school textbooks without number don't mention that the man owned slaves on his Mount Vernon estates at all, but he did and hunted down runaways as vehemently as any other plantation owner further south. Historian Mark Lloyd wrote, 'When I first learned that Washington ... owned slaves, I was devastated. I didn't want to have anything more to do with [him].' We should be wary of imposing twentieth-century attitudes on the past – but there were loud voices clamouring for an end to slavery even in Washington's day. He did at least set free his slaves in his will (the old Roman right of manumission) which none of the other slave-owning founding fathers did.

In a single paragraph, politician Mitchell Reiss demolishes Washington before going on to sing his praises: 'He was a former British military officer who rebelled against his sovereign.' This, as we have said, was the case for all those (about a third of the colonists) who took arms against the British. He could have been hanged for that alone. He was 'a revolutionary general who lost most of his battles'. An analysis of the War of Independence shows a preponderance of British victories and American defeats. It was ineptitude by the British generals and the combined might of the Colonists' allies in Europe that led to Yorktown. 'He was the only president elected unanimously (twice) but without any impassioned speeches, memorable writings or original political philosophy to his credit; a man with virtually no formal education ... an enigmatic paternal figure who had no offspring and whose lasting memorial is a spare, pale obelisk.'[1]

Reiss is wrong, however, when he claims that Washington had been impressed by Indian guerrilla warfare and imported that to his ragtag 'Army of the Continent'. On the contrary, the general imported a Prussian staff officer, Friedrich von Steuben, to try to teach the colonists how to fight in the European way; the project failed, which is why Washington avoided pitched battles with the British at any cost.

For all the heroism attributed to Washington during the war (and it was solely on this that his election as president rested) he was often unnecessarily gloomy. Days before he crossed the Delaware to trounce the Hessian Army on the far bank, he wrote, 'the game is pretty near up.' Less than six months before Cornwallis' surrender at Yorktown, he wrote, 'we are at the end of our tether.'

As president, he advocated avoidance of the outside world, regarding the United States as a pariah shunned by everybody. He created, although he denied doing so, an executive power every bit as arbitrary as that of the king (George III) he overthrew. Congress could advise, but policy lay in the hands of the president. And it could be argued that since the president was commander-in-chief of the armed forces, he wielded even more power than the British king, controlled as he was by a parliament that held the purse strings. In Washington's day perhaps this hardly mattered. In 1797, the United States Army was 840 strong; there was no navy. Later, as we shall see, that would change.

Worn out during his second term (the one he said he would never accept) Washington became the crabby old man with the bad wig we see on the one-dollar bill. His face was ravaged by smallpox and his dentures (made by Paul Revere) didn't fit. He only had one of his own teeth left. Under the glare of today's media spotlight, he wouldn't get elected to a parish council.

The infant American press accused him of being unable to control his cabinet, especially feisty Congressmen like John Adams, Thomas Jefferson and Alexander Hamilton. They also accused him of cosying up to the French, probably in gratitude for their help against the British during the war.

Let's let Tom Paine have the last word. As we have seen, Paine was a revolutionary Englishman who supported the Americans in their own revolution and risked his life for it. But by 1796, he wrote:

> As to you, Sir [Washington] treacherous in private friendship (for so you have been to me, and that in a day of danger) and a hypocrite in public life, the world will be puzzled to decide whether you are an apostate or an imposter ... Elevated to the chair of the Presidency, you assumed the merit of everything to yourself, and the natural ingratitude of your constitution began to appear.

John Adams 1797–1801

John Adams, who did so much to create the new United States, was born of the rigid Puritan stock of New England. In a speech he made after his retirement from the White House in 1802, he spoke glowingly of the Mayflower Compact, seen by some as a forerunner of the Declaration of Independence. He ignored the fact that the Compact was a spurious attempt to legitimize minority rule by alien white men. In a sense, so was the Declaration of Independence.

Some of what Adams stood for would be unacceptable today. He once boasted, 'My family, I believe, have cut down more trees in America than any other name.' He was referring to the taming of the wilderness which would make today's Greens howl in horror. He also brought in the Sedition Act, which made it illegal to criticize, by word or deed, the president and his administration.

On the other hand, he was the only member of the founding fathers not to own slaves and he had his Puritan origins to thank for that. He was also something of a snob. Because of his huge girth, he was known as 'His Rotundity' but this also accorded with his view that the president was essentially a king without a crown and should be treated accordingly.

There are, as always, two sides to a man like Adams. People loved him or hated him. And George Washington was a hard act to follow. As writer Daniel Forrester says, he could be 'combative, crusty, despised, bitter, tactless, a blowhard, condescending and egotistical'.[2] Despite all those things, he served as a diplomat for the infant American government and helped frame the Constitution. His vice president, Thomas Jefferson (see below), didn't like him and didn't much care who knew it:

> [Adams] is vain, irritable, and a bad calculator of the force ...
> of the motives which govern man ... He is as disinterested as
> the being which made him; he is profound in his views; and
> accurate in his judgement except when knowledge of the world
> is necessary to form a judgement.

Even a friend, fellow founding father Benjamin Franklin, wrote, '[Adams] means well for his Country, is always an honest man, often a wise one, but sometimes, and in some things, absolutely out of his senses.'

Alexander Hamilton went further:

> [Adams] does not possess the talents adapted to the
> administration of government and ... there are great and
> intrinsic defects in his character which unfit him for the
> office of chief magistrate ... He is often liable to paroxysms of
> anger, which deprive him of self-command and produce very
> outrageous behaviour to those who approach him.

He died, appropriately, on 4 July (Independence Day) 1826. How did he arrange that?

Thomas Jefferson 1801–09

Today, Thomas Jefferson stands high in the hall of American heroes, largely because of his fine words in the 1776 Declaration of Independence: 'We hold these truths to be self-evident, that all men are created equal etc.' This ignores the fact that the Declaration itself was a pseudo-legal smokescreen to disguise the reality that the War of Independence was a sordid squabble over trade. It also ignores the fact that most of it was pinched from Frenchmen Montesquieu and Rousseau and an Englishman, John Locke. And, of course, Jefferson did not actually mean 'all men' – he was not referring to Indians or to black slaves, sixty-six of whom he owned.

In his *Notes on Virginia* in 1785, Jefferson wrote, 'I advance it, therefore, as a suspicion only, that the blacks … are inferior to the whites in the endowments both of mind and body.' That didn't stop him fathering at least six children by the slave Sally Hemmings, according to DNA tests carried out in 1998.

He was not fond of female emancipation either. In response to a question in 1807, he said, 'The appointment of a woman to office is an innovation for which the public is not prepared; nor am I.'

Jefferson lived in an age when the party system was developing in the United States – the Federalists versus the Democrat-Republicans (confusingly to anybody outside that country). John Adams wasn't impressed by Jefferson's stance on it at all:

> It is with much reluctance that I am obliged to look upon [Jefferson] as a man whose mind is warped by prejudice and so blinded by ignorance as to be unfit for the office he holds. However wise and scientific as philosopher, as a politician he is a child and dupe of party.

Jefferson was not a public speaker like Adams and shied away from confrontation, preferring to write his polemics rather than face opposition in person. Brought up in the near-aristocratic atmosphere of the Virginian plantations and swanning through Williamsburg College, he had a sense of entitlement which only *some* later presidents had. When he was governor of Virginia in 1779, he ran in the face of an advancing British Army and left the colony leaderless for eight days.

Before his presidency and during it, Jefferson had a quiet and rather old-fashioned view of society. He had studied the Robinocracy in Britain and detested Walpole's espousal of business, banks and industry. Ironically, as leader of what would become the world's most industrially successful country, he wanted America to be an agricultural paradise with a rural population. This is not too surprising – the new nation was a wilderness at the time without the infrastructure to support industry.

At a time when God was still the be-all and end-all of the West, Jefferson veered towards atheism. His worship of Reason wasn't for everybody and landed the French Revolutionary Jacobins in all sorts of problems in the 1790s. And there was very little Reason in Jefferson's own Virginia, where paper money barely existed, coins were unusual and most trade took place via a Medieval bartering system. Even taxes were paid in tobacco. Forward-looking and Thomas Jefferson did not go hand in hand. As a philosopher he was inconsistent and blew with the wind.

Some writers have tried to praise Jefferson's legacy. Politician Alan S. Felzenberg claims that he founded the Democratic Party, 'the oldest continuous political party in the world', which ignores entirely a little thing called the Tory Party in Britain, which predates Jefferson's birth by seventy years. His casual protocol, letting guests sit where they liked at his dining table, greeting ambassadors in his slippers, shaking hands, is unremarkable today, but in the early nineteenth century, polite American society and the whole of Europe was appalled by it.

John Randolph of Roanoke wrote of Jefferson, 'I cannot live in this miserable, undone country where ... we are governed by the old red breeches of that prince of projectors, St Thomas of Cantingbury and surely, Becket himself never had more pilgrims at his shrine that the saint of Monticello.' We call such pilgrims today tourists and they are flocking to Jefferson's country house still.

James Madison Jnr 1809–17

Just as most British prime ministers had a background of public school (that's private in the US) and Oxbridge, many founding fathers and early presidents were raised on plantations and were baptized into the Church of England. Madison was shy and, at 5ft 4in, the shortest occupant of the White House. When he married Dolly Payne Todd, she wore the trousers and bossed everybody around, especially her husband. On his way to the presidency, Madison helped Adams bring in the Embargo Act. Designed to hit warring Britain and France with sanctions, it barely affected either nation but rebounded on New England merchants. As president, he fell for Napoleon's promise (rather like Hitler's to Chamberlain in the next century) to abandon the policy of pressing American sailors into naval service. Like Hitler, Napoleon lied.

Madison did not cause the war with Britain in 1812, but he let himself be bullied into it by the hawks in his cabinet and Congress. The American Navy had five ships (Britain's was the largest navy in the world with over 500) and its army was composed of state militiamen. It was his decision to invade Canada, a totally pointless exercise which ended in failure. By giving civilians the right to attack British ships, Madison not only created a war in which men, women and children were in the front line, but pushed New England (half the existing colonies) to threaten to leave the Union.

As historian Matthew Biekonski says, 'James Madison was not a very good president.' His treatment of Indians was barbaric, even by the standards of his own time, and, of course, he owned over 100 slaves, none of whom was ever freed. Henry Clay wrote of him in 1812, 'Mr Madison is wholly unfit for the storms of War ... he is not fit

for the rough and rude blasts which the conflict of nations generate.'
Fisher Ames had found him wishy-washy twenty years earlier: 'He is
also very timid and seems evidently to want any firmness and energy
of character.' This was borne out in August 1814 when the British
torched the Capitol, the White House and many other key government
buildings. Dolly Madison herself saved important documents from her
burning home; James had already left the city!

James Monroe 1817–25

James Monroe famously said, 'It is the knowledge that all men
have weaknesses and that many have vices that makes Government
necessary.' To which I would add it is the knowledge that all presidents
have weaknesses and that many have vices that makes government
difficult.

The last of the founding fathers to reach the White House and the last
of four Virginian plantation owners, Monroe was a spirited 'activist' (to
use a twenty-first-century term) against British control of the colonies.
He stole a mini arsenal from the governor's mansion (which would have
earned him a criminal record today) and joined the Continental Army
in 1776, fighting in several key engagements. Like later occupants of the
White House – Ulysses S. Grant, Teddy Roosevelt, Dwight Eisenhower
– he was a war hero. And, unlike Madison, he didn't run away from the
British destruction of Washington in 1814.

So, what's not to like? Aaron Burr wrote in 1815:

> Naturally dull and stupid, extremely illiterate; indecisive to
> a degree that would be incredible to one who did not know
> him; pusillanimous, and, of course, hypocritical. [Monroe]
> has no opinions on any subject and will always be under
> the government of most men; pretends, I am told, to some
> knowledge of military matters, but never commanded a
> platoon, nor was ever fit to command one.

The man will be forever linked with the 1823 Doctrine named after him. It was designed to keep European powers out of the Americas, but at the time, very little of the New World belonged to the United States. Canada (and Oregon) were British. The central and southern regions were still nominally owned by Spain. All lands west of the Mississippi belonged to the native inhabitants, the Indians. Today, the Monroe Doctrine is held up as a central plank of American foreign policy, but it was the first of the 'big stick' threats which saw later presidents grab Texas, Oregon, sections of the West Indies and many other regions of the world in the policy known as 'Manifest Destiny', that it was America's God-given right to encroach on these territories. Adolf Hitler had a similar idea in the 1930s; it led to the Second World War.

Chapter 9

Ministries and Talents

William Pitt, the Younger 1783–1801; 1804–06

William Pitt, son of the great Earl of Chatham, was a cartoonist's dream. He was only 24 when the king appointed him, increasingly desperate to fill the hole at Number 10 and anxious, at all costs, to avoid any more Whig mistakes. 'You are very young, Mr Pitt,' George had said at their first interview. 'Time alone, Your Majesty, will remedy that,' Pitt replied, which is a pretty good answer. But then, he was Chatham's son. When Edmund Burke heard Pitt's first speech in the Commons, he said, 'It is not a chip of the old block. It is the old block itself.' The king must have prayed that Burke was wrong.

Pitt's long and brilliant career coincided with the work of the great political cartoonists, Cruikshank and Gillray. Both men accentuated the new prime minister's upturned nose (not until the *Spitting Image*[1] model of Margaret Thatcher would such prominence be given to a proboscis). Modern spoofs on the man have included references in *Blackadder the Third*[2] to Pitt the Embryo, with a 10-year-old boy, complete with wig and breeches, holding forth in a rowdy and chaotic Commons only *slightly* more appalling than the real thing.

The younger Pitt was trained in debate and public speaking. Like his father a sickly child, he was educated privately, then attended Pembroke College, Cambridge and Lincoln's Inn, London. There was a brief and utterly ludicrous ministry formed between North, disgraced and unpopular, and Charles James Fox, anti-monarchy and wearing scarlet-heeled boots. It could not possibly have worked and after a few months, the king sent for Pitt. This was on 21 December 1783 and wags prophesied that it would be a 'mince pie ministry'; once the Christmas cakes were eaten, Pitt would be gone. His entire cabinet was made up of peers because virtually no commoner would serve. His carriage was overturned by a Whig-paid mob outside Brook's club. He was not a womanizer, had no known vices other than port (which would kill him in 1806). The poet Samuel Taylor Coleridge could find nothing good to say about him. 'He has no attachment to female society, no fondness for children, no perceptions of beauty of natural scenery, but he is fond of convivial indulgences ...'

Until the cataclysm of the French Revolution forced him to adopt a hard line, he spoke of reform. He supported William Wilberforce in his attack on the slave trade (although he only made one speech about it and he was dead before it was abolished).

The first crisis of Pitt's ministry came with the first (or was it?) outbreak of the king's madness. The trend among historians today is to call this bipolarism (which the elder Pitt probably suffered from) but this ignores the *physical* symptoms described by George's doctors. Bipolarism does not turn your urine purple – porphyria does. This was the diagnosis of the British Medical Association in the 1970s and I believe it to be the correct one.

Whatever the cause, the king was too ill to govern – and being chased around Windsor prior to being strait-jacketed by his doctors did little to alleviate his condition. All this was music to the ears of Pitt's rival, the Whig leader Charles James Fox, a bloated, larger-than-life rake in some ways from a different time. He died his hair purple, wore nankeen boots with red heels, had no judgement and gambled for England. He twice lost his entire fortune on the turn of a card. No wonder mad King George hated the sight of him as surely as he had once hated John Wilkes. Fox wanted to be prime minister and the king's collapse gave him his break. One of his gambling cronies was George, Prince of Wales, as off the wall as his father but without the old man's sense of duty. Fox immediately demanded that a Regency be declared as the king was incapable of ruling, confident that the Regent would immediately appoint Fox to the top job. But to Fox's disgust – and Pitt's relief – George recovered and all was restored.

Pitt's careful financial policy, with the development of Walpole's Sinking Fund and other tax cuts, was dented, however, by the war that followed the French Revolution. In essence, the Third Estate in France (by far the bulk of the population) overthrew the first two Estates – the Church and the aristocracy – after centuries of tyranny. The fact that this was true of every other European state, including Britain, did not deter the *sans-culottes* (the riffraff who wore ragged trousers rather than breeches) from taking to the barricades and marching to the palace of Versailles, where the king lived, demanding bread. As time went on, ever more deranged mob orators set up republican governments, executed the king and queen and offered, in 1791, to take the cause of revolution – *liberté, egalité, fraternité* – to any other country that wanted it.

Loose cannons like Charles James Fox, and proscribed traitors like Tom Paine, expressed support for the revolutionaries. Pitt, naturally, opposed them, but the reason for his declaration of war in 1793 had little to do with politics. It was all about trade – the French were refusing to let British merchantmen use the River Scheldt.

Pitt was no Chatham. He lacked his father's grasp of strategy and Napoleon – the 'sword of the revolution' – refused to fight a war in the colonies, focusing on Europe instead. With a strong economy as a result of the burgeoning Industrial Revolution, Pitt could mount coalition after coalition against *la bête noire*, paid for by British cash. He had to introduce paper money to do it, taking gold from people's bank accounts to fund the whole thing, but his popularity did not flag. When Pitt introduced paper money to pay for the war against France, rather than gold (which he used to pay the coalition governments in bribes), Gillray went into overdrive with the prime minister forcing himself on the 'old lady of Threadneedle Street' (the Bank of England) who is shrieking 'Murder! Murder! Rape! Murder! O, You Villain …' Half the country saw it that way too. Reversals and defeats bounced off Pitt, backed as he was by the king and an establishment terrified of Fox's increasingly unstable Whigs taking over.

It all fell apart, however, over Ireland. The French tried to whip up support in 'John Bull's other island' so that the Irish, implacable enemies of the English, would raise an army and give Pitt the headache of a war on two fronts. The actual attempt, by radical Wolfe Tone in 1798, was pathetic, but Pitt could not take the chance. He proposed that Ireland should become fully part of Britain, rather than the colony it was, by an Act of Union. The sweetener was to give the vote to Irish Catholics, and so to all Catholics. The other classifications, gender and property ownership, still applied but the king went apoplectic. He was head of the Church of England and could not countenance such a collapse of civilization. Pitt had to resign.

It was all going horribly wrong. The ex-prime minister was £40,000 in debt and had to sell his country estate. Worse, he had to agree to his government being run by the Speaker of the Commons, Henry Addington.

Henry Addington 1801–04

As George Thomson says, 'Shed a tear for Henry Addington! There he is, poor man, a thin and not very succulent sliver of premiership between two thick slices of Pitt.' It is unfortunate that we have a fixed view of leading politicians from their official portraits. Addington's was painted when he was 50; he is bald, his cheeks are gaunt, his skin wrinkled; he looks 90. And physical appearances are important in politicians, however much that ought not to be the case.

Addington was another in the long line of prime ministers who begged not to be given the top job, but George III had seen him commanding his yeomanry troop and was convinced that he would be good at ordering people about. 'Addington,' the king said, with his famous lack of grasp, 'you have saved the country.' He got a flash house in Richmond Park and seven prize cows from the royal herd of 'Farmer George'.

It didn't help that most MPs were miserable snobs and Addington's father was a humble quack (medicine had nothing like the status it has today) and he was a poor speaker, constantly berated by articulate gentlemen like George Canning.

During the truce of the Peace of Amiens, titled Britons flocked to Paris to see what the *bête noire* had done in the aftermath of revolution. Some of them were still there when war was declared again and could not leave for another ten years!

Pitt was back, although Addington became Viscount Sidmouth, one of the most high-handed and vicious Home Secretaries in history. He had served in no less than six administrations, as Lord Privy Seal and Lord President. As Canning quipped, 'He is like the smallpox. Everybody is obliged to have him once in their lives.'

All that remains of him now is the couplet 'Pitt is to Addington, as London is to Paddington.'

By the time Pitt returned to office he was already ill, and died, almost certainly of liver disease, in January 1806. The jury is still out on his last words. Was it the noble 'Oh, my country! How I leave my country' or 'I could just eat one of Bellamy's veal pies.' I hope it was the latter!

As I was writing this book, in the turbulent days of the overthrow of Boris Johnson and a vicious in-fighting for his successor (see Chapter 25), various politicians and journalists have called for a ministry of all the talents as the best solution. This filled me with dread, because the *actual* ministry of that name which followed Pitt's death, was an unmitigated disaster; for 'all the talents' read 'no talent at all'.

William Wyndham, Lord Grenville 1806–07

He was strikingly handsome and the son of a prime minister. He attended Eton (yawn!) and Christ Church, Oxford. He was also scruffy and his manners were appalling. But he was Pitt's cousin and in the days of nepotism and the Old School cravat, that counted for a great deal.

He was an MP at 22 and his wife, Anne Pitt, taught him how to dress properly. He backed Pitt's authoritarian regime against radicalism with gusto, kicking the French ambassador, Chauvelin, out of the country. He went along with the suspension of Habeas Corpus so that potential troublemakers could be held in custody without trial and helped to ban seditious meetings. It was the style at the time.

Oddly, Grenville backed Catholic emancipation, however, and was a disciple of Adam Smith, backing the notion of free trade which would dominate the economic debate in the first half of the nineteenth century. On Pitt's death, Grenville assumed the top job, on the condition that Fox was part of the team. The Whig leader said, 'We are three in a bed', referring to a coalition that was almost certain to fail. On his own admission, he couldn't bear to leave his books and garden for even one day in the House of Lords.

Grenville's successor, Lord Liverpool, got it right when he said, 'The most extraordinary character I ever knew ... not an ill-tempered man, but he has no feelings for others ... in his outward manner, offensive to the last degree, rapacious with respect to himself and his family.'

And back came the Duke of Portland after Grenville's resignation over Catholic Emancipation, on which the king would not budge. In one way, Portland was lucky – the increasingly boisterous press knew very little about him – and in those days, it was still possible to hide below the parapet. Rather like 'Silent Cal' Coolidge, the American president of a later era, he said little. He did not read state papers and bills either, often falling asleep on the job. The cabinet held meetings without him. He died of a stroke in 1809.

Spencer Perceval 1809–12

Shooting presidents became an American pastime in the nineteenth and twentieth centuries, but only once has a British prime minister been assassinated. It is a sad thing to say, but it was only John Bellingham's pistol ball that gave Spencer Perceval a place in the history books. He was one of the physically shortest occupants of Number 10, had nearly the most children and arguably the prettiest wife – a list of nearlies.

As a younger son of an aristocrat he lacked money. After Harrow and Trinity College, Cambridge, he took to law and lived over a carpet shop in Bedford Row in London. From 1796, he became involved in politics. He proved an able debater, taking on the brilliant Fox in the House. He was promoted to Attorney General but could not back either Pitt or Fox over Catholic Emancipation, of which he disapproved heartily. In the Ministry of All the Talents, he was Chancellor of the Exchequer, an 'honest little fellow'.

George III's descent into madness led to the Regency Act in 1811 and the Prince of Wales now called the shots. The Regent gave Perceval the top job and he unleashed the army and the full weight of the law against the outbreak of Luddism, which saw working men, losing their livelihood to machines, going on a wrecking spree. 'Great Enoch [the brand of huge hammers at the time] still shall lead the van. Stop him who dare. Stop him who can.' Perceval and the army could and hundreds were transported in convict ships to Botany Bay, Australia.

Sidney Smith wrote, 'you tell me he is faithful to Mrs Perceval and kind to the Master Percevals ... I should prefer that he whipped his boys and saved the country.'

In the end, it was not his politics that led to Perceval's murder. His killer was a deranged businessman who blamed the prime minister for his being imprisoned in Russia. On Monday, 11 May 1812, Bellingham shot him dead in the lobby of the Commons. He was hanged a week later, his plea of insanity ignored. Perceval's family was granted £50,000 by the House and £2,000 a year to follow.

Perceval's death, said Lord Holland, was 'a very fortunate event for the glory, happiness and independence of my country'.

Chapter 10

From Old Man Eloquent to the Worst President in History

John Quincy Adams 1825–29

Rather like Lord Palmerston in British history, John Quincy Adams – 'Old Man Eloquent' – was the first to be captured on camera. Portraits of presidents and prime ministers before the photographic age have a stolid sameness on canvas unless they are being lampooned by newspapers and satirists. As an old man, Quincy Adams stares at us out of the lens and he looks like the wrath of God.

Not a slave owner nor a Virginian, he hailed from Massachusetts and attended Harvard, fast developing into the 'Oxford' of the United States. From there, he became a lawyer, as did the vast majority of the other men who reached the White House. There were those, of course, who saw nepotism written all over him – John Quincy was the son of the second president of the United States, establishing a pattern which would be repeated in the Roosevelt (though not directly) and Bush families. Unlike the majority of presidents in the nineteenth century, Adams was widely travelled, serving his government in Russia, Britain and the Netherlands.

He was a Renaissance man, probably achieving less during his presidency than either before or after it. He was the last White House occupant not to be affiliated to any political party, at a time when the Republicans and the Democrats (then called, confusingly, Whigs) were crystallizing into the factions we know today. He married an English girl, Louisa Johnson, at All-Hallows-by-the-Tower, London, in 1797 and both families opposed the union. She always found Americans rather naïve and 'hick', but she was a great supporter to her husband and travelled everywhere with him.

Like the elder Pitt in Britain, John Quincy Adams collapsed in the chamber doing the job he loved. He died in a chamber in the House of Representatives in 1848.

But on the way, there was some argy-bargy. In the 1828 presidential campaign, none of the four candidates won a majority in the Electoral College[1] so the vote was re-run in the House of Representatives. Henry Clay, who had the lowest vote, threw in his lot with Quincy Adams who not only subsequently beat the front runner, Andrew Jackson, but proceeded to appoint Clay as his Secretary of State.

And he had his enemies. Martin van Buren, the future eighth president, wrote, 'Mr Adams' general personal demeanour was not prepossessing. He was on the contrary quite awkward ...' But Adams knew himself very well. 'I am a man of reserved, cold, austere and forbidding manners,' he wrote in 1819, 'my political adversaries say, a gloomy misanthropist and my personal enemies, an unsocial savage.' And he also knew he couldn't change. Like Winston Churchill 120 years later, he suffered from 'black dog' bouts of depression, which is a problem for the sufferer and those around him.

Adams' inaugural address was a disaster. Believing in a light touch from government, he advocated plans for a national university, a national observatory and huge public works schemes, which would not be seen until the days of Franklin Roosevelt in the 1930s. Nobody wanted any of this in 1825 and he was not re-elected.

Andrew Jackson 1829–37

What do you do with a president whose only two regrets were 'that I did not shoot Henry Clay and did not hang John C. Calhoun'?

What Donald Trump did was to hang the man's portrait in the Oval Office when he became president in 2017. At the same time, the Treasury Department wanted to take 'Old Hickory's' face off the

$20 bill. One of his biographers wrote, 'If you were his friend, you were his friend forever. If you were his enemy, God help you.'

Andrew Jackson was a rough frontiersman, who loathed the educated elite of New England and Virginia. Born in Tennessee, then bordering on Indian territory, he served as a boy messenger during the War of Independence and loathed the British as a result. The scars they gave him, on his head and hand, never healed. He gambled and drank, spending his grandfather's legacy in a single weekend. He married Rachel Robards in 1791 but she was already somebody else's wife and the marriage was adulterous and bigamous. In 1814, as commander of the Tennessee Militia, he defeated the Creek Indian tribe at Horseshoe Bend, killing over 1,000 of them and using their skins as decoration for his cavalry's reins.

In January 1813, he won the only battle of the 1812 war, which was an American victory, when General Pakenham's army was routed at New Orleans.[2] Jackson became a national hero, but the Speaker of the House of Representatives, Henry Clay, was unimpressed – 'I fail to see how the killing of 2,000 English persons in New Orleans qualifies a person for the difficult and complicated duties of the Presidency.' Thomas Jefferson agreed. In 1824, he wrote that Jackson was 'the most unfit man imaginable for the office'. As we have seen, the electoral college vote five years later went to John Quincy Adams rather than the populist Jackson.

This was the first election in the United States when a majority of white men had the vote. Cleverly using the growing newspaper media of the day, Jackson had lithographs printed of him in battle, the hero on the white horse, and the newly enfranchised male public fell for it. But the media has a habit, as Jackson found out, of biting back. His unfortunate marriage was smeared all over the *Cincinnati Gazette*: 'Ought a convicted adulteress and her paramour husband be placed in the highest offices of this free and Christian land?' The *Gazette* also claimed that Jackson's mother was a whore; it wasn't true, but when did little things like truth bother the Fourth Estate? Jackson got the

New Hampshire Patriot to attack his opponent Henry Clay, calling him 'a shyster, pettifogging in a bastard suit before a country squire' and claimed that Clay had pimped for the tsar while serving as Envoy to Russia. Followers of recent events in the US – and followers of Trump – won't be surprised to learn that Jackson won a landslide majority. If there's anything the American voting public likes, it is libel, slander and viciousness. There was one nearly blameless victim in all this – Rachel Jackson, slaughtered in the press, died of a heart attack. True to form, Jackson claimed that his enemies had murdered her.

The tone of the presidency was set by the party of celebration held at the White House. Thousands mobbed the place, windows and crockery were broken, ladies fainted. Jackson himself got out of there and went to a nearby inn! And it didn't get any better when the president packed federal agencies with his cronies. The headlines, however, were full of the Petticoat Affair. John Eaton was Secretary of War and he was knocking off the wife of a naval officer who died at sea during all this. Rumours spread that the man had committed suicide and the very sudden marriage of the widow and Eaton was *the* scandal in Washington, the wife of Vice President John C. Calhoun demanding that Eaton be kicked out. The media called Mrs Eaton 'The Doom of the Republic' and governmental business virtually ground to a halt.

Himself a slave owner, Jackson illegally destroyed anti-slavery posters and leaflets. He also passed the 1830 Indian Removal Act, which amounted to genocide for the Cherokee nation, the one indigenous tribe that had taken to Western farming, had their own alphabet and newspaper. The president was up-ending previous pledges to leave land west of the Mississippi to its original inhabitants. He ignored a Supreme Court decision that the Removal Act was illegal and it led to the 'trail of tears', a sad exodus of starving Indians to Oklahoma. Thousands died – no wonder the Cherokee called Jackson 'the Devil'.

In the press at the time, the president was often lampooned as a donkey ('jackass') and this became the proud symbol of the new Democratic party that Jackson set up. He won the next election with it.

When he tried to close down the Bank of the United States because he saw it (rightly) as a moneymaking behemoth for the benefit of the few, there was uproar. Screaming matches took place in the Senate and Henry Clay warned that Jackson was aiming for arbitrary power, trying to make himself a dictator. The Senate censured him, the only time in American history that that has happened, and still Jackson ignored it. As a sign of the times, when he stood down, he left Washington in a steam-driven locomotive (March 1837).

Astonishingly, later presidents Lincoln and F.D. Roosevelt admired the man. It is less astonishing that Donald Trump did too. Ironically, under Barack Obama, Jackson's face on the $20 bill was to be replaced by that of Harriet Tubman who rescued fugitive slaves on the 'Underground Railroad'. It still hasn't happened.

Martin van Buren 1837–41

Martin van Buren has more nicknames than any other president. He was 'the little magician', the 'red fox' and the 'American Talleyrand', named after the crafty old survivalist French politician who served Louis XVI, the Revolutionary governments, Napoleon and Louis XVIII over a thirty-year period.

He was the first president to be born after the Revolution and belonged to the earliest colonial group in New England, the Dutch. With no formal education after the age of 14, van Buren nonetheless passed the Bar exams and became Attorney General of New York State. A dandy in dress and manners, his time at the state capital was called the 'Albany Regency'.

Despite his obvious talents as a politician, van Buren nailed his colours to Jackson's mast and was made vice president in 1833, 'as close to the president as a blistering plaster', one critic said. Four years later, he was president and presided over – and had no answers to – the grim economic recession of 1837. The press had a field day, calling him 'Van Ruin'. He also heaped trouble on the Indians, implementing the Indian

Removal Act of 1830 that led to untold misery for America's native population. Van Buren was also criticized for not helping the Texans in their bid to break away from Mexican control.

John C. Calhoun summed him up:

> [van Buren] is not … of the race of the lion or the tiger; he belonged to a lower order – the fox; and it would be in vain to expect that he could command the respect or acquire the confidence of those who had so little admiration for the qualities by which he was distinguished.

William Henry Harrison March–April 1841

If Andrew Bonar Law is the forgotten prime minister, the description surely fits William Harrison better. It wasn't his fault; he died of pneumonia only a month into office, but then, he was already 68 at the time. As journalist Emma Burnell wrote, '[Harrison] is probably most famous as the president who died of machismo.' The press carped about his age (see Trump and Biden), so he delivered his inaugural address, nearly two hours of it, in the rain without an overcoat.

He was Virginian aristocracy, a return to the previous generation and his father had signed the Declaration of Independence. He joined the army and fought the Shawnee under their great chief Tecumseh, beating him by sheer weight of numbers at Tippecanoe. This became his nickname when he ran for president. The election slogan in 1840, with John Tyler as his running mate, was the catchy 'Tippecanoe and Tyler too'. He has come down to us as someone who didn't take his job too seriously. Martin van Buren wrote, 'The President is the most extraordinary man I ever saw. He does not seem to realize the vast importance of his education. He is as tickled with the Presidency as is a young woman with a new bonnet.' John C. Calhoun was ruder. 'It is almost distressing to see him. He is now his 69th year with the full share of infirmity belonging to that age … yet, as unconscious as a child of his difficulties and those of his country, he seems to enjoy his elevation as a mere affair of personal vanity.' William L. Massey, future war secretary, said in 1841. 'I have not seen old "Tip", but all represent him as merry as a cricket, careless of the future, garrulous in the display of obscene stories, thoroughly intent with the spirit of lechery.'

This was the first election where a convention was set up to appoint nominees. Noticeably, the gentlemen of the press were given front-row seats and they have never been absent since. Bizarrely, the press got it wrong; Harrison, son of a plantation owner, was billed as the man of the people and van Buren, the son of an innkeeper, as an elitist New Englander (Kennedy had the same image in 1960). The press also pushed the fact that Harrison liked a drink (specifically cider) and, long before the country's hysterical temperance movement and the ludicrous Volstead Act banning alcohol, booze became a political weapon of the press. Flag-waving, ticker-tape parties – everything that typifies modern American electioneering – appeared for the first time and have never gone away.

John Tyler 1841–45

In the famous last word stakes, John Tyler ranks high. 'I shall neither retire ignominiously nor be forgotten'; he managed both. He was known as 'His Accidency'. because he only got the top job through the death of Harrison. The writer Charles Dickens, who had no experience of presidents, found him agreeable and gentlemanly, despite the fact that he was at war with everybody. John Quincy Adams told it like it was. 'Tyler is a political sectarian of the slave-driving, Virginian, Jeffersonian school, principled against all improvements, with all the interests and passions, with vices of slavery rooted in his moral and political constitution, with talents not above mediocrity.'

In his own time, few people had much time for him. His wife, gossips whispered, was thirty years younger than he was and, like Palmerston in Britain, he fathered his last child in his seventies. His prominent Roman nose gave him a look of condescending superiority over everybody else. Undoubtedly a clever lad, he passed his Virginia bar exams at the age of 19. He was a slave owner, but never spoke over what was becoming a burning issue among the states.

When Harrison died, there was no precedent for what should happen. Tyler assumed the mantle of president, as he was already a number two to the dead man.[3] He never had a vice president of his own. He clashed continually with the Whigs, vetoing bill after bill until there were open discussions about impeachment. When loud and drunken celebrations were held in Washington when he left office in March 1845, he quipped, 'They cannot say now that I am a president without a party.'

His death, following a stroke in January 1862, took place during the Civil War. As a Virginia slave owner, he was buried in the 'bars and stars', the Confederate flag, and the North regarded him as a traitor.

James Knox Polk 1845–49

Brian Klaas, professor of politics at University College, London, calls James K. Polk 'the most consequential president you've never heard of', which says it all. John Quincy Adams went for him. 'Polk is the leader of the Administration of the House,' he wrote in 1834, 'and is just qualified for an eminent County Court lawyer … He has no wit, no literature, no point of argument, no gracefulness of delivery, no language of eloquence, no philosophy, no pathos, no felicitous impromptus.' Come on, now, John, what do you *really* think of James Polk? Seargent S. Prentiss was more succinct, but less withering ten years later. '[Polk] is a blighted burr that has fallen from the mane of the warhorse of the Hermitage.'[4]

Polk hugely increased the size of the United States, but he did it without thinking of the cost. Taking slavery further west merely built up the problems that led to the Civil War. Grabbing territory from European powers meant that United States had few friends in

the nineteenth century – the 'splendid isolation' of future presidents
was not entirely a conscious and deliberate policy. A slavish follower
of Jackson, Polk came to be known as 'young Hickory'. As governor
of Tennessee in 1839 he was a disaster and he was not re-elected. It
astonished everyone, Polk included, when he was nominated for the
presidency by the Democrats.

Polk's metier in office was odd. On three mornings of the week, he
received visitors at the White House with no appointment, listening to
grievances and gripes which achieved nothing. One of the intruders
barged his way in and insisted that Polk make him a brigadier general
in the army. There was no presidential protection squad, the Secret
Service, until 1865. He had no sense of humour and was a charmless
host; a contemporary said that he was 'a victim of the use of water as
a beverage'.

A keen exponent of Manifest Destiny, he pushed the physical
boundaries of the States and continued to make life intolerable for the
Indians. When all this led to an ongoing war with Mexico over Texas,
rising politicians like Abraham Lincoln accused the president of abuse
of power and behaving like a tyrant. Thirteen thousand Americans
died in the war, as well as 25,000 Mexicans. Given the population at
the time, the Mexican War was on a par with Vietnam, only far worse.

Zachary Taylor 1849–50

The idea of being president, Zachary Taylor wrote in 1846, 'never
entered my head, nor is it likely to enter the head of any sane person.'
He got that right! Unlike almost everyone else who reached the White
House, Taylor had no involvement in politics at lower levels, was largely
self-educated and had virtually no interest in politics.

While in office, Horace Mann wrote. '[Taylor] really is almost
simple-minded old man. He has the least show or pretension about
him of any man I ever saw; talks as artlessly as a child about affairs of
state, and does not seem to pretend to a knowledge of anything of which

he is ignorant.' Civil War general Winfield Scott, while recognizing the man's courage, said, 'General Taylor's mind has not been enlarged or refreshed by reading or much converse with the world. Rigidity of ideas was the consequence …'

Taylor became a soldier, fighting largely against Indian tribes, where he earned the nickname 'Old Rough and Ready' for his sharing the hardships of his men. In the war with Mexico, his successes earned him fame and people began to think of him as a potential president. He hardly looked the part. He detested uniform (his heavy body wasn't right for it), and one fellow officer said of him that 'on horseback [he] looks like a toad'. When Taylor was nominated by the Whig convention, he hadn't been there and only heard about it six weeks later!

In July 1850, having overdone the Independence Day celebrations, Taylor having gorged on cherries and iced milk, the president fell ill and died of a bacterial infection five days later. There was talk of poisoning by pro-slavery Southerners furious that the slave-owning Southerner had done nothing for their cause. His body was exhumed in 1991 but no cause of death could be found. The likeliest outcome was that it was the medicine of the day that finished him off.

As broadcaster Michael Crick says, '[Taylor] was out of his depth, one of a string of mediocrities to occupy the White House.'

Millard Fillmore 1850–53

'I had not the advantage of a classical education,' Millard Fillmore wrote of himself two years after leaving office, 'and no man should, in my judgement, accept a degree that he cannot read.' The ex-president had been offered an honorary degree by Oxford University, then (ludicrously) still written in Latin.

But with Fillmore, I'm afraid, here is another president you've never heard of. Unless, that is, you were or still are caught up in the vicious arguments for and against slavery in the mid years of the nineteenth century. Charles Sumner wrote in 1850, 'Other presidents may be forgotten; but the name signed to the Fugitive Slave Bill can never be forgotten ... better by far for [Fillmore] had he never been born.' After leaving office, he stood briefly for the American party or 'Know Nothings', who opposed immigration and would have rallied round Trump's recent 'Make America Great Again' slogan. Fillmore only carried Maryland with eight votes.

In 1963, the Millard Fillmore Society was formed to celebrate his anonymity, handing out medals to honour 'mediocrity to combat the rising tide of over achievers'.

The son of a poor farmer, Fillmore was a grossly working-class president, apprenticed to a clothier at the age of 13. He learned to read, as did thousands of others, from the Bible. He fell for and married Abigail Powers, a teacher who became the only First Lady to work both before and after her husband's term of office. She built up the first library in the White House. Insecurity over his origins haunted him all his life, despite acceptance by the New York Bar. He became the Whig congressman for Buffalo in 1837.

Fillmore was chosen as running mate for Zachary Taylor – a Northern lawyer and self-made man alongside the slave-owning war hero. In this capacity, he promised anything to anybody, courting the popular vote as a man of the people. The problem was that President Taylor's right-hand man was not Fillmore but William Seward and Fillmore hated the man with a passion. With Taylor's death on Independence Day (another one?), however, Fillmore was in the White House, as surprised by this as everybody else. The entire cabinet resigned (which was customary on a president's death or his leaving office), and (this was not customary) Fillmore accepted them all.

There was no principle in Fillmore. He was a man of compromise and blew with the wind, but he caught a cold over the Fugitive Slave Act, building on an earlier one from 1793. Abigail told him not to sign it, but he went ahead anyway. From now on, any slave escaping to a Free State had to be hunted down and brought back. Today, this redneck line would be unthinkable, along with the use of the 'n' word but in the 1850s, 'nigger' was simply a descriptive term for a black man. That said, the president's policy was seen at the time to be over harsh. There were revolts in free states and Fillmore threatened to send in troops to restore order. Slave catching became a lucrative extension of bounty hunting.

Today, Fillmore's name has been removed from the tablets of the great and good at the University of Buffalo, which he founded. From rags to woke oblivion is not much of a legacy.

Franklin Pierce 1853–57

'Frank's a good fellow,' said a resident of New Hampshire in 1852, 'but when it comes to the whole United States, I daresay that Frank Pierce is going to spread damned thin.' Teddy Roosevelt was more direct over thirty years later. 'Pierce was a small politician of low capacity and mean surroundings ... he was ever ready to do any work the slavery leaders set him.' The writer Nathaniel Hawthorne, however, presented a more enigmatic view. 'He is deep, deep, deep.'

Pierce tried to keep the Democrats together and the States together over slavery. He failed. He was the son of Revolutionary War hero Benjamin Franklin and met Hawthorne at Bowdoin College, Maine, where he did as little work as possible. He was a heavy drinker and outdoors sporty type and his marriage to mousey little Jane Appleton, a teetotaller, surprised almost everybody. She hated Washington, and all three of her sons died in childhood.

Pierce was pro-South, a crony of Jefferson Davis, who went on to become president of the Confederacy, and with Jane staying away as much as possible, the president essentially lived as a bachelor in the White House. The local press called him 'doughface' (a Northerner with Southern sympathies).

Keen to emulate his military father before he was elected, Pierce was given a brigadier's rank in the Mexican War. His horse bolted and the general ruptured himself on the pommel of his saddle. In a later engagement, he twisted his knee; both times he missed the fighting.

At the Convention of 1852, it took forty-nine ballots to vote Pierce in. He wasn't there himself and was only pressured into it by friends. Jane fainted when the couple got the news. The press campaign at the time was vicious; Pierce was accused of being anti-Catholic and a drunk, but despite this he won the election.

His remaining son was killed in a train crash shortly after and his wife did not attend the inauguration. Neither did Pierce use the Bible as part of the ceremony, believing that God had abandoned him. Two years later, the president was sending troops into Massachusetts to drag escaped slaves back to Virginia. He also backed the Kansas–Nebraska Act of 1854, which led to violent clashes between Abolitionists and pro-slavers in what came to be known as 'Bloody Kansas'. It was this act that led to the creation of a new Republican Party pledged to abolish slavery. He became the only president not to be re-selected as a nominee by his own party.

With Jane dying in 1863, Pierce took to serious drinking and died of cirrhosis of the liver in October 1869. However you look at Franklin Pierce, it is difficult to see the depths that Nathaniel Hawthorne wrote about. In the rankings of presidents (itself something of a national industry) he is very near the bottom.

James Buchanan Jnr 1857–61

In numerous recent surveys in the United States, James Buchanan usually comes a resounding bottom in terms of success, popularity and legacy. George Templeton Strong didn't mince his words when he wrote in 1861:

> Old James Buchanan [he was 69] stands lowest, I think, in the dirty catalogue of treasonable mischief makers. For without the excuse of bad Southern blood … he has somehow slid into

the position of boss-traitor and master-devil of the gang. He
seems to me the basest specimen of the human race ever raised
on this continent.

Which is telling it like it was.

The race question, the place of slavery – 'the peculiar institution'
as it was called – has hung over American history like a damp fog. It
led to a bloody civil war immediately after Buchanan's presidency and
has never gone away, so that the United States today is one of the most
divided nations on Earth. When Buchanan said, 'I am the last President
of the United States,' he had a point.

The average lawyer who served in the war of 1812 had a squint,
which meant that in conversation he tilted his head to one side;
several of the portraits and photographs show this angle clearly. It
unnerved most people. A champion of state rights and a believer
in Manifest Destiny, he loathed abolitionists with a passion. After
several attempts at office, flirting with both Democrats and Whigs,
he finally won the conventions ballot after seventeen counts and got
to the White House.

In office, he supported the South and blasted the new Republican
Party. As a bachelor, Buchanan was rumoured to be 'gay' (that word meant
a heterosexual prostitute in the 1850s) and he was linked romantically
with William Rufus King of Alabama. There is no evidence for this,
but rumour was always more compelling than hard fact, especially
when it comes to the presidency. His First Lady, necessary for social
functions, was his niece, Harriet Lane, and he packed family members
into any conceivable administrative post.

Buchanan had no answers to the economic crisis of 1857, but he
outraged liberal America and the abolitionists with his support of the
Dred Scott case. Scott was a slave taken by his master to Wisconsin,
a free state. In the legal battle that followed, Scott lost, thanks to the
geriatric Chief Justice Roger Taney, on the grounds that the Fifth
Amendment to the Constitution allowed slave owners to take their

'property' anywhere; the 'black man had no rights that a white man need observe'.

In the ongoing hoo-ha over slavery in Kansas, Buchanan backed the pro-slavers, using his influence and handing out bungs to Congressman to follow suit. Early in 1860, his administration faced corruption charges from a congressional committee, but, as all too often in American history, the president himself got away with it. When the Republicans put Abraham Lincoln forward as their candidate, a real dividing line appeared to be drawn. Lincoln presented as an abolitionist (which he wasn't) and a certain amount of panic set in. Two months after Buchanan left office, the Civil War erupted. At the time, several people referred to it as 'Buchanan's War' for obvious reasons. He had failed to placate the warring factions by 'doubling down', as we would say today, on the side of the pro-slavers.

He died of pneumonia in 1868.

Chapter 11

Tories: Ultra and Liberal

Robert Banks Jenkinson, Lord Liverpool 1812–27

Benjamin Disraeli never met a predecessor he liked. He found Lord Liverpool boring – 'the arch mediocrity', he called him.

A product of Charterhouse and Christ Church, Oxford, Robert Jenkinson's political career was shaped by the fact that he was on the Grand Tour in Paris in 1789 when the mob stormed the Bastille prison. Not for him the radical excesses of Fox and Tom Paine; he remained an orthodox conservative all his life. MP for the pocket borough of Appleby, famous only for its horse fair, his maiden speech was awful; the young man was shy and awkward, traits that never left him.

When Pitt fell in 1801, Jenkinson became Foreign Secretary. When Pitt returned, he was Home Secretary and now sat in the Lords as Lord Hawkesbury.

Under Perceval, Jenkinson inherited his father's title of Earl of Liverpool and on Perceval's assassination, the Prince Regent asked him to take the top job. His cabinet was bursting with egos – Canning, Castlereagh and Brougham – and it was quite remarkable that he could control them at all. Castlereagh, in particular, was a problem. Apart from the man's insufferable arrogance, it was a quirk of the constitution that put him centre stage. As an Irish peer, he could sit in the Commons. Consequently, he became the government's mouthpiece on everything, while all other ministers were in the slightly more dignified Lords. When the Manchester and Salford Yeomanry tried to break up a peaceful meeting of radicals in St Peter's Fields, Manchester, in the summer of 1819, eleven people were killed and over 400 injured. The government supported the magistrates, the police, the yeomanry and the army, all of whom were involved in crowd control that day. Despite the fact that Castlereagh was Foreign Secretary at the time, he became associated with the forces of cruel reaction. The cartoonist George Cruikshank, echoing the views of many ordinary people, portrayed the Yeomanry as butchers, with axes rather than swords in their hands.

The Romantic poet Percy Shelley wrote *The Masque of Anarchy* in response to 'Peterloo': 'I met Murder on the way – he had a mask like Castlereagh ...' and Shelley advocated revolution: 'Rise like Lions after Slumber In invanquishable number ... Ye are many, they are few.' *The Times* put its journalistic head over the parapet making a supportive fuss over the victims of Peterloo. Its editor, Thomas Barnes, was summoned to parliament to explain himself. Obviously, they were too polite to him, because Barnes continued to attack the government over its bad handling of the situation.

By 1827, by which time there were younger, more reformist voices in the cabinet, Liverpool was ill. He sniffed ether whenever he made a speech in the House and died from a stroke in February. Incidentally, he was said to have the longest neck in England.

George Canning 1827

In the course of writing this book, the forty-four-day ministry of Liz Truss came and went. Today's press went into overdrive – hers was the shortest premiership since George Canning, ignoring three factors. First, neither Canning nor Truss had the shortest premiership; the Earl of Bath did. Canning's ministry lasted nearly three times as long as Truss's and the only reason it was short was because he died of pneumonia.

Canning had an unfortunate beginning. There was no silver spoon for him. His father was a journalist and died young. His mother was a failed actress (at a time when most actresses were, in the phrase of the time, 'no better than they should be') and Canning himself, born in Dublin in 1770, seemed doomed to follow a rocky road. His uncle,

Stratford Canning, however, was a city slicker and paid for the boy's education at Eton and Christ Church, Oxford.

Canning was, as a young politician, a professional Irishman, joining London's Irish Club. He also crossed the floor of the House and joined the Tories. Called to the Bar, Canning also became one of two MPs for Newport, Isle of Wight, in 1794. He was a dazzling debater à la Fox and made enemies through his over-the-top histrionics. He may or may not have had an affair with the notorious and smelly Caroline of Brunswick, the Prince of Wales's jilted wife, who was still making a nuisance of herself around court.

As an Irishman, he supported Catholic Emancipation, but all he got from Pitt's second term in office was the Treasurership of the Navy. It was now that Canning clashed with Castlereagh to the extent that they fought a duel. Canning missed with his pistol and Castlereagh's ball grazed Canning's thigh. He was patched up and, as gentlemen, they shook hands and said no more about it.

Spencer Perceval's arrival at Number 10 saw Canning resign rather than serve under him. He was hoping for the top job himself; as a 'friend' said, 'He considers politics as a game and has no regard for principle if it interferes with his object of achieving power.'

There is no doubt that George Canning was one of the most jealous men ever to hold high office and he quarrelled with almost everybody. It was Caroline of Brunswick who made life difficult for him in 1821. The 'old, mad, despised' George III had died in 1820. The lavish coronation of George IV, at a time of industrial discontent, caused outrage. It was the last time that the king's champion, in full armour, clattered into Westminster Abbey to throw down the gauntlet on behalf of his liege lord. All very colourful, anachronistic and expensive. But Caroline was still, nominally, George's wife, so now she was legally Queen of England. She demanded entry to the Abbey and the doors were locked against her. The treason trial that followed led to the Caroline riots in London and Canning resigned.

Disenchanted with British politics, he was about to leave the country as Governor-General of India, when Castlereagh, under huge strain in the Commons and possibly about to be outed as a homosexual, picking up soldiers in St James's Park, committed suicide. The last man the king wanted to see at the Foreign Office (or indeed *any* office on British soil) was George Canning, who had backed his ghastly ex-queen so openly. Wiser counsel prevailed, however, and Canning was appointed.

Now, the man's genius showed itself. The king came to like him, he controlled the Commons, won hearts and minds with his dazzling speeches. In terms of Europe, he famously said, 'For Europe, read England.' After the overthrow of Napoleon, the *ancien régime* tried to reassert itself, shrinking France to its pre-revolutionary size and grabbing what territory it could. Any whiff of revolt, any interest in democracy, was stifled immediately by force. Britain stood aloof from all that; after all, its parliament was the second oldest in the world. Englishmen took pride that they had rights that no one else possessed – no one seriously included America in such conversations.

Canning took a gamble and sided with the South American colonies of Spain that now broke with the mother country. As he said, 'I called the New world into existence to redress the balance of the Old.' Liverpool's stroke meant that Canning, the most liberal of the 'Liberal Tories' would probably now become prime minister. He was 57 and already ill, taking ever larger doses of laudanum. He was unpopular with his party. It was obvious that Wellington despised him for his free trade, pro-Catholic sentiments, but Robert Peel, the Home Secretary, was a liberal himself – he nevertheless resigned rather than serve under Canning.

In pain from lumbago, he collapsed at the Duke of Devonshire's house in Chiswick on 8 August. The ever-compassionate Wellington wrote later, 'Mr Canning's death will not do all the good it might have done at a later period. But it is still a great public advantage.'

It certainly was for him.

Lord Grenville said, 'the Tories, idiots that they were, hunted [Canning] to his death with their besotted and ignorant hostility.'

Frederick Robinson, Viscount Goderich 1827–28

'Goody Goderich' as the pamphleteer William Cobbett called him, should never have been prime minister, nor indeed held any of his other jobs.

Born to a wealthy Yorkshire family in October 1782, Goderich attended Harrow and St John's College, Cambridge. He entered parliament in 1806 and in 1815, as the Corn Laws were brought in to protect British farmers (and push up the price of bread); Goderich backed the government's move and the mob smashed the windows of his London house. Liverpool made him Chancellor of the Exchequer, much to everyone's astonishment. 'Why Fred Robinson is in the Cabinet,' one MP wrote, 'I don't know, nor do I recollect to whom he is supposedly more particularly to belong.' His budgets were jolly affairs, however, long before such things were forensically scrutinized by press or public and he came to be known as 'Prosperity Robinson', partly because he used the 'p' word far too often in the House.

Under Canning, Goderich became a viscount and made a dismal job as Secretary for War and the Colonies. George IV chose him as Canning's replacement simply because he was a 'yes man' and the king interfered in cabinet selection too, which effectively undermined the prime minister's power. He simply wasn't up to the job, could not control his squabbling party and resigned in a flood of tears, the king lending the 'blubbering fool' his handkerchief. In the months he was in office, he never attended a single parliamentary session; a unique record.

Disraeli, of course, had the usual vicious *bon mot* which summed Goderich up. He was 'a transient and embarrassed phantom'. And Harold Wilson, a future prime minister himself, wrote, '[Robinson] ... tends to be treated as a figure in the Downing Street joke-book.'

Arthur Wellesley, Duke of Wellington 1828–30

Arthur Wellesley, Britain's most brilliant soldier, became one of its worst prime ministers.

'The beau' as he was known by fellow officers because of his snappy dress sense, was the son of an Irish peer. He attended Eton (which he hated) and then, because there was no such thing in Britain, had to go to France (Angers) to attend a military academy.

In 1807, he was given command of the army in Spain, protecting Portugal from a French invasion. For six years, he carried out a brilliant series of campaigns in the Peninsula, beating the French every time. His defeat of Napoleon at Waterloo in June 1815 made him the most famous soldier in the world and a grateful nation gave him a fine London house, £500,000 cash and the title of Duke. They even named tan-topped hunting boots after him.

He did not get on with his wife, chased other women and detested his two sons. Before he got the top job, scandal hit with the publication of *The Memoirs of Harriet Wilson*. The woman claimed to have bedded half the aristocracy and several of them shelled out wads of cash to keep her quiet. Not so Wellington; his 'Publish and be damned' left her speechless. Although he had always been a political soldier (he was briefly Chief Secretary for Ireland) his failure as a politician was that he expected his wishes to be obeyed as commands, as they had been in the Peninsula. Of his cabinet, he said, 'An extraordinary affair. I gave them their orders and they wanted to stay and discuss them!' Unwilling to serve under the far-too-liberal Canning, Wellington resigned from the cabinet and also from his post as commander-in-chief. He was not too surprised when the king sent for Goderich – 'Our lord and master hates Peel and me', but he was cajoled into taking the commandership back.

George IV sent for Wellington when Goderich had come crying to him. 'Arthur,' he said. 'The cabinet is defunct.' There is no doubt that the king exhibited the same symptoms of insanity as his father. For instance, he told the story so often that he had come to believe it, that *he* had fought at Waterloo and that Wellington was only there to back him up.

Wellington was under no illusions. He disliked party politics and the ninnies he had to deal with in the House. The press made no bones about this, the new *Manchester Guardian*, not yet transformed into its more left-wing leanings of today, wrote that the prime minister had a 'strong bias to arbitrary power, utter ignorance of the principle of philosophical legislation, inveterate prejudices, mediocre abilities, unteachable disposition.'

However, he was shrewd enough to continue Canning's policy of Catholic Emancipation (opposed by half his party) and gave the Home Office to Robert Peel, the best and most reforming Home Secretary of the century. Wellington's standing as a national hero meant that he could control George IV – 'The king stands in awe of him.' In the fiery debates over Emancipation, Lord Winchelsea insulted Wellington who challenged him to a duel. It was still illegal of course, but he was Wellington and no one felt inclined to remind him of the law. Both men deliberately shot wide on Battersea Field (the press beefed up the story with cartoons over the next few days with Wellington's head as a crab's claw) and honour was satisfied. Wellington raised his hat, Winchelsea apologized and no harm was done.

Events in France made this whole position highly relevant. Having succeeded in toppling their king and government in 1789, the French did it again, kicking out Charles X and bringing in the 'bourgeois king', Louis Philippe. George IV's death, which coincided with all this, meant a general election, as the constitution then demanded. Wellington seized on this as a chance to leave politics, but he was not allowed to go quietly.

The mood now was for the electoral reform that radicals had been demanding since the 1770s. The American Revolution and both French Revolutions, as well as the finding of freedom by Greece and South American states, encouraged reformers to believe that true democracy was just around the corner. With (rich, male) Catholics now having the vote, the mob was on the rampage. Lord Grey, of the Whigs, was now prime minister, but Wellington spoke against reform in the House. The most 'ultra' of the Ultras, the reactionary group of the Tories, was hanged in effigy in Seven Dials. Stones were thrown at his windows in Apsley House too, but his butler dispersed the mob with his blunderbuss.

Wellington would, briefly, come back, for a few months in 1832, when the new king, William IV, who had even less grasp of politics than his elder brother, sacked Grey. 'His Highness, the Dictator,' Grey said, 'is concentrating in himself all the power of the state.' Wellington was Prime Minister, First Lord of the Treasury, Foreign Secretary, Home Secretary and Minister of War!

Increasingly deaf[1] and more than a little out of touch (the electorate had doubled in 1832) the duke was only too glad to hand over affairs of state to Lord Melbourne. He continued in the shadows as a distinguished elder statesman for another twenty years. When pigeons were crapping all over visitors to Prince Albert's Crystal Palace during the Great Exhibition in 1851 it was Wellington to whom Victoria turned. His answer was simple and expedient. 'Try sparrowhawks, Ma'am,' he said.

Chapter 12

Reform!

Charles, 2nd Earl Grey 1830–34

'There is no one more decided against annual parliaments, universal suffrage and the ballot than I am. My object is not to favour, but to put an end to such hopes and projects.'

All in all, it didn't look too hopeful. Here was the man on whom thousands pinned their hopes, leader of the more progressive party, the Whigs, warning everybody, in essence, that reform was not going to happen. Everybody, from Tom Paine and John Wilkes in the 1760s to William Cobbett and the Chartists in the 1830s, was clamouring for an end to the jobbery, bigotry, wealth and arrogance of the landed aristocracy and gentry. The Industrial Revolution, well underway long before the Americans broke away, had made the lot of the poor worse, not better. Everybody now moved to the relentless thump of the machines. Those who tried to stop the 'progress', the Luddites, were imprisoned and transported to Australia. Those entrepreneurs who brought in the machines, quickly acquired land which gave them status and they became the new masters, filling the Commons in ever greater numbers. But pressure for change to a lopsided and unfair political system had been building for seventy years and it was Charles Grey who was in the hot seat when the country had finally had enough.

His beginnings were conventional enough. He went to Eton and Trinity College, Cambridge and entered the Commons as a moderate Tory. As time went on, he became a moderate Whig, seeing reform, controlled and modified, as the obvious antidote to the revolution spouted by pro-French Jacobins and many Fleet Street journals like *The Black Dwarf* and the polemical outbursts of Cobbett.

Addington was impressed by Grey's maiden speech, but then, Addington was easily impressed. The newcomer opposed Pitt's repressive measures before 1806 and hard-line Six Acts that were bought in after Peterloo to stamp out sedition. He did not approve of the union with Ireland and wanted the civil list (the Prince of Wales's pocket money granted by parliament) to be halved.

After 1800, however, he attended parliament less and less, marrying and raising fifteen children in the family estate at Howick, Northumberland. Known as something of a rake in the London clubs, knocking off (along with several other people) the flirty Georgiana, Duchess of Devonshire, he was now Mr Boring, the family man.

Fox, however, persuaded him to join the Ministry of All the Talents. He endeared himself to today's chattering classes by abolishing the Slave Trade. Even so, there were strings to this; compensation had to be paid to slave owners (like the Gladstones, of whom more later) and the *ownership* of slaves, as opposed to the *trade*, did not end until 1833.

Despite the peerage he inherited from his father, Grey was always something of an outsider, especially in royal circles. He openly criticized the king's dismissal of a former mistress (or was she his wife?), Maria Fitzherbert, and called George's current squeeze, Lady Hertford, 'an unseen and pestilent influence that lurked behind the throne'.

In 1830 everything changed. Wellington's Tories lost the election and the new king, William IV, sent for Grey. He had not held office for nearly a quarter of a century and barely knew the men in his cabinet. They were, to a man, wealthy aristocrats, owning more land, people said, than any earlier power group. The wigs of earlier generations had gone and breeches were only worn for ceremonies. George 'Beau' Brummel, the fashionista friend of the Prince Regent, had made trousers fashionable and *everybody* wore them now. The Lords still wore top hats, but the Commons did not, and frock coats were invariably dark and drab.

Grey's Reform Bill had to be debated, clipped and trimmed several times before it saw the light of day as the first reforming act of the nineteenth century. It kicked out the anomaly of the rotten boroughs, reduced the number of pocket boroughs and saw industrial cities like Birmingham and Manchester enfranchised for the first time. The electorate, still based on *man*hood suffrage and property, doubled in what many, like Wellington, saw as the end of civilization.

'The revolution is made,' the duke moaned, '... power is transferred from one class of society, the gentlemen of England, professing the faith of the Church of England, to another class of society, the shop-keepers, being Dissenters from the Church, many of them Socinians [humanists], other atheists.' It is as well that the Beau did not live to see the still further changes in 1867, 1884 and 1918. What he would have made of 'votes for women', God only knows!

It was tough going. The Second Reading only passed by one vote and there was rioting in the streets, the mob pelting Wellington's house and carriage with stones and excrement. Lord Brougham, the Lord Chancellor, had drunk so much port during his speech that he could not stand up! The first Bill failed; so did a second in the Lords (always the obstacle to anything new). 'Radical Jack' Lord Durham ranted and raved at Grey (who happened to be his father-in-law) in cabinet meetings. Lord Melbourne, present at the time, was amazed that Grey didn't knock him down.

Against his natural instincts, the king agreed to create enough yes-men peers to force the Bill through, although when Wellington told him he couldn't form a government, he did not have to. On the final day of the vote, many Tory peers stayed away.

Grey's work was done and he resigned in July 1834, bald but still 'the best dressed and handsomest man in England' according to the diarist William Creevy. He had promised that the Reform Act would be a once and for all change.

As we would say today – 'Yeah, Right.'

William Lamb, 2nd Viscount Melbourne 1834, 1835–39, 1839–41

William Lamb wasn't of the old school of Whig landowners. Despite his beetling brows, he was strikingly handsome, attended Eton and Cambridge and, rather bizarrely, Glasgow University. He said of the latter, 'The truth is that the Scotch [*sic*] universities are very much calculated to make a man vain, impatient and pedantic …' He can't have been concentrating very much at Cambridge, then!

He became MP for Leominster, a disciple of Fox and supporter, like the more dissolute Whigs, of the French Revolution. His marriage was a nightmare. Caroline Ponsonby was 'profligate, romantic and comical'. He was 'good-natured, eccentric and not nice'. Their only child was mentally ill. It was Caroline's affair with Lord Byron – 'mad, bad and dangerous to know' – that became the talk of London and made a fool out of the cuckolded Lamb. Byron himself was the product of Harrow and Trinity College, Cambridge but he was constantly broke, was almost certainly sleeping with his sister and was eventually kicked out of the House of Lords. His poetry hardly compensated for all that.

Lamb resigned his Commons seat in 1812, the year in which Byron's *Childe Harold* hit the bookstalls and the poet became a 'magnet attracting every nymphomaniac in London'.

Four years later, Lamb was back in the Commons under George Canning. He inherited the title Lord Melbourne in 1828, the year that Caroline died. It was in Ireland that Melbourne had a fling with a married woman (the first of several) whose husband agreed to keep quiet as long as he got a bishopric out of it. The case came to court, however, and Melbourne got off on the grounds of lack of evidence. The problem with citing adultery in divorce cases, known then by the euphemism of 'criminal conversation' is that they often relied on the tittle-tattle of disgruntled servants, whose word was often dodgy.

Under Grey, Melbourne was Home Secretary. He was anti-reform, despising, as Wellington did, the nation of shopkeepers *some* of whom now got the vote. He was, in this context, the man who sent the Tolpuddle labourers to Botany Bay. These men were only trying to form a trade union for agricultural workers, but appalled farmers accused them of sedition and Melbourne had them sentenced under the Mutiny Act of 1797. Unwittingly, this gave the Labour Party (undreamt of in the 1830s) an excuse for an annual knees-up to mark the occasion. 'Jack' Durham believed that the king's choice of Melbourne for prime minister was a good one because he was 'the only man of whom none of us would be jealous'.

Robert Peel was at Number 10 briefly but his majority was too small and he resigned, replaced by Melbourne again. He carefully controlled the patronage conferred by his own office and, indirectly, the king's. 'Confound it,' one critic said, 'does he now want a Garter for his *other* leg?' Then, scandal struck again, in the form of 'criminal conversation' with Caroline Norton. This raven-haired beauty was *much* more attractive than the ex-Mrs Lamb and the Irish peer's wife he had had a fling with in Dublin. Her husband, however, brought an action against the prime minister.

Caroline lived at Storey's Gate near the Houses of Parliament and Melbourne called in to see her on his way home. Again, he got off, having the same 'Teflon' qualities attributed to several later prime ministers – and presidents. The court may have bought the word of the gorgeous Mrs Norton that nothing untoward had occurred, but Melbourne's brother knew better. 'Do not let William think himself invulnerable for having got off again this time. No man's luck can go further!'

The death of William IV in 1837 brought an end to the *ancien régime* with its wigs and perukes, its card-sharpery, jobbery and political wasteland. The monarch was now 18-year-old Victoria, the first queen to reign in her own right since Anne died in 1714 when Walpole was a young cabinet minister and there was no such recognized office as prime minister and no grace and favour house in Downing Street.

Victoria was strong willed but took the advice of Melbourne, now the elder statesman and there is no doubt that she fell a little in love with him; behind her back, she was known as 'Mrs Melbourne'. He, however, was too experienced and worldly wise to reciprocate. But he continued to advise the queen until her marriage to Albert of Saxe-Coburg Gotha in 1841. He died of a stroke seven years later.

In one respect, Melbourne created a system which would last for a century and a half. In debating the Corn Laws, brought in to protect British farmers from foreign competition in 1815, he said to his cabinet, 'Now, is it to lower the price of corn, or isn't it? It is not much matter which we say, but mind, we must all say *the same*.' This was the collective responsibility of the cabinet, a central tenet of all three major parties until *very* recently.

Boris Johnson could have done with some of that.

Robert Peel, 2nd Baronet 1834–35, 1841–46

Robert Peel was one of a new breed of politicians, a child of the Industrial Revolution. His father was a calico printer and he was born in Bury, Lancashire, in 1788. He never quite lost his 'working-class' accent and his enemies (and there were many of them, even in his own party) never let him forget it. He was with Byron and Palmerston (another future prime minister) at Harrow and went on to Christ Church, Oxford where he got a double first in Classics and Mathematics. The Classics bit was essential for any would-be gentleman of quality (Boris Johnson was recently an anachronistic product of this sort of thinking) but his grasp of figures meant that, unusually in a Tory statesman, he understood the economy.

He entered politics in 1809 for the pocket borough of Cashel, Tipperary and got the Secretaryship of Ireland under Liverpool. At this stage, he was a staunch conservative, opposed to change and giving too much, if any, more freedom to the working class. In 1830, when the French Revolution threatened briefly to explode in Britain and rioters in Bristol roamed the streets under their fictional leader, Captain Swing, he spoke of 'that class of People which has neither property nor sense' and was stocking up on rifles to defend his home in Staffordshire. His Irish policy, firmly with the Protestant landowning ascendancy, earned him the nickname 'Orange Peel'.

As Home Secretary from 1822, however, he showed another side of his character. He slashed the 100 Medieval crimes that carried the death sentence and introduced the Metropolitan police force, which became the model of such forces not just around the country but the world.

Peel's marriage, to the beautiful Julia Floyd, produced seven children and attracted no scandal whatsoever. Peel had no sense of humour and was always formal with his cabinet colleagues. The Irish tub-thumper Daniel O'Connell described Peel's smile as 'like the silver plate on a coffin'. Wellington couldn't stand him. 'How are we to get on? I have no small talk and Peel has no manners.'

After the seismic Reform Act of 1832, during which Peel was out of office, he returned in 1834. He was regarded as a fine mind and an honourable man by both parties; whenever he stood up to speak, there was a respectful silence. He was on holiday in Italy when the king sent for him to form a ministry to replace Grey. A cotton-spinner's son was at Number 10 and there were raised eyebrows and suckings-in of breath everywhere. He was only in office for 100 days (fewer than Canning but more than Truss) and when in opposition again reformed the old Tory party to become the new Conservatives. Reform for reform's sake (the Whig and Radical mentality) was out of the question, but sensible, moderate reform for a great industrial power made sense. This was enshrined in Peel's Tamworth Manifesto, a speech he made to the Commons and which was partly written by Thomas Barnes, editor of *The Times*.

By 1839, with Melbourne's party apparently stagnant and with no more reformist ideas, the new queen asked Peel to form another ministry. He plunged headlong into the Bedchamber Crisis, which sounds considerably juicier than it actually was. He asked that, in the interests of impartiality, the queen would dismiss half her Whig-friendly ladies-in-waiting and appoint a few Tory ones. She refused and Peel would not bend, so Melbourne staggered on until 1841. 'He is shy with me,' Victoria wrote of Peel, 'and makes me shy with him.' The ever-conciliatory Albert, himself new on the scene as the queen's consort, smoothed things over and feisty Victoria backed down.

Peel's ministry was beset with problems, not least agitation over the unfair and obsolete Corn Laws and rise of the Chartists, who demanded six points so radical that one of them, annual parliaments, has still not been enacted today. Corn prices were modified in Peel's budget of 1842, one of the best of the century and the boom of 'railway mania' was allowing business to improve in all directions and at speed.

Then came the famine. 'Rotten potatoes,' grumbled Wellington, 'have put Peel in his damned fright.' Because of the high cost of seed corn, Irish farmers, often barely subsisting on meagre allotments, had gone over to potato growing. In three successive harvests in 1844 and 1845, the 'praties' were hit by a blight, turned black in the ground and could not be dug, let alone eaten. English absentee landlords did nothing for their tenants and nearly a million died from starvation. Nearly the same number emigrated, some via Liverpool to work as navvies on the railways, others to the United States where they found work in the police and the army (the very institutions they had hated at home) and made sure that the grudges they bore were passed on to their descendants – including the current incumbent at the White House, Joe Biden.

Peel sent food and cash, but it was all too little too late. But it did make him realize that, for the solvency of *all* farmers, the Corn Laws had to go. The debates were fierce, headed in the Commons by Disraeli, determined himself to 'climb to the top of the greasy pole'. He led the Young England movement, patriotic, romantic and almost completely impractical. They spoke for Protection (i.e., strict government control of wages and prices) which would have frozen capitalism in a ghastly time warp. What few people other than Peel knew was that Disraeli had once written a nauseating, cloying letter to the prime minister asking for a cabinet job. Peel carried this letter in his coat during the Corn

Law debates. When Sidney Herbert, a cabinet colleague, asked him why he did not produce this letter and stop Disraeli in his tracks, he said, 'I never wrestle with a chimney sweep.'

In the meantime, Daniel M'Naghten, a Scots maniac, tried to assassinate Peel but only succeeded in killing his secretary. Peel got his Corn Law Bill through, but his enemies were itching to remove him and he lost a motion on a minor Bill days later. In those days, such a situation led to an offer of resignation from the prime minister and Queen Victoria accepted it. By this time, she had grown fond of the cotton spinner (his was the only politician's house she ever visited during her long reign) and she was reluctant to part with him.

Never a party man, Peel got up the noses of most Tories when he wrote:

> to be ... the tool of a party ... to adopt the opinions of men
> who have not access to your knowledge and could not benefit
> by it if they had, who spend their time in eating and drinking
> and hunting, shooting and gambling, horse-racing and so forth
> ... would be an odious servitude to which I will never submit.

It cost him his job.

In 1850, Peel died after a fall from his horse on Constitution Hill. The Tory squirearchy were not sad for long – he was not a good rider; never really one of them.

Chapter 13

From War to the Gilded Age

Abraham Lincoln 1861–65

From the worst to the best in a few chronological weeks. If James Buchanan routinely appears at the bottom of presidential surveys, Abraham Lincoln – Honest Abe – is invariably at the top.

Lincoln is one of those presidents who transcends history, largely because he was the first of four (to date) who have been assassinated. But we have to see his murder in Ford's Theatre, Washington, in April 1865 by the unstable John Wilkes Booth in context. As one Southerner wrote at the time, 'It was a Sunday. He should have been in church.'

The hagiography surrounding the man from a log cabin in Kentucky with little formal education is astonishing, with 16,000 books written on him. Count Leo Tolstoy, the Russian supporter of the oppressed, wrote, 'The greatness of Napoleon, Caesar or Washington is moonlight by the sun of Lincoln. His example is universal and will last a thousand years.' John Wilkes Booth, of course, thought differently even before he shot him. 'Lincoln's appearance, his pedigree, his coarse low jokes and anecdotes, his vulgar similes, and his frivolity are a disgrace to the seat he holds. Other brains rule the country. *He* is made the tool ... to crush out slavery by robbery, repine, slaughter and bought armies.'

Today, Abraham Lincoln would have got nowhere near the White House on looks alone. At 6ft 4in he towered over everybody, especially his wife, Mary Todd, and commander of the Union Army, George A. McLellan. His trousers were too short, as were his sleeves and his clothes were scruffy and patched. He eventually grew a beard (not an attractive one) to cover his scrawny neck. He did not take a good photograph. Like many holders of high office, Lincoln suffered from depression, and even in studio portraits, he looks gloomy and sad. As a child he had malaria (twice), frostbite, was kicked by a horse and beaten by his father. As an adult, he was beaten by his unstable wife (when she wasn't spending outrageous sums of public money on her clothes and silverware). Even when delivering the famous Gettysburg Address, he was suffering from the onset of smallpox. The address itself, eulogized today, largely because of Lincoln's murder, lasted only two minutes, and *The Times* wrote of 'the luckless satires of that poor President Lincoln'.

His sense of humour didn't help. When asked on his wedding day (he failed to turn up on the first date appointed) where he was going for his honeymoon, he said, 'To hell, I reckon.' But he also had a reputation as a teller of tall frontier tales that refined gentlemen like Booth hated. As a young politician, Lincoln could be unpopular, even in Illinois, which he represented, and in Washington he was regarded as an upstart. Life with Mary wasn't a bundle of laughs, either. In 1858, he reached prominence in the Lincoln–Douglas debates over slavery. The 'Wee Giant' Stephen Douglas was only 5ft tall. Both men were superb orators, but Douglas won. He lost, however, in the Electoral College vote for the presidency in 1860.

By the time of Lincoln's inauguration, seven states, led by South Carolina, always the most opposed to Washington control, had seceded from the Union. As journalist Julia Langdon points out, at Lincoln's second inauguration four years later, $5 billion had been spent on the war and there were 600,000 dead.

And although Lincoln came to believe passionately that slavery should be abolished, he hadn't always thought that way. In the debates with Douglas, he said, 'I am not, nor have ever been, in favour of bringing about the social and political equality of the white and black races ... I am not, nor have ever been, in favour of making voters or jurors of Negroes.' Like all politicians, and indeed people generally, Lincoln called blacks 'niggers'. It was descriptive, rather than racist, whatever today's opinions may be. He also wanted to send blacks back to Africa, the 'free state' of Liberia, which, when it was tried out, turned out to be a disaster.

The formidable ex-slave, Frederick Douglass, who actually admired Lincoln, was, nevertheless, aware of his shortcomings. In April 1876, he reminded an audience that Lincoln was a white president (when were they not, other than Barack Obama?) and that his presidency was 'entirely devoted to the welfare of white men'.

In terms of scandal, Abraham Lincoln does emerge squeaky clean, especially by comparison with many others in this book. But to see him as a plaster saint and martyr is to do him an injustice. The lyrics of a song from the 1950s America sung by black actor, activist and bass baritone Paul Robeson say, 'He went down to his grave to free the slave.'

Lincoln is far more complicated than that.

Andrew Johnson 1865–69

Thaddeus Steven knew his Bible. In 1866 he wrote:

> In Egypt, the Lord sent frogs, locusts, murrain [a disease of cattle], lice and finally demanded the blood of the first-born of all the oppressors … We have been oppressed by the taxes and debts and He has sent us worse than lice and has afflicted us with Andrew Johnson.

Two years later, General William Tecumseh Sherman knew his Shakespeare. '[Johnson] never heeds any advice. He attempts to govern after he has lost the means to govern. He is like a General fighting without an army – he is like Lear roaring at the wild storm, bareheaded and helpless.'

Another figure near the bottom of the heap in presidential listings, Johnson suffered (as did his near namesake a century later) by comparison with the previous incumbent of the White House. If Lincoln was a saint, Johnson was the devil incarnate. From a poor background, the future president is often portrayed as the only truly working-class man ever to reach the White House, ignoring Lincoln's grimly poor childhood and the lowly beginnings of … wait for it … Bill Clinton! It was his wife, Eliza McCardle, who taught Johnson to read and write and he became a better-than-average speaker in local Tennessee politics.

As senator and president, he backed the common man, annoying the old plantation aristocracy whose cause he indirectly supported. Lincoln made him his running mate and vice president in 1865 to try to heal the divided union, but it backfired spectacularly. He was undoubtedly drunk at his inauguration, which wasn't a good start and he had to be helped to his chair. As president, Johnson opposed Congress's wishes to bring about black equality. Slaves had been freed under the Proclamation of 1863 but that was a long way from racial equality. The president was also keen to heal America, still reeling from its loss of manpower and money, by being unduly lenient to the South. So the so-called 'Reconstruction' era was nothing of the sort. Ex-Confederate soldiers were given land grants, 'carpet-baggers' were allowed to rook honest people of their small-holdings and, most terrifying of all, General Nathan Bedford Forrest ignored the whole point of the previous few years and set up the vicious brotherhood of the Ku Klux Klan, an attempt to overthrow Appomattox.[1] Johnson vetoed all of Congress's attempts at compromise and harmony, rendering the huge loss of life during the war as an irrelevance and a waste of time. In his speeches, the 'I' word was used extensively and his opponents were 'traitors'.

When Johnson proposed that military districts be set up to override civil authority, Congress finally snapped and slapped the president with eleven articles of impeachment. In the event, after rows in the corridors of the Capitol and the press of the day going into overdrive, the impeachment vote failed by one. The 'Teflon' nature of presidents never ceases to amaze.

However, Johnson was shaken by the attack on him, from his own party as well as his opponents and he backed off active intervention – which explains the Sherman quotation above. With the same childish small-mindedness shown by both Adamses and Donald Trump, he refused to attend the inauguration of his successor.

Hiram Ulysses Simpson Grant 1869–77

At the end of the First World War, Henry Adams wrote,

> That, two thousand years after Alexander the Great and Julius Caesar, a man like Grant should be called ... the highest president of the most advanced evolution, made evolution ludicrous. The progress of evolution from President Washington to President Grant was alone evidence to upset Darwin.

Today, Ulysses S. Grant (he quickly dropped the Hiram) is a hugely controversial president. Novelist and broadcaster Germaine Greer calls him the most corrupt of the lot and yet, in opinion polls, he is never lower than halfway and in some is as high as seventh. He was descended from the earliest Puritan settlers in the Massachusetts Bay colony, which gave the family status, if no money. In fact, Grant's father was a tanner, so Ulysses is surely another contender for a 'man of the people' president. He was wrongly enlisted as 'U.S. Grant' at the military academy at West Point on the Hudson and was known there as 'Uncle Sam' as a result.

He was a good horseman, but a poor student, finishing towards the bottom of his class. At 5ft 2in, he was too short even for the cavalry, but had reached a sneaky 5ft 7in by the time of his graduation, almost certainly with the aid of very thick-soled boots! Grant's parents were abolitionists, but he married Julia Dent, a slave owner's daughter, against their wishes. He did well in the Mexican war and learned how to fight. In the Civil War itself, Lincoln allegedly said, 'I wish some of you would tell me the brand of whiskey that Grant drinks. I would like to send a barrel of it to every one of my other generals.' This story was widely circulated, especially by the press, but Lincoln's own comment was 'That would have been very good if I had said it.'

Grant's business ventures in the 1850s, including farming, were a disaster. The eruption of the Civil War was the making of him but his drinking was a problem. Securing victory after victory, he was made lieutenant general by Lincoln and given command of the Northern armies.

With the South having bled to death against the superior money and equipment (but not generalship) of the North, Grant and his wife were invited to the theatre in April 1865 by the president. But the Grants disliked Mary Lincoln and declined; that may have saved his life. When the general was running for president during Andrew Johnson's term of office, he pushed through General Order No. 11, which amounted to a pogrom against Jews who Grant saw as war profiteers. Jews were expelled from all areas under his jurisdiction. Despite this (or because of it?) Grant won the presidency and took office in March 1869, at 46 the youngest man to do so. The problem before him was Reconstruction.

The South had lost and a golden romanticism spread over it, from the KKK itself through 'good ol' boys drinkin' whiskey and rye' to *Gone With the Wind* and *Birth of a Nation* (which led to the resurgence of the Klan in the 1920s). The North wanted to establish rights for black Americans (wholly ignored in the original Constitution) which became the Thirteenth, Fourteenth and Fifteenth Amendments. It was in this context that Grant's reputation as a corrupt exploiter of the white South took hold. The gold scam of September 1869, which implied the government was effectively manipulating the market, caused chaos. Grant himself was probably not involved but he and his extended family made money out of it, nevertheless. It was the first of many 'Black Fridays' to plague economies around the world.

The president clashed with the press, especially the renowned Horace Greeley, owner of the *New York Tribune* who backed liberal Republicans opposed to Grant. 'Grantism' was the paper's word for over-harsh treatment of the South. For the first time, blacks voted in the Southern states, only to have their rights curtailed again by later administrations.

If anything, Grant's reputation has slumped since his death, from throat cancer, in 1885. It would have taken a brilliant president to 'fix' America after the Civil War; Ulysses S. Grant was not that man.

Rutherford Birchard Hayes 1877–81

Sometimes, in politics, you cannot win. Rutherford B. Hayes certainly didn't. Berated by North and South, he was known as 'His Fraudulency'. William Lloyd Garrison, the veteran abolitionist, wrote in 1878, '[Hayes], we are told, sits in his magisterial chair, severe, smiling, complacent and confident that the best way to protect sheep from being devoured is to give them over to the custody of the wolves.' James A. Garfield, himself a future president, said, 'The policy of the President has turned out to be a giveaway from the beginning. He has nolled [avoided] suits, discontinued prosecutions, offered conciliation everywhere in the South while they have spent their time in whetting their knives for any Republican they can find.'

Hayes came to power in what many historians see as the dodgiest election in American history, even worse than the 2020 Trumpian debacle which saw an unruly mob physically attack the Capitol building and its staff. He effectively gave in to the South and set up the infamous 'Jim Crow' laws designed to keep 'the negro' in his place. All this while his wife, 'Lemonade' Lucy Webb, would never allow alcohol in the White House. As one disgruntled guest wrote, 'The water flowed like champagne.'

Hayes followed the frequent path of law to politics to the White House, attending Harvard Law School. He was a minor war hero, with four dead horses and five bullet wounds to show for it. As representative for Ohio from 1864, he didn't shine. As Governor of Ohio, ditto. The Republican Convention of 1876, the year of the country's centenary was split between arch rivals and Hayes was a compromise man in the middle. At election level and in the Electoral College, Hayes's count was questioned (the same had happened to John Quincy Adams, Benjamin Harrison and would happen to George W. Bush and Donald Trump). There were cries of a stolen election (see Trump) and somebody fired a bullet through Hayes's parlour window. In the end, the 'Hayes compromise' saw him get the White House by one vote, on condition that Federal troops be removed from the South. So 'His Fraudulency' and 'Rutherfraud Hayes' it was. 'Jim Crow' segregation spread all over what had been the Confederacy, and Hayes did nothing about it.

Because of the structure of US government, Hayes could not push through the legislation he wanted to – Congress blocked him at every turn, even among his own Republicans. As the Gilded Age lit America, the tiny few, the Rockefellers, the Carnegies, the Vanderbilts, became obscenely rich on the backs of their workers. Wages were cut, trade unions outlawed, troops sent into trouble spots, all with the president's backing.

He promised to secure one term and he did, living in retirement in Fremont, Ohio, until his death in 1893.

James Abram Garfield March–September 1881

A man who dies a violent death usually emerges as a martyr and a saint. Both Abraham Lincoln and John Kennedy fit this pattern; James Garfield doesn't. Before Garfield was assassinated in September 1881, Ulysses S. Grant wrote, 'I am completely disgusted with Garfield's course … [he] has shown that he is not possessed of the backbone of an angleworm.' And after it, Henry Adams said, 'The cynical impudence with which the reformers have tried to manufacture an ideal statesman out of the late shady politician [Garfield] beats anything in novel writing.' Because he was in power for such a short time, he is usually omitted from the ranking of presidents.

Another – and the last – product of a log cabin, he was deeply religious and largely self-taught. He trained as a lawyer. Typical of the conflicted minds of whites in the 1850s, he hated slavery, but wrote in 1865 that he had 'a strong feeling of repugnance when I think of the negro being made our political equal'. He served with distinction in the Union Army and became Senator for Ohio. He got the White House almost by accident and had few political ambitions at the time. Reforming both the corrupt postal service and the civil service, Garfield's work was cut short by his murder. Henry Adams's view (expressed above) carries some weight, however. It is all too easy to paint greatness on to a blank canvas, and any number of presidents have found it necessary to change tack on idealistic issues when sitting in the Oval Office.

Chester Alan Arthur 1881–85

Mark Twain, as always, was very tongue-in-cheek about it. 'I am but one in 55 million,' he wrote in 1883. 'Still, in the opinion of this one fifty-five millionth of the country's population, it would be hard to better President Arthur's administration. But don't decide until you hear from the rest.' Harriet Blaine was less convinced the previous year. 'Flowers and wine and food, and slow pacing with a lady on his arm and a quotation from Thackeray or Dickens or an old Jane Miller ... make up [Arthur's] book of life.' Politician Roscoe Gambling came off the fence entirely. 'I have but one annoyance with the administration of President Arthur, and that is, that, in contrast with it, the administration of Hayes becomes respectable, if not heroic.'

Arthur didn't want the job; that much was clear. But having got it, he milked it for all it was worth. He floated to the top on the 'spoils system', whereby posts in the corridors of power at all levels of American politics were filled with cronies, family members and hangers-on, often in exchange for cash (Britain had a similar system too). Politics courted the gilded rich and got votes from the poor by giving them backhanders in the form of a few dollars. As Arthur himself wrote, 'Political leaders had organised gangs of ruffians at their command and could impose obedience at caucuses ... ballot boxes were stuffed almost openly.' Arthur was part of all this in New York.

Chester – Chet to his family and friends – married Ellen Herndon of Virginia in 1859 and got a key post in New York, which saw his salary leap from $12,000 to $50,000 (more than £1 million today). He bought a flash house on Lexington Avenue, drank good wine and smoked expensive cigars. It wasn't his fault that the deranged, disappointed office-seeker Charles Guiteau screamed as he shot James Garfield, 'I am a Stalwart [Republican extremist] and Arthur will be president.'

The prospect horrified people. 'Chet Arthur, president of the US! Good God!'

Then he saw the light. 'For the Vice Presidency,' he said from the Oval Office, 'I was indebted to Mr Conkling. For the Presidency of the United States, my debt is to the Almighty.' He never had a vice president of his own. Reform of the civil service became his obsession, based on the precedent of Gladstone's reorganization in Britain; perhaps Arthur didn't realize that the GOM (Grand Old Man) had failed utterly with the Foreign Office – the very group with which Americans had to deal.

Any incoming president has to cope with the failures of his predecessors. The corruption of Grant's administration and the ineptitude of Hayes's needed to be fixed. Gussying up the White House (see Chapter 7) was just the outward show of that. Nobody, in the Gilded Age, seemed to notice that the president was putting gold wallpaper up everywhere, 'the flowers, the damask, the silver, the attendants, all showing the latest style'. And this, at a time when the huddled masses were flocking into Ellis Island, desperate for a living wage. As a recent historian has put it, 'Chester Arthur was the closest thing to Jacqueline Kennedy that Washington would see until Jacqueline Kennedy.'

Arthur himself had his suits made by a London tailor, earning him the nickname 'the Dude'. He was a showman, riding in an open top carriage despite the Lincoln and Garfield experience, tipping his hat to all and sundry.

He was frequently outgunned by Congress who stopped the more modernizing of his policies such as civil rights. White Americans had already fought a war over the black issue – most of them believed reform had gone far enough. He clashed with Congress over Indian rights in the West, Chinese immigration, and the need to control the lawlessness of the cowboys West of the Pecos. It was a laudable stand to take, but scandalous in that he allowed all three to fail. Only certain huddled masses were allowed in in future.

Opponents pointed out that Arthur's right to hold the top job should be removed because he was born in Canada, which effectively made him a British citizen. He burned all his papers before he left office and retired on grounds of ill health (he had kidney trouble) before the end of his term. He hated the press. One paper wrote 'A Chat with Chet' but he gave nothing away. 'I hope you are not interviewing me – I believe that is the word – or intending to quote what I have been saying.' Future presidents would have to learn to live with the Fourth Estate; they weren't going away.

Stephen Grover Cleveland 1885–89, 1893–97

Benjamin Tillman, governor of South Carolina, didn't like Grover Cleveland. He was known as 'Pitchfork Ben' because in 1894 he promised to run one into Cleveland's body. That year, he wrote, 'When Judas betrayed Christ, his heart was not blacker than this scoundrel, Cleveland, in deceiving the democracy. He is an old bag of beef and I am going to Washington with a pitchfork and prod him in his old fat ribs.'

In years of Republican dominance, Cleveland is the only Democrat to reach the White House between 1856 and 1912. The family of Puritans came from Cleveland, England in 1633, and Grover's great-grandfather had fought at Bunker Hill. They didn't come much more 'all American' than that. Entering law as a career, Cleveland was High Sheriff of Erie County, New York, where he came to be known as the 'Hangman of Buffalo'. He is the only president of the United States who was once a public executioner.

In the election of 1885, Cleveland's opponents could not fault the man's honesty or his determination to fight the corruption with which American politics was riddled, So they attacked him personally. Over his illegitimate child, they chanted, 'Ma! Ma! Where's my Pa? Gone to the White House. Ha! Ha! Ha!' He also avoided service in the Civil War, putting in a substitute instead; while legal, this left a nasty taste in the mouth.

In office, Cleveland had little idea of how to cope. He distanced himself from Congress, believing that he had no right to interfere with legislation – 'If a botch is made at the other end of [Pennsylvania] Avenue, I don't mean to be party to it.' Many of the measures adopted in his first term were rubber-stamped by him; there is no hard evidence he ever read them. Cleveland hated crowds, glad-handing and the press – all three vital by the 1890s for a successful president. He couldn't even make much capital out of the fact that he married Frances Folsom, the only such ceremony at the White House in history. She was young enough, opponents rumoured, to be his daughter.

In the run up to the next election, Cleveland was accused of being 'the British candidate' with the British ambassador in Washington, Lionel Sackville-West, writing gushing letters of support (which was *well* out of an envoy's remit). Irish-American voters, ever keen to blame Britain for their troubles, voted accordingly. Cleveland was out.

Cleveland's second term in office was hit by economic recession, bank closures and the rise of paper money as opposed to gold. The man who had long attacked corruption now used it himself, using his patronage shamelessly and withdrawing it from would-be opponents. Never a good public speaker, he rather let the cat out of the bag with his 'while the people should patriotically support their government, its functions do not include the support of the people.' This smacked of the mantra in Britain much later, in the twentieth century – 'Bugger you, Jack; I'm all right!' When Pullman railway workers went on a strike in 1894, Cleveland, without the usual invitation of the state governor, sent troops into Chicago to put it down. He didn't stand again.

His book, *Presidential Problems* (1904), told his readers nothing they didn't know already.

Benjamin Harrison 1889–93

'Harrison was a plain little man, white as to hair and beard, who kept his elbows to himself at dinner ...' William Allen White remembered in 1928. 'He was as glacial as a Siberian stripped of his furs.' Thomas

Collier Platt wrote in 1910. In Harrison's own time, Walter Wellman said, 'We have one of the smallest presidents the US has ever known. Harrison is narrow, unresponsive and oh, so cold. As one senator says, "It's like talking to a hitching post".'

Benjamin's grandfather had been president (see Chapter 10) and the dynastic qualities surrounding many aspects of the White House, while offering a comfort of continuity for some, show appalling nepotism to others (see Adams, Roosevelt, etc.). Because of this, Harrison's nickname was 'Grandfather's Hat'. He fought bravely in the Civil War, became a lawyer and married Caroline Scott in 1853. In the run up to the election, he only gave speeches from his home, 'the Front Porch Campaigner', the press called him. He was accused of buying votes to win the popular vote and the Electoral College result.

The Harrisons came to the White House with a menagerie – dogs, a goat and two opossums. Despite the chilliness of his disposition, the place was a bustling family home in his presidency, with plain food – steak and flapjacks – replacing the usual haute cuisine. As a Presbyterian, he didn't work on Sundays. Like Gladstone, Harrison had himself recorded on a wax cylinder singing the praises of the first Pan American Congress, which he set up in 1889. You can hear a remastered version of this on YouTube and it's terrible. When the people of Chile overthrew their government in 1891, the new regime was hostile to the United States. Harrison was hostile back and the press accused him of warmongering.

When he stood for re-election the following year, one senator said, 'There are two serious objections to Harrison's renomination; first, no one cares anything for him personally; second, no one, as far as I know, thinks he could be elected if nominated.' The senator was right; the human iceberg lost.

William McKinley Jnr 1897–1901

Joseph Cameron wrote, 'McKinley keeps his ear to the ground so close that he gets it full of grasshoppers much of the time.' Theodore

Roosevelt, who would follow him to the White House and was the man's vice president, was more scathing. 'McKinley has about as much backbone as a chocolate éclair.'

Of the very common Scots-Irish descent (over time, hundreds of thousands of the Gaelic fringe have fled Britain for a better life), William McKinley's education was patchy, but he had the good luck to serve as ADC to Rutherford Hayes in the Civil War. After that he became an attorney in Ohio. He became governor of the state and got embroiled in a financial scandal which his friends said was carelessness, not corruption. Yeah, right!

In the run for the presidency, McKinley followed Harrison's Front Porch style, never leaving his state at a time when travelling by train and going walkabout was becoming the norm. In terms of the media, however, McKinley's term was the first in which a dedicated press room was set up covering presidential activity in a way that had never happened before. It was a two-edged sword, of course. As historian David Torrance says, 'McKinley was of the view that America's commander-in-chief had to be seen to be believed.'

Dragged into a conflict he disagreed with, the president sent the battleship USS *Maine* to Cuba to watch over the rebellion there against Spanish overlordship. The *Maine* blew up, hit by a mine, and 266 American sailors died. The press went berserk, led by William Randolph Hearst, the richest and mouthiest of the press barons who dominated the media. This resulted in US expansion in Pacific and Caribbean areas, no doubt a delight to the Manifest Destiny and Monroe Doctrine rump of hard liners, but it created more trouble than it was worth; an influx of 'uncivilised' Puerto Ricans and near nuclear war in the Cuban missile crisis. In 1898, the president grabbed Hawaii, too. 'We need Hawaii just as much and good deal more than we did California,' which can't have endeared him to Californians.

Leon Czolgosz's bullet put an end to it all on 6 September 1901; McKinley became the third president to be assassinated.

Chapter 14

Very Odd People

Lord John Russell 1846–52, 1865–66

'The Russells,' by the family's own observation, 'are very odd people' but in some ways all four of the prime ministers in the middle years of the nineteenth century fit the phrase perfectly well.

At 5ft 4¾in tall, Lord John Russell was the shortest of all the prime ministers and it seems odd to think of him potentially standing alongside his American counterpart in the 1860s; Abraham Lincoln was a foot taller even without his stovepipe hat! Russell explained his shortness by saying that he had been taller, but helping to force through the Reform Bill had ground him down.

Westminster School was followed by Edinburgh University and European travel including a visit to Wellington's lines at Torres Vedras in the Peninsula and a chat with the exiled Napoleon on Elba. According to one account, having been bored rigid by the story of the Russell family, the former emperor went into the corner of the room for a pee.

Russell's health was never good and, as MP for the pocket borough (although the term was no longer openly used) of Tavistock, he was out of the Commons as often as he was in. His reputation as something of a 'Jack the Lad' is overblown; two titled ladies turned down his offer of marriage. He tried his hand at writing, but his drama and his poetry were described by Disraeli (of course) as 'feeble'. He was touchy and expected praise for the most humdrum 'achievements' and fell foul of William IV who thought that Russell had plans to undermine the Church of England, already in decline because of the six-dayness of industry.

It was the potato famine that gave Russell his opportunity. A free trader, he didn't have his master's grasp of economics and when the

Chartists held their largest rally on Kennington Common in 1848 (the first such political event to be photographed), Russell was barricaded behind his extensive library in his town house. There was, supposedly, an attempt to assassinate the prime minister, but evidence on this is pretty thin.

He then crossed his own Foreign Secretary, 'this terrible milord' Palmerston, who always behaved like a one-man government. Russell sacked Palmerston who promptly voted against the government over a minor Bill and Russell fell. 'The complaint is,' his brother told him, 'that you were not sufficiently Prime Minister' and the capital letters said it all. From the days when Grey demanded total support from his cabinet, Russell's was a series of loose cannons. Like Peel, people found him aloof. Like Peel (at first) the queen didn't like him. More precisely, she didn't like his wife, the former Fanny Elliot and was appalled when Russell turned down an invitation to Balmoral, her new hidey-hole in the Highlands.

Along with Aberdeen (see below) Russell, now in a coalition, handled the Crimean War (1854–56) badly and was sent to Vienna to carve out the details of a peace treaty with Russia. He failed in that too. About the only vague glimmer of hope for Russell's career was that he was present at Willis's Tea Rooms in London, along with Palmerston, where, in effect, the Whigs became the Liberals and a great party was founded. In the same year, as Palmerston's Foreign Secretary, he came out in support of Italian unification, without consulting his boss or his colleagues. Luckily for him, that chimed with popular opinion (whose new hero, Giuseppe Garibaldi, had a biscuit and a snazzy range of red shirts named after him).

The *Alabama* incident was 'one of those things' that occur historically, although a lot of the blame was dumped at Russell's door. Many commentators, then and since, have maintained that the American Civil War was a long time coming (see Chapter 10) and senior politicians like Russell and Gladstone (see Chapters 14 and 15) believed that the South would win. The *Alabama* attacked Lincoln's gunboats, but because it had been built and launched in Birkenhead, it was the British government that had to shell out $15 million in compensation.

Palmerston's death in 1865 brought Russell to Number 10 again. A further extension of the vote was being demanded and Russell was no longer the man (if he ever had been) to push this through. In the event, Disraeli (of all people!) beat him to it. Russell doesn't emerge well from the political maelstrom. He was spiteful, vindictive and jealous, without any of the qualities of a great statesman. He died at Richmond in May 1878, aged 86.

Edward Stanley, 14th Earl of Derby 1852, 1858–59, 1866–68

A glance at the dates when Derby held office is probably all we need to know about his abilities. His family had been political intriguers since the Middle Ages. The future prime minister was one of the most scholarly to live at Number 10. His translation of Homer's *Iliad* ran to six volumes. He was also a keen gambler, as were many of 'the fancy', betting ridiculous sums on the outcomes of horse races and bare-knuckle boxing bouts.

He carried on the Whig tradition of wearing blue and buff (the party colours from the late seventeenth century) but, unusually for a gentleman, went on a Grand Tour of the United States rather than Europe. As an MP in the 1820s, he came to be known, because of his occasional brilliance, as 'the Rupert of Debate'.[1]

He was nevertheless a ditherer. The politics of the previous fifty years had eroded the old Tory/Whig boundaries. He once said that he was 'a protectionist in the country, neutral in a small town and a Free Trader in the cities'. All very smarmy and duplicitous, but it didn't play well with the voters who were unsure on whose side he was.

Under Grey, Derby was Chief Secretary for Ireland and he clashed at once with Daniel O'Connell, the Irish leader, over the place of the Protestant Church in Ireland. He crossed to the Tories and served under Peel, but, finding the prime minister's free trade ideas too radical for him, he resigned and took up his hereditary seat in the Lords. He now backed Disraeli and his friend Lord George Bentinck, in a new, short-lived Protectionist party. He was asked by the queen to form a government, especially as he was now an earl, but he only lasted months before Aberdeen defeated him. He even forgot to kiss the queen's hand when she gave him the job – what an ingrate! Derby was all too happy to spend his time at turf meetings and weekend country pigeon shoots.

Palmerston's death brought Derby back to Number 10, but his gout was now a major problem, and it was Disraeli, his 'hatchet man' who was actually the driving force in government. The Second Reform Act (1867) rightly belongs to him. Eighteen months after leaving office for the last time, Derby died in October 1869.

George Hamilton Gordon, 4th Earl of Aberdeen 1852–55

The causes of the Crimean War (1853–56) are complicated but from the British perspective, straightforward. Russia was flexing its muscles to threaten the eastern Mediterranean and with it Egypt and the overland route to British India, already, in the cliché of the time, 'the jewel in the crown'. Unfortunately, Lord Aberdeen was the nearest thing we have had to a pacificist at Number 10 and that led to dither and confusion.

Yet it all began fairly well. He went to Harrow, second only to Eton as a proving ground for prime ministers and allegedly had a pillow fight there with the future Lord Palmerston. Appalled by the condition of his Scots estates, he became an 'improving landlord' – a nineteenth-century trend – for the benefit of his tenants. When his wife died young in 1812, Aberdeen wore the black of mourning for the rest of his life.

He was ambassador to Vienna in 1813 and witnessed first-hand the horrors of the battlefield after Leipzig, the 'battle of all the nations' where Napoleon was decisively beaten for the first time. When his brother was killed at Waterloo two years later, it put Aberdeen off war forever.

His reputation in parliament was that of a dour Scots Presbyterian – 'more of a scarecrow than ever,' said Lady Lyttleton, 'and as stiff as timber.' In his work with France, building fences that many thought should not be built, he coined the phrase '*entente cordiale*'.

With Peel's death, Aberdeen was leader of the Free Trade Conservatives (Peelites) and was chosen as prime minister of a motley government of Peelites, Whigs and Radicals. Peel had been the first prime minister not to be chosen by the monarch; from now on, the top job would go to a man who had the majority of his party behind him. Aberdeen's problem was that almost everybody in his cabinet had more personality than he did – Gladstone, Palmerston and Russell were all champing at the bit.

By March 1854, the prime minister had little choice but to declare war on Russia. A wave of Russophobia swept the country and Aberdeen gave in to it. The *Morning Post* was the biggest warmonger of the lot and it was rumoured that it was being fed cabinet leaks by Palmerston, outraged by Aberdeen's dithering. The war didn't go well. For the first time in history, Britain and France were allies, but cooperation was not a word that either nation understood. The third ally, Turkey, proved militarily weak and the commissariat and supply weaknesses in the British Army were soon exposed. The country exulted in the charge of the Light Brigade at Balaclava in October but the inescapable fact was that the charge was a shambles and should never have happened in the first place. Most of the aid sent to soldiers suffering from cholera and frostbite came from private sources and charitable institutions, not the government. The war itself – and the inadequacy of the army – weren't Aberdeen's fault, but as prime minister, he carried the can. Forced to resign, he was given a KG and went quietly, dying in St James's in December 1860 at the age of 76.

Henry John Temple, 3rd Viscount Palmerston 1855–58, 1859–65

'PAM', 'Lord Cupid', 'this terrible milord' was a larger-than-life politician who ran rings around most of his contemporaries, oozed charm and had a reputation as a womanizer second to none. The contemporary press invariably showed him as a Jack the Lad, with a cocky straw in his mouth. Since 1841, *Punch, or the London Charivari* had been lampooning famous figures, prime ministers among them. Although the whole slant of the weekly was one of comedy, the journalists who wrote for it didn't miss a trick and there's nothing better than ridicule for deflating even the most pompous occupant of Number 10. You have to recognize the tongue-in-cheek snidery of *Punch* to get the full benefit. Of the new alliance with France in the Crimean War, the magazine wrote, 'And there were England and France together, with nothing but good fellowship and give-and-take jest, and good humour ... between them. And as it is in 1854, so may it ever be!'

They'd already had a pop at Aberdeen – 'It's very hard, and so it is, to be misinterpreted by a set of low press-writers, Ill-informed and discontented ...' But Palmerston got away with it. Colonel Sibthorpe, a real-life 'disgusted of Tunbridge Wells' figure, found the entire cabinet 'underhand, low, dirty, mean, cowardly, unworthy of Englishmen' *except* PAM! I wonder what Palmerston had on him ...

Born at Romsey, Hampshire, in 1784, Palmerston went to Harrow and Edinburgh University before settling down at St John's, Cambridge. His first Commons seat was for Newport, Isle of Wight, in 1807, but he got it on condition that he never set foot on the island. He never did. He dashed through a series of minor government posts and then through a series of fashionable London ladies whose 'salons' were the most-attended venues of the season. Lady Jersey, Princess Lieven (Palmerston's Russian was very good) and Lady Cowper all fell for the dashing buck. It was his relationship with Emily Cowper (Melbourne's sister) that led to *The Times* calling him 'Lord Cupid'.

In 1811, Goderich offered Palmerston the chancellorship but the king didn't like him and stopped it. Throughout the 1820s, Palmerston drifted ever further left from the Tories to the liberal Tories to the Whigs, so that Grey made him his Foreign Secretary. He was a martinet and did not suffer fools gladly – foreign fools not at all. Ambassador after ambassador stood trembling on his carpet as 'this terrible milord' berated them. Not for him the niceties of diplomacy: 'Diplomats and protocols are very good things but there are no better peace-keepers than well-appointed three-deckers.' In Palmerston's day, the British Navy and its army were the envy of the world; both of them had trounced Napoleon. He was personally responsible for setting up an independent Belgium in 1830; although that friendship would cause chaos and untold slaughter in the years ahead, Palmerston can hardly be blamed for that.

Out of office with the fall of Melbourne, he hunted on his Broadlands estate and bribed the incumbent of the seat of Tiverton to the tune of £2,000 to stand aside and let Palmerston back in. At 55, in 1839, he married his mistress, Emily Cowper and the feisty pair were the darlings of London polite society.

Palmerston, however, could not keep it in his breeches. In the year of his marriage, he tried it on with one of the queen's ladies-in-waiting. The story went that 'Lord Pumicestone' got the wrong bedroom in Windsor Castle by mistake, but nobody believed that! Victoria and Albert (always more straitlaced than she was) were horrified, as they were by the man's foreign policy. Because of Albert and her own German ancestry, the queen had always had a more Eurocentric outlook than most of her subjects, Palmerston included. He was a true-blue Englishman as he proved in 1850 over the Don Pacifico affair.

Don Pacifico was a Portuguese Jew who lived in Gibraltar, which effectively made him a British citizen. When the Greeks burned down Pacifico's house in Athens (largely because he was a Jew) the merchant appealed to the British Foreign Office. Today, such a complaint would be all over the press and social media but the government would *do* nothing. Palmerston sent the fleet! The admiral in command moored his warships in Piraeus harbour and threatened to flatten the place until the Greek government coughed up £6,400 in damages, *far* more than the man's house was worth.

Parliament was outraged but Palmerston shut them all up with his magnificent three-hour *Civis Romanus Sum* speech, reminding his fellow MPs (all of whom had a Classical education) that the rights of a citizen were as important now as they had been in the days of ancient Rome.

Between them, Victoria and Albert contrived to topple Palmerston, whom they saw as a loose cannon. Not for the first or last time, the royals were seriously out of tune with their subjects and anyway, Palmerston was soon back as Home Secretary under Aberdeen. When the Scot lost a vote of no confidence, Palmerston was at Number 10. 'The aged charlatan,' said the radical John Bright, 'has at length attained the great object of his long and unscrupulous ambition.' Palmerston himself said, 'I am, for the moment, *l'inevitable.*'

Benjamin Disraeli, who by now had proved himself to be probably the worst Chancellor of the Exchequer of the century, had an axe to grind when he wrote, 'this old painted pantaloon, very deaf, very blind and with false teeth' about the new man in the top job that he himself coveted. Like a whirlwind, however, Palmerston ended the Crimean War, sending reinforcements and supplies and forcing the Russians to do what they always do when war turns against them: burn their own territory. The Russian naval base in Sebastopol was finally flattened by the Royal Navy and the Royal Engineers.

'P's popularity is wonderful' Lord Shaftesbury wrote. The old man handled conflict with China, Persia (Iran and Iraq) and the Indian Mutiny with cool, rational flair. The loudmouths of the Commons, Bright and Cobden, lost their seats.

The Orsini bomb plot saw Palmerston out of office briefly. Like the *Alabama* in the next year, the bomb was made in London and it was used potentially to kill the French emperor, Napoleon III. Palmerston's Conspiracy to Murder Bill was defeated and he resigned.

He was back by June 1859, still riding to the House every day at 75 and was said to have fathered a child at 81, although in fact he was dead by then. He was cited in a divorce case at 79. His Chancellor of the Exchequer, William Gladstone, sent him so many resignation letters that Palmerston was afraid the burning of them would burn down Broadlands.

Palmerston's devil-may-care attitude to world events would never be seen again at Number 10. John Bright summed him up. 'Palmerston likes to drive the wheel close to the edge and show dexterously he can avoid falling over the precipice.'

In domestic policy, he was less impressive, but stubborn and cantankerous in the extreme. When the Scots asked for a national day of prayer in the teeth of a severe cholera epidemic, he told them to improve Edinburgh's sanitation. He maintained that children were born good and were only lured into lives of crime by bent adults. Loonies attacked him for impugning original sin. Some accused him of treating Heaven 'like a foreign power'.

Chapter 15

Old Gladeye v Dizzy

T wo men dominated the political scene in Britain in the second half of the nineteenth century. Their politics, although born in the same party, were worlds apart. Their education could not have been more different. Their morality was chalk and cheese. And on a personal note, they hated each other. They were Benjamin Disraeli and William Gladstone, and, like many others in this book, we shall not look upon their like again. Whole libraries have been written on these two; we will cut to the chase.

Benjamin Disraeli, Earl of Beaconsfield 1868, 1874–80

Disraeli was an outsider from the start and, with the possible exception of Ramsay MacDonald, the least likely to climb to the 'top of the greasy pole' of politics (the phrase is his). His family were Sephardic Jews who had fled the Inquisition from Spain and settled in London. His father, Isaac, still spelled his name D'Israeli even though there had not been a country called Israel since ancient times. Isaac was a scholar, an author and a bibliophile – qualities and enthusiasms he passed on to his son.

The boy, born in December 1804, went to a Unitarian school and converted to Christianity (specifically the Church of England) when he was 12. Without this, Disraeli could not have stood for parliament before 1858 when the Jewish Disabilities Act made this possible for the first time. The Disraelis lived in fashionable, bookish Bloomsbury and the young man, apprenticed as an articled clerk in a solicitor's office, had no university education nor public-school background. That alone might have barred him from office.

Nothing daunted, he went on the Grand Tour reserved for gentlemen and threw in, because of his Bohemian background, Cairo and Jerusalem, as well as the usual classical haunts of Greece and Rome. When he came back, he was flamboyance personified, his ringlets carefully macassared, his 'kicksies' (trousers) a garish check. His jacket dangled with chains, which in the 1820s gave him the appearance of a freak. He was a gift to the cartoonists of *Punch*, however, who portrayed him in a huge array of costumes.

He founded a newspaper, *The Representative,* which quickly failed, leaving his publisher out of pocket to the tune of £26,000. He invested in South American mining which lost him a personal fortune he never *quite* got back. He had a nervous breakdown in 1826.

In this slough of despair and failure, he wrote a novel, *Vivian Grey,* published anonymously and having a dig at John Murray, his former publisher. We have heard several of Disraeli's waspish jibes already in this book; the chip on his shoulder was colossal. Two more books followed, *The Young Duke* and *Contarini Fleming* which netted Disraeli a reasonable income, though not enough to offset his losses. Disraeli's fiction is unreadable today; I never got beyond page three of his later and most famous novel *Sybil or the Two Nations.* It did him no favours of course that he was a contemporary of Dickens, Wilkie Collins and Carlyle and hard on the heels of Walter Scott, *real* writers with huge fanbases.

He now became interested in politics – 'Toryism is dead and I cannot condescend to be a Whig,' he said with an arrogance bordering on inanity. He picked up women rather as Lord Byron had, dazzled as they were by his appearance and sparkling conversation. He tried seven times in all to get into the Commons, switching from Tory to Whig as the mood took him. That alone should have ended any hope of success. He had failed at journalism. He had failed in business. How could he succeed in politics? He even had the nerve to reply to Melbourne, who asked him what he wanted to be, 'Prime Minister.' Melbourne chuckled, 'No chance at all.'

In 1837, Disraeli finally won a seat for Maidstone in Kent. He married Mrs Wyndham Lewis, having ditched an earlier mistress, Henrietta Sykes (a married lady) and this gave him a steady income and a Park Lane address. Mrs Disraeli was stoically loyal, though hardly the brightest apple in the barrel, never knowing who came first, the Greeks or the Romans (hint – it was the Greeks!)

In the 'hungry 40s' (a modern term) when Peel was grabbing Free Trade by the scruff of its neck, Disraeli founded the Young England movement – 'I am neither a Whig nor Tory. My politics are described by one word, England' – which actually made him a Tory by 1840s standards. Peel's Conservatism appealed to him, although he would rather die than admit it – 'Tory men and Whig measures' as he put it.

Disraeli's maiden speech in the Commons was dreadful. To shouts, wolf-whistles and laughter, he famously said, 'Though I sit down now, the time will come when you will hear me.'

That time came quickly because in 1846, Peel threw out the Corn Laws. Disraeli, whose request for a seat in Peel's coalition had been turned down, led the Protectionist group, damning Free Trade.

By 1848, Disraeli was prepared to admit that, 'protection was not only dead, it was damned.' His financial backer and crony in the Lords, George Bentinck, was dead too. Disraeli had borrowed a colossal sum from his lordship to buy his country estate at Hughenden in Buckinghamshire, a debt he never repaid.

Perhaps because memories are short, perhaps because Disraeli had such charisma, Lord Derby made him Chancellor of the Exchequer in 1852. Today, the job, with the house in Downing Street next door to the prime minister, is seen as the most important job in the cabinet. In the 1850s, that was the Foreign Office; the Exchequer was strictly a utility job – somebody had to do it. And Disraeli did it badly. His figures didn't add up and proved as chaotic as his personal finances. William Gladstone, a mathematical genius whose figures *always* added up, tore into him, quite rightly, in the Commons. And from that day, a vendetta was born. Derby's government fell.

By the late 1860s, the political mood of the country had changed. Palmerston was dead and the Whigs and Peelites had formed a new party, the Liberals, with Gladstone at their head. The working class were deemed to have grown up and to have lost their links with the armed and dangerous radicals of the Chartist years. There was a further demand to extend the franchise. It was to be limited to the towns, but the electorate would double. There was too much opposition to Gladstone's over-zealous reforms, however, and his government fell. Into the breach stepped Derby and Disraeli who pushed the Second Reform Act through with Disraeli's skill at debate. In fact, 1867, the 'leap in the dark' as Derby called it, was a more extreme measure than Gladstone's and once Disraeli had dropped his 'fancy franchise' idea, which would have given *two* votes to university graduates, the idea seemed relatively acceptable.

By 1868, Derby was too ill to carry on in politics, so Disraeli led the Conservative party and the nation. Many were in shock. Even so, he was no match for Gladstone, who couldn't forgive him for 1867 and having 'dished the Whigs' and the Conservatives lost a debate over the disestablishment of the Irish church. Gladstone was in and Disraeli was out.

The 'Grand Old Man's' first ministry was the most far-reaching and comprehensive shake-up the country had ever known, and in some ways it created modern Britain. But, as Disraeli in opposition said, it left the cabinet 'a range of exhausted volcanoes'. The 1874 election was a disaster for the Liberals, and Disraeli was at Number 10 again.

Part of the success of Disraeli's ministry was his relationship with the queen. Albert had died in 1861 and Victoria had become 'the widow at Windsor', behaving so peculiarly in her grief that she chaired Privy Council meetings in a different room from her councillors. Disraeli was one of the men (Albert's Highland servant John Brown was the other) who brought her out of reclusion into the limelight again. Disraeli knew that royalty responded to flattery and he laid it on with a trowel. He sent her presents and nauseating little poems which would have most of us reaching for the sick-bag. When a book of her childlike water colours was published, Disraeli beamed with pride – 'we authors, Ma'am'. Above all, he *explained* complex issues to her. Realizing that her intellect was not of the first order and *well* below his, he talked her through the Byzantine entanglements of domestic and foreign policy. He condescended, but she didn't notice.

His other claim to fame was his brilliance with words. In most books of quotations, his speeches outweigh those of all other prime ministers put together. More than any other factor, his own personality explains why, in the years ahead, labouring men in flat caps voted Tory; on paper, the Tories did nothing for them.

More than any other prime minister except perhaps Clement Attlee, Disraeli pushed through a series of domestic reforms, which actually complemented Gladstone's of the first ministry, and created the modern state. He improved education and public health, he galvanized local government. He pushed through the Artisans Dwellings Act, the Public Health Act, the Agricultural Holdings Act and another Education Act, all of which were socially helpful but equally guaranteed to bore generations of schoolchildren who later had to learn this stuff for tests. But all this was church vestry stuff. What Disraeli saw himself as, first and foremost, was an international statesman, famous throughout the world.

He pushed through the purchase of the Suez Canal from the French and the Khedive of Egypt, securing a personal loan from his friend the multi-millionaire Lord Rothschild. It cost £4 million, and gave Britain a *huge* advantage over rivals in the round-the-world import/ export trade. 'What security?' Rothschild had asked him. 'The British Government,' Disraeli said. In a move that she loved, Disraeli made the queen Empress of India by act of parliament. He also carried on affairs now that his wife was dead but by the mid-1870s he was crippled by gout, walked with a stick and had kidney problems.

His finest hour came, arguably, in 1877. By 1871, the Russians had rebuilt Sebastopol and their warships prowled the Black Sea. They declared war on Turkey who, against all the odds, stopped the Russian advance in its tracks and a congress was called at Berlin, now the capital of a newly united Germany, under the 'honest brokership' of its 'iron' chancellor, Otto von Bismarck. The Liberals, under Gladstone, were anti-Turkey, everybody else was anti-Russian. As Disraeli said, there were twelve men in his cabinet and seven different views as to what to do with the 'Eastern Question'. The prime minister sent the fleet to the Bosphorus and put Indian troops on stand-by. It was the sort of gunboat diplomacy displayed by Palmerston; it worked, but it was reckless.

At Berlin, 'Dizzy' stole the show. His private secretary persuaded him not to address the notables present in French (still, astonishingly, the language of diplomacy), because he was so bad at it. There was a huge boost of sales of Disraeli's novels and von Bismarck was hugely impressed by him. '*Der alter Jude, das ist der Mann*' (the old Jew, he is the man). In the negotiations, Turkey got virtually all its territory back and Britain got Cyprus as an important naval base in the Mediterranean.

Disraeli brought back 'peace with honour' but most of the grunt work had been done by his Foreign Secretary, Lord Salisbury. The outsider who had often been called 'ol' clo' (old clothes) behind his back because of the number of Jews selling second-hand gear in the East End was now a KG and at the pinnacle of his success.

Then it all went wrong. The British Army was in trouble in Afghanistan and a maverick imperialist, Bartle Frere, had engineered a war against the Zulu in South Africa and an entire regiment – the 24th Foot – was wiped out at Isandlwana. None of this was Disraeli's fault, but the man at Number 10 by definition carried the can, as we have seen so often before.

Gladstone swept to victory and Disraeli finished a novel, *Endymion*, for which he was paid an astonishing £10,000 (over £5 million today), the highest advance ever for a work of fiction. It is worth noting that future prime ministers got similar amounts for their post-career memoirs, also often works of fiction.

Having referred to Palmerston as an old pantaloon, Disraeli now took to wearing rouge to camouflage his grey pallor and his gout troubled him more. He was still rewriting the Hansard proofs at Hughenden when he died of pneumonia in April 1881 – 'I will not go down to posterity talking bad grammar.' Flags flew at half mast. London's clubs drew their blinds.

The queen sent a bouquet of primroses, according to her his favourite flower, which was an unprecedented flattery from a monarch to a subject. The Primrose League, complete with its yellow enamel badges, outlived the prime minister by sixty years.

By definition, because he outlived him, Gladstone has the last word: 'As he lived, so he died – all display, without reality or genuineness.'

William Ewart Gladstone 1868–74, 1880–85, 1886, 1892–94

William Gladstone is the 'come-back kid' with four terms in office. He was a professional Scotsman (rather like Bute and just as unpopular with some people for that reason) which is odd because he was born in Liverpool and attended an English public school, Eton and Christ Church, Oxford. Yet we have the man's voice recorded on one of the marvels of his age, wax cylinder, and he has a decided Scots brogue.

He was born in December 1809 to a Lancashire merchant family which makes him just as middle class as Disraeli. Because much of the family wealth came from slave plantations and sugar in the West Indies, some people have tried to airbrush him from the pages of history. When compensation was paid to slave owners for the loss of their property, the Gladstones became richer still.

At Oxford, he became president of the union, often seen as a first step to greatness and, like his hero Peel, got a double first in Classics and Maths. At 23, he was MP for Newark for the Tory party. He took on a succession of junior ministerial posts and married Catherine Glynne, who was a feisty woman in her own right and took a cold bath every day for reasons that made sense to her. They had eight children.

With Peel in office in 1841, this 'hope of the stern unbending Tories' became president of the Board of Trade. The 'Parliamentary Train Act' of 1844 was Gladstone's idea, providing cheap travel for the masses in third-class railway carriages. When Peel fell in 1846, Gladstone did too but he was soon back as MP for Oxford University. As a Peelite under Aberdeen, he became Chancellor of the Exchequer, one of the best in history. He trashed Disraeli's attempts to do the same job and planned to abolish income tax, which had been brought in as a temporary emergency measure by Pitt and as a permanent one by Peel, because he believed it to be morally wrong. 'Get your figures up [together] thoroughly,' was his advice to anybody who asked, 'and then give them up as if the whole world was interested in them.' In the House, he was a whirlwind, his electrifying speeches delivered by a young man in a hurry, flailing his arms like a windmill – he was still doing that at 82. His budget speeches were usually three hours long, but nobody missed a word.

Out of office again in 1855, he wrote a three-volume translation of Homer's *Iliad*, claiming a non-existent link with Christianity which infected most of his policy. It looked as though his career was over but, as Aberdeen said, 'he is terrible on the rebound.'

As he aged, Gladstone mellowed. In the 1830s, the only reform he backed was the removal of child labour in the mines; by 1859 he was willing to join the Whigs under Palmerston to espouse a whole range of changes (which actually appalled Palmerston himself). He was Palmerston's chancellor, back at Number 11, with a speech lasting four hours (during which he gulped a concoction of sherry and raw egg). He was constantly at loggerheads with almost everybody in cabinet meetings. Palmerston told the queen that if he had a choice of losing Portsmouth, Plymouth (his major naval bases) and Gladstone, he would choose the latter.

Income tax was down to 4d in the £1, annoying Karl Marx whose *Communist Manifesto* of 1848 was based on the fact that 'the poor were getting poorer'. Gladstone became MP for Lanark. 'At last, my friends,

I am come among you. And I am come unmuzzled.' He was referring
to the death of Palmerston, whose powerful views were at odds with
further reforms of the franchise. The essayist Thomas Carlyle thought
he was 'the representative of the multitudinous cants of the age'.

Oddly, for a man with God on his side, Gladstone sided with the
South in the American Civil War, impressed by Jefferson Davis's
creation of an army, a navy and a nation. People suddenly remembered
that the Gladstones had once owned slaves.

He was on holiday in Italy when Disraeli and Derby stole the 1867
Reform Bill and made it their own, probably the most glaring piece of
political chicanery of the century. Gladstone and Russell's Bill would
have given the vote to an extra 400,000 men; now over a million had
it, the vaguely named 'urban artisans' who were the backbone of the
Industrial Revolution.

But the voting public proved more fickle after 1867 than before.
Expecting gratitude from the new voters, Disraeli was horrified to find
that they voted in droves for the Liberals. Gladstone's obsession with
God emerges everywhere. Until the 1830s he had toyed with a career
in the Church. Now he was convinced that, 'The Almighty seems to
sustain and spare me for some purpose of His own.'

But the new prime minister played the royal card very badly. As
we have seen, after Albert's death, Victoria became a little unhinged.
Disraeli handled it well – 'He is full of poetry,' she gushed, 'romance
and chivalry' – whereas Gladstone 'treats me as if I were a public
meeting.' The pseudo-Scotsman couldn't translate his usual long words
into short, understandable ones and the queen, exposed and alone,
loathed him for it.

The First Ministry saw a whirlwind of reforms. The Protestant
Church of Ireland was dismantled (Gladstone's personal crusade) and
an unworkable Land Act forced through. The Civil Service, as much a
useless behemoth as it has become again today, was reformed, although,
tellingly, the Foreign Office resisted any change at all. The army was
overhauled, the 150-year-old purchase of commission scrapped in

favour of written examinations – Wellington, no doubt, spun in his grave! – and there was a limit on the opening hours of pubs in an attempt to reduce drunkenness. This is an interesting – and early – example of minority pressure groups, in this case the Temperance Movement, bullying everybody else into change. It spectacularly backfired, however, and the 1874 election saw a landslide swing to Disraeli and the Conservatives. 'We have been borne down,' Gladstone whinged, 'in a torrent of gin and beer.'

In 1876, just before Disraeli's success at the Congress of Berlin, the Turks massacred 12,000 Christians in Bulgaria. Gladstone was appalled and came thundering back out of semi-retirement, demanding that the Turks be kicked out of Europe (i.e., Constantinople) 'bag and baggage'. Had he been prime minister at the time, he might have sent a Palmerstonian gunboat. Cabinet minister William Harcourt wrote privately, 'Gladstone and Dizzy seem to cap one another in folly and imprudence and I don't know which has made the greater ass of himself.'

When the Zulu War went wrong in 1879, Gladstone made the fatuous analogy of their king, Cetewayo, as 'the noble savage', ignoring the fact that he had had two relatives murdered to take the throne in the first place. But England now was the England of the underdog – the Italians under Garibaldi in 1859; the Confederacy in the American Civil War; the massacred Christians in Bulgaria; the Zulu in South Africa – and they voted for Gladstone en masse in 1880.

Gladstone had come out roaring on the campaign trail in Midlothian. While Disraeli was ill and crippled, the 'Grand Old Man' as he was now to become, was fit as a fiddle and shook hands and kissed babies (the first politician to go 'walkabout', now essential for electoral success) and ranted about the injustice, the lack of freedom and the inhumanity of the Tories. None of it was true, but it sounded good and people fell for it.

The reality of Midlothian was that most of Gladstone's listeners still didn't have the vote and the Liberals had done almost nothing for the plight of the working man. Even so, porcelain companies went into overdrive, providing the chattering classes with plates depicting Gladstone and his 'missus', not to be eaten off but placed proudly on the parlour wall. The same companies provided pictures of Disraeli too – Lord Beaconsfield as he now was – but at the bottom of a chamber pot! The queen was appalled at the 1880 result – 'the People's William' was back.

But the ministry was not to be as successful as the first. In the Commons, the 'Fourth Party' emerged under the arrogant Randolph Churchill, he of the heavy moustache and hand-on-hip which became several MPs' trademark stance for a few years. Churchill was undoubtedly clever and quipped that Gladstone's penchant for personally hacking down trees on his Hawarden estate in North Wales was as destructive as his policies. 'The forest laments,' he said, like an accidental forerunner of the Green Party, 'in order that Mr Gladstone may perspire.'

The Irish Question came back to bite Gladstone where it hurt. His Church Act had missed the point, his Land Act was a failure because of the intransigence of the landlords. The result was the rise of Charles Stuart Parnell's Land League and the murder of Lord Frederick Cavendish, Chief Secretary for Ireland, in Phoenix Park, Dublin, in 1882.

In terms of foreign policy, the prime minister timed it badly. The Mahdi was a Muslim mystic leader who promised to drive the Christians out of the Sudan, where the British had ended slavery years before. Gladstone sent General Charles Gordon, as much of a religious fanatic as the Mahdi, to evacuate Europeans from Khartoum. But Gordon disobeyed orders and made a fight of it. Gladstone, under pressure from press and public, sent a relief column but it arrived two days too late to save Gordon, who was murdered by the 'Fuzzy-Wuzzies' who followed the Mahdi. Overnight, the GOM (the Grand Old Man) became, in the eyes of the people and the newspapers, the MOG (Murderer of Gordon).

Despite what amounted to an obsession with Ireland, Gladstone had tried to sit on that particular fence for as long as he could. Now, however, he went over to Parnell's position of a demand for Home Rule – an independent Eire. This split the Liberal Party with a younger, breakaway group led by 'Radical Joe' Chamberlain (father of the future prime minister, Neville) refusing to serve under the Old Man. The sticking point was Ulster – which was largely Protestant and had no wish to follow the Catholic south into republican independence. 'Ulster will fight,' Randolph Churchill warned, 'and Ulster will be right.' As Lord Salisbury said, 'The Mahdi pretends to be half-mad but is very sane; Randolph occupies exactly the converse position.'

But Churchill described the situation perfectly – the Liberal party was 'shivered into fragments to gratify the ambitions of an old man in a hurry.' Yet Gladstone won the 1892 election and the queen was stuck with him once more – 'a deluded, excited man of eighty-two.' She was furious when the GOM was given a state funeral and even more so when her own sons acted as pall-bearers for his coffin.

By the age of Disraeli and Gladstone, there were two clear 'armed camps' in Fleet Street. One of the Grand Old Man's most ardent supporters was William Stead of the *Pall Mall Gazette,* who split society by 'buying' a 13-year-old girl to expose the horrors of child prostitution. Stead wanted to create a national newspaper in Gladstone's own Christian image, a beacon of light in an amoral world. 'I have received the highest compliments,' Stead wrote in his diary, 'from Mr Gladstone.' The American press was so impressed by Stead that the *New York Sun* wrote, 'in the years between 1884 and 1888 Stead came nearer to governing Great Britain than any other man in the kingdom,' which is an extraordinary misconception probably because it was part of the journalist's obituary in 1912. He went down with the *Titanic*.

There was one 'Question', however, which barely surfaced. Today, it would fill the front and centre pages of every newspaper in the world, dominate the rolling news on television and produce some vicious comments (and a few good jokes) on social media. That was Gladstone's sexuality. He had a strong sex-drive which clearly Mrs Gladstone couldn't cope with and he regularly visited prostitutes. She knew all about it and probably tolerated the whole thing to have a few nights off! He, of course, denied that anything improper went on (he was trying to get them to see the light of Christianity) but, nevertheless, whipped himself in his study when he got home to atone to his God. Mistresses aside, I can't think of a prime minister in British history (except perhaps David Lloyd George) who pushed this particular boundary as far as Gladstone. His 'peculiar night work' (Catherine Gladstone's phrase) led to a blackmail case in 1853. The blackmailer went down and Gladstone carried on regardless.

Today, his career would have ended there and then.

Most of the vitriol heaped on Gladstone comes, inevitably, from Disraeli, and the Tory press took it up with relish. 'He has not a single redeeming defect' and, extracting the Michael from Gladstone himself, 'A sophisticated rhetorician, inebriated with the exuberance of his own verbosity and gifted with an egotistical imagination that can at times command an interminable and inconsistent series of arguments to malign his opponents and glorify himself.' ... 'that unprincipled maniac Gladstone ... never a gentleman.'

Henry Labouchère didn't like him either. 'He did not object to the old man always having a card up his sleeve, but he did object to his insinuating that the Almighty had put it there.'

Chapter 16

The Barnum Circus

Theodore 'Teddy' Roosevelt Jnr 1901–09

Along with Washington and Lincoln, Teddy Roosevelt is up there with the greats among American presidents, largely because his persona is so much larger than life. Rather like Winston Churchill in Britain, he was a rip-roaring ex-soldier and war hero, who won hearts and minds wherever he went. But some people saw through him. William McKinley, his boss in the 1890s, wrote, 'I am afraid he is too pugnacious … I want peace and I am told that … Theodore is always getting into rows with everybody.' William James was more analytical. '[Roosevelt] is still mentally in the Sturm and Drang period of early adolescence [he] gushes over war as the ideal condition of human society … and treats peace as a condition of blubber-like and swollen ignobility.'

As befits an over-the-top politician, he had a number of nicknames: 'T.R.'; 'Bull Moose'; 'Teddy Bear' (after whom the cuddly toy was named); and was often referred to by his enemies as 'that damned cowboy'. He was a PR man's dream, 5ft 10in tall and broad with it, a full head of hair, huge fashionable moustache, gold-rimmed pince-nez and pearly white teeth (his own – see Washington). He 'worked out', as we'd say today; riding, fishing, hunting, swimming, boxing and ju-jitsu were his regular routines and he'd invite the press to watch him do it all. His British opposite number at Number 10, Arthur Balfour, made do with cocktail parties and attending the Bayreuth Festival.

Roosevelt also had a mind like a razor, reading up to three books a day and devouring government papers in his stride. He wrote thirty-eight books and more than 150,000 letters. Mark Twain did not approve. He claimed that Teddy was a 'show off', the 'Tom Sawyer of the political world', believing that America was 'a vast Barnum Circus with him for a clown and the whole world for an audience'.

Making a name for himself in the corrupt politics of big business in New York and standing up to that corruption, the deaths of his wife Alice Lee and his mother on the same day, left him bereft and he moved to Dakota and set up a cattle ranch. On his return to New York, he married Edith Carrow, who would go on to produce five children. When he championed an expanded navy, the *Washington Post* said, 'Well done ... nobly spoken ... Theodore Roosevelt, you have found your place at last.'

The problem with the big stick policy of American foreign affairs was that it needed some force behind it. In 1898, the US Army was only 28,000 strong (fewer than Wellington had had with him at Waterloo over eighty years earlier). Roosevelt raised a cavalry regiment, the Rough Riders, and they gained immortality by charging up San Juan Hill in the Cuban war, turning the man into an international hero. He was a 'shoo in' to stand for the Republican Party in New York State, but even his own party managers were afraid where that would lead. Sure enough, when he won the election, one of them said, 'I can't do what I want with him. He's as wilful as Hell.'

On the assassination of McKinley, Roosevelt became the country's youngest president at 42. He redesigned the White House, working (in the absence of the Oval Office not built until 1909) in what is today the Roosevelt Room in the West Wing. Some saw his obsessive work rate as an example of paranoia and a power complex. The novelist Henry James said that T.R. stood for 'Theodore Rex'. This despite the fact that his domestic policy, the square deal, was doing a great job to end the monopolies of the very rich in favour of the common man. His big stick foreign policy, which he claimed was for the good of the whole world, was a rather dodgy claim. The Panama Canal was built essentially for America, fast challenging Britain as the world's leading imperial and naval power. The 'Roosevelt Corollary' to the Monroe Doctrine gave the United States the right to interfere in the Americas

Right: Lord North, the prime minister who lost America. Contemporary anonymous caricature approximately 1778, redrafted by author.

Below left: Andrew Jackson seen as a king by American cartoonists. His use of the veto to override Congress was seen as an example of British-style tyranny. C. 1830, redrafted by author.

Below right: Arthur Wellesley, Duke of Wellington, was a far better soldier than he was politician. He gave his name to fashionable hunting boots, not the rubber 'wellies' we wear today. C.1820, redrafted by author.

President Ulysses S. Grant sheds crocodile tears over the loss of the Jewish vote. He had banned Jews from the army twenty years earlier. Tenniel cartoon, *Punch* 1884, redrafted by author.

William Gladstone as a music hall act in 1891. 'The idol of the working classes for whom he did so little.' Tenniel cartoon, *Punch* 1891, redrafted by author.

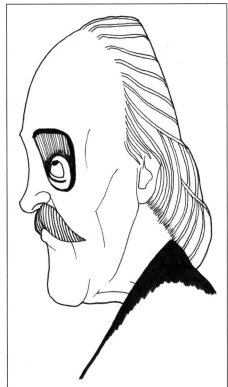

Above left: Benjamin Disraeli, Lord Beaconsfield, climbed to the top of the greasy pole. For a middle-class Jew, this was almost impossible in Victorian England. Tenniel cartoon, *Punch* c.1874, redrafted by author.

Above right: Arthur Balfour in retirement in the Art Deco style. 1920's caricature, redrafted by author.

Right: The cowboy president Teddy Roosevelt speaks softly and wields the big stick. *Punch* c.1905, redrafted by author.

Above left: Could he be any cuter? The Welsh wizard David Lloyd George keeping his hands to himself. Caricature from *Punch* c.1920, redrafted by author.

Above right: Woodrow Wilson offers the olive branch of the League of Nations after the First World War. *Punch* 1919, redrafted by author.

Left: President Taft as a music hall turn discovering he is not going to have an encore at the White House. Redrafted by author.

Above: Franklin Delano Roosevelt creates economically vital New Deal for the American people, but he was accused of destroying the Constitution to do it. 1935, redrafted by author.

Right: Winston Churchill looked like everybody's baby all his life. This cartoon from *Punch* (redrafted by author) shows him as Chancellor of the Exchequer in the 1920s.

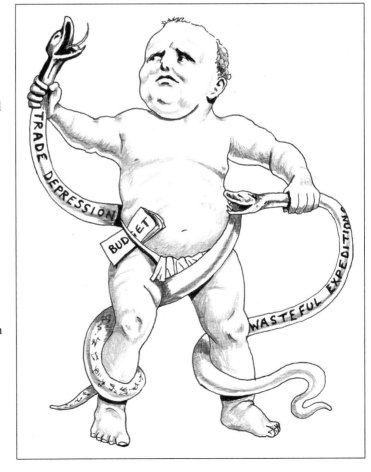

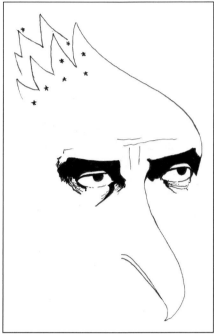

Above left: He had never had it so good! Harold Macmillan as 'Supermac', creating prosperity for all. You'll really believe a prime minister can fly. British cartoon c.1961, redrafted by author.

Above right: Lyndon Baines Johnson, the hawk who refused to take troops out of Vietnam. American cartoon c.1965, redrafted by author.

Left: Richard Nixon, aka Tricky Dickie, will forever be remembered for Watergate. This caricature shows his iconic pose throughout his presidency. Redrafted by author.

Above: Margaret Thatcher as a rabid old bat. The vampire theme was popular among satirists in the context of the Tory Party. Original cartoon, redrafted by author.

Above: 'Demon-eyesing' Tony Blair. This Conservative poster was banned by the media as exceeding the code of fair standards. The caption was 'New Labour, New Danger' and the campaign was dreamt up by the Saatchi brothers' PR company in 1997. Redrafted by author.

Left: George W. Bush, one of several dynasties of American presidents. Caricature c.2003, redrafted by author.

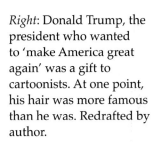

Right: Donald Trump, the president who wanted to 'make America great again' was a gift to cartoonists. At one point, his hair was more famous than he was. Redrafted by author.

generally. Later generations would see this on a par with Hitler's policy of *Lebensraum* (living space) as an excuse to march into somebody else's territory. Odd, perhaps, that the president should get the Nobel Peace Prize for his intermediary role in ending the Russo–Japanese War of 1904–05. Rudyard Kipling's poem *The White Man's Burden* was written specifically for Roosevelt, a personal friend, even though today both men have come under criticism for imperialist jingoism.

When the president invited Booker T. Washington, a black man, to dinner at the White House, the South were universally outraged. Nevertheless, Roosevelt held to the claim of virtually all his predecessors that blacks were 'altogether inferior to the whites'. This was apparent when the 10th Cavalry, the Buffalo soldiers, were accused of wounding whites in Brownsville, Texas in 1906. There is no hard evidence against them, but the president had them all cashiered anyway. One of them had ridden behind him up San Juan Hill.

Having left the White House, honouring Washington's decision in the dawn of time not to run for a third term, Roosevelt went on safari and travelled extensively elsewhere. He met David Lloyd George in England, and the pair, both larger than life, got on famously. Back home, he was standing again as the leader of the 'Bull Moose' Party when he was shot in the chest. The bullet's impact was deadened by his glasses case and a sheaf of notes, and he went on to deliver his speech before going to hospital.

He died years later in January 1919, peacefully in his bed. His vice president, Thomas Marshall, wrote, 'Death had to take Roosevelt sleeping, for if he had been awake, there would have been a fight.'

Teddy became the fourth president along with Washington, Jefferson and Lincoln, to be carved into the rock face of Mount Rushmore in Dakota.

William Howard Taft 1909–13

Most people liked the colossal William Taft (he weighed over 20 stone), but those who knew him well knew that he was out of his depth. 'I am afraid,' he once said, 'I am a constant disappointment to my party.' Teddy Roosevelt, in whose cabinet Taft served, wrote, 'He has not the slightest idea of what is necessary if this country is to make social and industrial progress.' And it didn't help that his heart was never really in the job. 'Politics,' he once famously said, 'make me sick.'

He was a lawyer from a wealthy family in Ohio, all of them steeped in various ways in the law. It was his wife, Nellie Herron, who pushed him into politics. For several years he served as a judge in a variety of capacities until William McKinley offered him the job of running the Philippines. After that, his friend Roosevelt gave him the Secretaryship of War.

Taft hated political campaigning – 'the most uncomfortable four months of my life' – but won the nomination and election and entered the White House in March 1909. Snow drove the inauguration ceremony indoors. 'After the Lord Mayor's cart ...' There was nothing wrong with Taft's presidency, but he was not Teddy Roosevelt. He lacked the man's charisma and failed to follow his policies, even though the Bull Moose expected him to. In particular, he was wholly hung up on the literal wording of the Constitution and did virtually nothing to extend the civil rights of black citizens. Roosevelt was so disappointed by the man's conservative timidity that he set up, as we have seen, the rival Bull Moose Party. Taft only carried two states in the 1912 election, out-popularized by Roosevelt and outsmarted by the Democrats' Woodrow Wilson.

Leaving the White House, he said, 'I'm glad to be going. This is the lonesomest place in the world.'

Thomas Woodrow Wilson 1913–21

Winston Churchill got it nearly right when he said of Woodrow Wilson in 1929, 'The spacious philanthropy which he exhaled upon Europe stopped quite sharply at the coast to his own country. Peace and goodwill among all nations abroad, but no truck with the Republican

Party at home.' Years earlier, before Churchill's 'philanthropy' comment became apparent, the newspaperman William Randolph Hearst wrote, 'Wilson is a perfect jackrabbit of politics, perched upon his little hillock of expediency, with ears and nostrils distended, keenly alert to every scent or sound, and ready to run and double in any direction.'

In a profession in which appearance has come to be everything, Woodrow Wilson looks like a particularly malevolent accountant or perhaps dentist. His narrow, shifty eyes behind the rimless specs are untrusting and untrustworthy. The famous Fourteen Points, which was Wilson's plan for the resettlement of Europe after the disaster of the First World War, was laudable and sensible and his international reputation rests on that. Inside America, however, he is less of a hero.

James W. Loewen has made an extensive study of how badly American history has been taught in American state schools. As he says, 'What we did not learn about Woodrow Wilson is even more remarkable.' Continuing the Manifest Destiny policy of his predecessors, Wilson sent troops into neighbouring countries more often than at any time in history: Mexico in 1914 and 1916; Haiti in 1915; the Dominican Republic in 1916; Cuba in 1917; and Panama in 1918. Troops in Nicaragua forced regime change and a treaty preferable to the United States. He sent cash, ships and a ground force to help White Russia in the civil war against the Bolsheviks between 1918 and 1920. This was none of America's business, but it marked the start of the anti-communist obsession that dominated the whole of the twentieth century and still lingers today. Wilson's defenders claimed at the time, and some still try it on today, that all the countries involved were in dire straits politically and economically and invited America to help them. This, as Henry Ford once said about history, is 'bunk'. In the case of Mexico, the president sent troops without Congress's consent. Such was the outrage, by both sides in the Mexican conflict, and from the Americans themselves, that he was forced to order these troops out. In Haiti, the United States Marines routinely killed civilians and forced them to build roads. Over 3,000 died in the anti-American revolt.

As for communism, he made a speech in Billings, Montana, in which he said, 'There are apostles of Lenin in our own midst. I cannot imagine what it means to be an apostle of Lenin. It means to be an apostle of the night, of chaos, of disorder.' Say 'hello' to the Senator McCarthy of his generation.

'At home,' says Loewen, 'Wilson's racial policies disgraced the office he held.' Ever since Lincoln, with one notable exception, successive presidents had extended, albeit slowly and hesitantly, the civil rights of black people. So we are not criticising Wilson's stance from our own twenty-first-century viewpoint, but from the contemporary views of millions of Americans. Wilson hailed from Princeton University, the only major college that didn't accept black students. He told stories about 'darkies' in cabinet meetings and was encouraged in this by his second wife, Edith Galt. Even though Congress wouldn't back him, Wilson used his executive prerogative to oust blacks from office and put black sailors in the navy to work in the galleys and boiler rooms. He once had African American leaders thrown out of the Oval Office by his security team. When he had a private viewing of D.W. Griffith's outrageously racist film *Birth of a Nation*, he wrote, 'It is like writing history with lightning, and my only regret is that it is also true.' Under Wilson's watch, a new KKK emerged in the 1920s, infinitely larger than the original organization had been. Lynchings became the norm.

Wilson's racism extended far beyond blacks. He referred to the modern terminology creeping in – African-Americans, Chinese-Americans, and so on – 'Any man,' he said, 'who carries a hyphen about with him carries a dagger that he is ready to plunge into the vitals of this Republic, whenever he gets ready.' James Loewen goes so far as to say that under Wilson, the United States came closer to a police state than at any time in its history. Helen Keller wrote of Wilson that he was 'the greatest individual disappointment the world has ever known'.

A lawyer by training, he obtained a PhD at Johns Hopkins University and taught history, no doubt with a racial bias, at Bryn Mawr College, Pennsylvania. He later became president (chancellor) of Princeton and

'Tom' as he was universally known became the more formal 'Woodrow', his mother's maiden name. Inevitably wearing a frock coat and top hat, he looked the part of a distinguished academic, so different from the run-of-the-mill politician. For several years, newspaper cartoonists showed him in gown and mortar board. In the run-up to election to the White House, Wilson promised the same old guff about saving America from the evils of big business, even though it was big business that employed the people it was supposedly exploiting.

He chose his cabinet badly. Most of them were Southerners pledged to keeping the black man in his 'Jim Crow' place. That said, outside the context of race, Wilson's dramatic reforms were generally sound and not unlike the social legislation undertaken by Asquith's Liberal government in Britain before the First World War.

Unfortunately, Roy Hattersley, former deputy leader of the British Labour Party, buys into the foreign policy myth that Wilson only reluctantly got involved in America's near neighbours' controversies. 'He was profoundly antagonistic to the idea of empire,' says Hattersley. And that is just plain wrong.

In the spirit of splendid isolation, Wilson did his level best to keep out of the First World War (F.D. Roosevelt would do the same twenty years later). When the German Navy used their U-boats to sink American ships, with 1,198 loss of life on board the *Lusitania* in 1915, the president caved into his country's outrage and declared war. Even so, it was not until the winter of 1917 that American troops arrived and they only amounted to a single division, hardly likely to make any impact on the German war effort.

Wilson's Fourteen Points were a genuine attempt to settle Europe in 1918–19. This, of course, from a president who was at the same time getting militarily involved in Russia's internal affairs. But they were also, given the slaughter involved over the last few years, wholly impractical. The French president, Georges Clemenceau, ridiculed Wilson by saying 'Why fourteen? The good Lord required only ten.' In the end, the most important of the points – the creation of a League of Nations to settle international disputes amicably – was an excellent ideal, but failed abysmally. With the rise of dictator Mussolini in Italy in the 1930s, the League did nothing; Wilson can't be blamed for that.

The president fell ill towards the end of 1919 with a series of strokes that left him partially paralysed. He retired to a short and unsuccessful legal career. As for Princeton, which once held out against black students, because of his racism, the Woodrow Wilson School of Government on its campus has now been renamed. And nobody today mentions the press's nickname for Wilson: 'Peck's Bad Boy'. The divorcee Mary Allen Peck was his mistress. This tells us more about the changing nature of scandal and the topsy-turvy attitudes of the twenty-first century than it does about Woodrow Wilson.

Warren Gamadiel Harding 1921–3

Warren G. Harding (not surprisingly, he didn't make much of his middle name) is one of the few presidents (or prime ministers, come to that) who reflected publicly on his own job. 'This is a hell of a job! I have no trouble with my enemies. I can take care of my enemies all right. But my damn friends, my God – damned friends ... they're the ones who keep me walking the floor nights!'

William Gibbs McAdoo (Woodrow Wilson's son-in-law), had thoughts about him in a little more depth by 1931:

> [Harding] was a good fellow in the ordinary locker-room, poker game sense of that term. Far too much of a good fellow, in fact, to be entrusted with great authority ... His speeches left the impression of an army of pompous phrases moving over the landscape in search of an idea. Sometimes these meandering words would actually capture a struggling thought and bear it triumphantly, a prisoner in their midst, until it died of servitude and overwork.

Two years after that, Alice Roosevelt Longworth (Teddy's daughter) cut to the chase. 'Harding was not a bad man. He was just a slob.'

He was also extraordinarily popular (see Trump). His vote for president was so huge it was described as 'an earthquake' by a member of Woodrow Wilson's outgoing staff. When he died in office three years later, over 3 million Americans turned out to watch the train carry his body back to Ohio. Three of the principal mourners were Thomas Edison (all things electrical), Henry Ford (cars as long as they were black) and Harvey Firestone (tyres, which were also black).

Then the truth came out. In 1927, Nan Britton wrote *The President's Daughter*, the first kiss and tell account ever written about a president. She was Harding's mistress and the pair routinely had sex in a cupboard off the Oval Office (see Bill Clinton). DNA tests carried out in 2015 prove the truth of this. At the time, the Republican Party gave her $20,000 hush money.

She was not the only mistress to be bought off. Jess Smith, one of Harding's aides, was kept pretty busy for three years trying to keep a whole string of women out of the limelight. He even bribed the editor of the *Washington Post* (long before it became holier-than-thou over Watergate) to keep his mouth shut.

Bizarrely, the president was the first to be a newspaper editor before he got the top job. This gave him unparalleled access to the media (which helped in the *Washington Post* context) and a PR team savvy in respect of photo opportunities. He was the first president to broadcast via the radio to the nation. 'He was a handsome dog,' one of his opponents admitted, immediately followed by, 'I distrusted him.' His native Ohio had unaccountably become the 'presidential state' – seven of the twelve presidents since 1869 had come from there, but Harding was the last to date. He was charming and avoided controversy in state politics, despite accusing Woodrow Wilson of having mishandled the war. He backed votes for women and opposed strong liquor, although he drank himself, because these were the popular ideas of the day, kowtowing to the press in a way which more conservative Americans found disgusting. Harding's drinking, at a time when the temperance movement had convinced everybody that the Volstead Act, prohibiting liquor, was essential (see Boris Johnson and climate change) was, to say the least, unfortunate. So was his gambling problem. At one point, in late-night card sessions with his 'Poker Cabinet', he lost the whole china tea service brought to the White House under Benjamin Harrison. Harding had a bungalow built especially for pressmen opposite his home. They were there when the president was sitting on his porch with his current squeeze, Carrie Phillips, and Mrs Harding threw various bits of furniture at her.

The race card emerged, accusing Harding of having black blood (totally untrue) and leaflets were distributed with pictures of the White House and the caption 'Uncle Tom's cabin?' after the famous book that Abraham Lincoln once may have said started the Civil War.

Although Harding's cabinet was allegedly composed of 'great minds', several of these were corrupt Ohio officials, a number involved in financial scams. There were at least five major frauds in three years which involved the cabinet. If Harding didn't know about them, he should have. The president's predilection for women was focused on a house of ill repute in K Street, ostensibly a headquarters for lobbyists, but there was another house which Jess Smith shared with the Attorney General Henry Doherty, which had a pink taffeta bedroom. Smith shot himself in the head in 1923 and there were rumours in the press that he had been murdered by the Harding administration because he knew too much. Harding himself was full of self-doubts, admitting to an academic visitor, 'I am not fit for this office and never should have been here.' He died on a goodwill tour of the States in August 1923, rumours flying around that his wife, Florence – the 'Duchess' – had conspired with the family doctor to poison him. He wrote excruciatingly bad poetry in love letters to various women, released in the 1960s, including the little snippet that he referred to his penis as 'Jerry'. James Buchanan may have been the worst president in history, but Warren Harding was the most scandalous.

Calvin Coolidge 1923–29

'Silent Cal' didn't impress many people. 'Mr Coolidge's genius for inactivity,' wrote Walter Lippmann in 1928, 'is developed to a very high point. It is far from being an indolent inactivity. It is a grim, determined, alert inactivity which keeps Mr Coolidge occupied constantly.'

He was aware, however, of the power of ugly rumour that surrounds every president. 'I have noticed that nothing I never said ever did me any harm.' He was also prone to George W. Bush-style gaffs (which is probably why he said so little) – 'When more and more people are out of work, unemployment results.'

Journalist Edward Lowey wrote that he was 'a politician who does not, will not and seemingly cannot talk'. That makes him unique. The story is probably apocryphal (though it's a good one), that a dinner guest once said to him, 'Mr. President, I made a bet that I could get more than two words out of you.' Coolidge's reply was, 'You lose.' More cruelly, the writer Dorothy Parker, when told of the president's death, asked, 'How could they tell?'

In fact, Coolidge regularly broadcast on the radio, smiled for press photos and even dressed as cowboy, with Stetson and chaps for a visit to Dakota in 1927. And in that, of course, nobody wins. One journalist griped, 'The President of the United States has become a pitiful puppet of publicity.' He failed to control the rise of the new Klan, even though he claimed that he detested racism and he welcomed Prohibition, despite believing in 'small government'. The Volstead Act was one of the most blatant examples of arbitrary government in American history.

You will be astonished to hear that he became a lawyer and from there went into local politics in Massachusetts. He was sulky and difficulty in his marriage to Grace Goodhue, but she became a perfect dazzling foil to his glumness. As a senator and even vice president to Harding, he was often alone, physically sitting apart from his colleagues in a corner of the dining room. He didn't have his own apartment but had to live in the Willard Hotel. When the place caught fire, Coolidge tried to go back in when it was safe. He was stopped at the door. 'I am vice president,' he explained. 'Vice president of what?' the fireman asked.

Once in the White House, Coolidge carried on Harding's work, but the corruption of the cabinet still lurked. Harold Ickes wasn't impressed. 'If the country has reached the state where Coolidge is the right sort of person for president, then any office boy is qualified to be chief executive.' Since both the president and his Treasury Secretary, Andrew Mellon, were men of few words, it was rumoured that their conversations consisted only of pauses. Successful economist though he was, his lifestyle was frugal to the point of boring meanness; he napped in the afternoon and went to bed early, delegating work to others. As H.L. Menken wrote, '[Coolidge's] ideal day is one in which nothing whatever happens.' Oddly, he had a practical joker streak which bordered on the imbecilic, such as ringing bells for staff then hiding under his desk or behind the curtains. He'd probably be sectioned for that today.

Herbert Clark Hoover 1929–33

For six years, Coolidge complained, 'Hoover has given me unsolicited advice – all of it bad.'

Negatives abound about Herbert Hoover. The shanty towns of the Great Depression were called 'Hoovervilles' for years after his term of office and a wag altered the scriptures – 'Hoover is my shepherd. I am in want.' The impressive dam he ordered built on the Colorado River was not named after him for twelve years, and even then it had to be done by a Congressional resolution.

Hoover was the first president born west of the Mississippi (in Iowa) and was a highly successful engineer and businessman in the 1920s. His spelling was atrocious and didn't get much better later in life (he famously misspelt F.D. Roosevelt's surname, but then who hasn't?) He met Lou Henry, Stanford University's first female geology graduate, and married her in 1899. She was possibly the most erudite of all First Ladies. Between them, the couple translated Georgius Agricola's, sixteenth-century mining treatise; it took them five years. So impressed were the British with Hoover's work for Belgian refugees at the outbreak of war in 1914 that they offered him a peerage if he took British citizenship; he declined, becoming known as the 'Great Humanitarian'. Under Harding, he was Secretary of Commerce and the 'Undersecretary of Everything Else'.

As president, Hoover chose good men over experienced ones, and this didn't pay off. Modernizing, he closed the White House stables and put a phone in the Oval Office. His day was full – work from 8.30 a.m. to 6.00 p.m., after which he and Lou entertained. With little political experience, however, Hoover soon fell foul of Congress over tariff reform. And no one in the White House had any answers to the Wall Street Crash in October 1929. The ripples spread around the world now that a more or less global economy was in place, and nobody else had any answers either. The slump hit Britain hard, and in Germany it gave rise to Hitler's Nazi party. Many countries pulled out of American investment and two successive years of drought hit agriculture. There were marches on the White House and the Capitol building. By 1932, unemployment was over 23 per cent. The collapse of banks followed and the depression was laid at Hoover's door.

But it was the ban on booze that spelled Hoover's end, just as Gladstone had once said of an election defeat in 1874, 'We have been borne down by a torrent of gin and beer.' The dumping of thousands of gallons of liquor and the rise of the Speakeasies and organized crime were greeted with horror by respectable America. It was ironic that Hoover became the first president to set up opinion polls and for the first time, people could make their views known in large numbers in perfect anonymity. Against the dazzling smile of F.D. Roosevelt, with his cheerful outlook and the band playing *Happy Days Are Here Again*,

Hoover stood no chance. The Electoral College gave FDR 472 votes; Hoover got fifty-nine.

The Wall Street Crash would probably have toppled any president, but equally, Hoover wasn't up to the job. In one respected opinion poll, ranking presidents, he ends up lower than 'Tricky Dicky' Nixon.

Chapter 17

From Splendid Isolation to Tipperary

Robert Arthur Talbot Gascoyne-Cecil, 3rd Marquis of Salisbury 1885, 1886–92, 1895–1902

The Cecils had been at the forefront of politics for centuries. William, Lord Burghley had been the chief adviser of Elizabeth I. None of them, however, had to face the free press. From 1851, the tax on newspaper advertising was cut and the *Telegraph*, the *Manchester Guardian* and *The Scotsman* became 1d dailies. The failings of prime ministers could now be read by millions over breakfast.

Robert Gascoyne-Cecil was born at Hatfield House in May 1830 and went to Eton where he was so badly bullied, his family took him out. He went on to Christ Church, Oxford, but only got a fourth-class honours degree in Maths; Peel and Gladstone, he was not! As MP for Stamford, Lincolnshire, he had not married very well and his income (from his father) was small. He supplanted this with Tory articles for the *Quarterly* and *Saturday Review*, highbrow journals read by the cognoscenti.

He opposed the entry of Jews into parliament and fought hard to keep the right of Anglicans only to attend Oxbridge. He was far more honourable when it came to foreign policy, pursuing an almost Gladstonian Christianity and sense of moral outrage.

He served under Derby but resigned over the 'leap in the dark' the following year. By 1868, he was in the Lords as Viscount Cranbourne, then Marquis of Salisbury under Disraeli. He wasn't happy, referring to having to work with him again as 'like a nightmare'.

Salisbury was a scholar, a universal man, out of politics. He had a state-of-the-art photo laboratory at Hatfield and made a speech entirely in Latin (off the cuff) when made MP for Oxford University. Under Disraeli, he was sent to Constantinople to deal with the Bulgarian massacre crisis, but since the Sultan was mad as a tree, his progress was limited. The leader of the 'sublime Porte' refused to read any papers with black ink on them and had a morbid fear of candles.

The Russian threat to Constantinople brought out the best in Salisbury and he was very much the factotum behind Disraeli's dazzling success at the Congress of Berlin. He was bored by the endless hobnobbing, however, and drove miles out of his way to attend an Anglican service in Dresden. What he enjoyed most was talking electromagnetism with the German physicist Hermann Helmholtz.

On Disraeli's death, Salisbury became leader of the Conservatives in the Lords and prime minister four years later. He wasn't keen on the job and never lived at Number 10. If needs must, he used his town house in Arlington Street.

In this short-lived ministry and the next one, he retained his Foreign Office job. He added to African colonies at a time when there was an unseemly squabble among European countries in the scramble for Africa. Everyone wanted a piece of the action (even though, economically, Africa was a white elephant) and Britain got what would become Rhodesia (now Zimbabwe); its capital was called Salisbury.

Out of office against Gladstone's Home Rule storm, he rode his bike on the Hatfield estate and dabbled in science, becoming president of the British Association in 1894. Back in office in 1895, he steered the Foreign Office well, avoiding clashes with the United States over Venezuela, and France over Fashoda; both incidents could have led to war. He also coined the phrase 'splendid isolation' which referred, not to the empire, but to Europe.

By 1899, the prime minister's mind wasn't as sharp as it had been. Neither was his eyesight. He famously confused the new king, Edward VII, for one of his generals, Sir Redvers Buller, when given a signed photograph. His memory was going too. Yet his hold over cabinet and country remained strong.

The Boer War still leaves a nasty taste in the mouth to this day. The Boers were Dutch farmers who had settled areas of South Africa since the seventeenth century, but they clashed with the British who were after the same territory. A handful of farmers bought up in the Veldt should have been no match for what was perceived to be the finest army in Europe, but a series of incompetent generals (Buller among them), led to losses and failure. Salisbury was 70 by now and gratefully passed the Foreign Office to Lord Lansdowne. When the war broke out in 1899, he referred to it as 'Joe's war' (Joe was his pushy subordinate, Joseph Chamberlain). Salisbury seems to have been very conflicted over the key issues of his day. He backed trades unions and the right to strike but detested Socialism, which gave all that a philosophical focus. He disliked compulsory education, brought in in 1886, but insisted that it should be free.

The Conservatives won the 'khaki' election of September 1900 but the front man now was Joseph Chamberlain, tipped for top office, and Salisbury was fading. He died at Hatfield in August 1903. He once said, 'If you believe the doctors, nothing is wholesome. If you believe the theologians, nothing is innocent. If you believe the soldiers, nothing is safe. They all required to have their strong wine diluted by a very large admixture of insipid common sense.'

Archibald Philip Primrose, 5th Earl of Rosebery 1894–95

Primrose was born in London in May 1847. Like so many of his predecessors, he went to Eton and Christ Church, Oxford, and became the Earl of Rosebery in 1868. His ambitions were apparently to own a Derby winner (twice), marry an heiress (Hannah de Rothschild in 1878) and become prime minister (1894). As a song of a few years ago nearly said, 'three out of three ain't bad'.

Family squabbles abounded. Along with most of the aristocracy, Rosebery's mother, the Duchess of Cleveland, was anti-Semitic and refused to attend the wedding into the Rothschild clan. The Jewish press, incidentally, also opposed the marriage, perhaps because they had heard the rumour that when Rosebery wanted his in-laws to go to bed, he would say 'To your tents, O Israel.'

Primrose was undoubtedly a snob. He mixed with fellow aristocrats at Oxford and spent so much time and money on the horses that the university gave him an ultimatum; the turf, or a degree. He chose the turf. By 1878, his income was around £130,000 (almost £13.5 million today). He owned three huge country estates, a house in Berkeley Square and a villa in Naples. One night in Newmarket he won £1,300 at baccarat, officially an illegal game.

Nevertheless, Rosebery, as he was by then, masterminded Gladstone's Midlothian campaign. Rather as Gladstone espoused all things Scots with very little reason, Rosebery pushed his northern British ancestry too (his father was Lord Dalmeny). Rosebery left for Australia, where he persistently referred to the British Empire as 'a Commonwealth of nations' (fine today; not so good for the 1880s).

Back in England, he served as Commissioner of Works in 1884 and Foreign Secretary next time around. He was intensely loyal to Gladstone, even though he found the GOM's Irish obsession a little wearing. He worked hard for social reform as chairman of the newly formed London County Council (1889) but continued to live sumptuously all over the place.

John Buchan, administrator and author, saw Rosebery as 'the Calvinist of seventeenth-century Scotland' with a deep religious streak. He loved books and racing, but he was a gloomy individual, especially after the death of his wife. His insomnia worsened as he grew older. The queen thought he was being 'dangerously radical, almost communistic' (but then, without Disraeli to advise her, what did she know?).

After much agonizing, he agreed to be Foreign Secretary under Gladstone in 1892, but he wasn't well. Henry Labouchère's vicious weekly *Truth*[1] attacked him with a vengeance. Rosebery's inclinations were imperialist, but he understood a basic principle, which the

Americans would forget (if they ever knew it) in the next century – 'We cannot afford to be the Knight Errant of the world, careering about to address grievances and help the weak.'

Gladstone couldn't last forever (or so the Conservatives and half the Liberal Party hoped), and two men were seen as his likely successor. One was William Harcourt, the other Rosebery. The problem was that Rosebery was in the Lords, and whereas that had been the norm it was now expected that the prime minister should sit in the Lower House.

In the end, Rosebery got the top job, but he wasn't universally popular, even in his own party, which remained split over Irish Home Rule and sniping between disappointed office seekers. The Rosebery– Harcourt alliance didn't work and the party lost the election of 1895. Now out for good, Rosebery summed up his situation perfectly: 'There are two supreme pleasures in life. One is ideal, the other real. The ideal is when a man receives the seals of office from his sovereign. The real pleasure comes when he hands them back.'

He said, years later, when out of the limelight, 'I always detested politics ... When I found myself in this evil-smelling bog, I was always trying to extricate myself.' He narrowly missed the arrival of the *Daily Mail*, 'brash and breezy' as it called itself, owned by Alfred Harmsworth. It was deliberately based on American journalese and staid Britain was aghast.

He died after a stroke in May 1929.

Arthur James Balfour 1902–05

The Midlothian Question began to encroach ever more after the appointment of Arthur Balfour to the top job. He was born in July 1848, the son of a laird. His mother was Salisbury's sister and Rosebery's Scottish estate was just down the road. I will not embarrass both of us by telling you where Balfour went to school, but refreshingly, he continued to Cambridge, where he read philosophy and science.

Young Arthur, with large, drooping eyes and interests in music and china was seen as rather effeminate – 'decadent' was the word at the time. His nickname at Eton had been 'Pretty Fanny'.

The only love affair of his life ended when his fiancée, Marie Littleton, died of typhoid in 1875. He may have had flings after that, but they were short lived and discreet. The Balfours were a mixed bunch. One brother drank himself to death; another was a mountaineer killed in 1882; yet a third forged cheques and was exiled to Australia. Arthur's father had been an MP, however, and died when the boy was 6, leaving him a small fortune ($£4$ million – almost $£400$ million today).

In 1874, he was elected Tory MP for Hertford and joined the tiny 'Fourth Party' breakaway group led by Randolph Churchill. He was well known in the Bohemian literary circles in London and developed a reputation as an intriguer.

In 1887, Salisbury gave him the job of Chief Secretary for Ireland, never a sinecure considering the violence in 'John Bull's Other Island'. He stepped up to the plate, condemned by the rebels as 'Bloody Balfour' for his firm measures against them, keeping the infant Irish Republican Brotherhood firmly under wraps.

Interestingly, he got the mood of the politicians right. The Commons was becoming full of young men who were professionals. They were greedy and ambitious and had little or no interest in their constituents or their country. The House of Lords was decrepit and increasingly irrelevant, but a second chamber was deemed to be important, and Balfour had no answers on this score.

In 1895, still in opposition, he became president of the Society for Psychical Research, which for nearly fifty years had been trying to answer the supernatural question posed in Victorian drawing rooms: 'Is anyone there?'

Decline in Salisbury's health as the century turned saw Balfour taking over the top job. He didn't get on well with the new king. With hindsight, Edward VII was a sensible, even useful, addition to the monarchy, but at the time, he was 'Rum-tum', a hugely overweight gambler and womaniser with unfortunate, dissolute friends. Balfour was far more straitlaced.

Britain's position as workshop of the world was fading fast. The United States and, more importantly, an aggressive Germany under the Kaiser, was challenging and overtaking British industrial output. Tariff reform was on everybody's lips and Balfour's government was disunited over it.

In terms of the empire, Balfour set up a committee of Imperial Defence, coordinating the military and naval elements of the largest empire the world had ever known, including Canada, Australia, New Zealand, India and a lot of Africa and other dependencies. The Conservatives were an exhausted force by 1905 and were defeated in the election of the next year. Balfour resigned.

His political career wasn't over as he became advisor in various capacities to later prime ministers. He died in March 1930. 'I do not think,' he said, 'so far as I can judge, in the absence of actual experience, that I am at all afraid of dying.'

He was the first avowed atheist at Number 10.

Henry Campbell-Bannerman 1905–08

The Midlothian question lumbered on. Henry Campbell was born in Glasgow in 1836, but at least he went to school in Scotland and it was a day school! His Tory father was a draper, but one with political ambitions, who received a knighthood for the party. And sent his son on a very belated Grand Tour and then to Glasgow University and Trinity College, Cambridge.

In 1868, he became MP for Stirling, which he held for forty years. The death of a rich uncle, James Bannerman, came with a country estate on condition that he added the Bannerman to the Campbell. He went through a number of government posts, and when he got

Ireland, his secretary reminded him how deeply unpopular Scotsmen were there; he gave him a revolver!

Irish Americans called for the head of the Prince of Wales and offered serious money to hitmen to do the job. CB, as he was now known, was years ahead of his time and would have found favour in many elements of the Gaelic fringe; he believed in Home Rule for Ireland, Scotland and England.

It was the Boer War that threatened to split the Liberal Party. Chamberlain seriously underestimated the willingness and ability of the Boers to fight and the country, like CB, was horrified at the prospect of women and children being rounded up in barbed wire concentration camps. CB was now facing, from his own party, Herbert Asquith, Richard Haldane and Edward Grey, experienced and dodgy politicians with large followings in both Houses. They tried to force him into the Lords, but he held firm, despite having to allow Grey into his cabinet at the Foreign Office. Balfour resigned in December 1905, and the Liberals won a stonking majority weeks later.

His party was hopelessly divided over Ireland, the Boer War fallout and the rise of the political left, a new problem for the twentieth century. Arthur Balfour said of him, 'Campbell-Bannerman is a mere cork, dancing on a torrent which he cannot control.' It is to CB's credit that he kept it all together, but he was not a well man. His wife, Charlotte, died of diabetes in August 1906 and he had heart problems. He was in secret talks with the French over a tight military alliance over an impending Armageddon that CB believed, rightly, would one day erupt. What had been splendid isolation under Salisbury, with Britain presiding magisterially over an 'empire on which the sun never sets' was turning into ever increasing European involvement, which, historically, had rarely ended well.

Henry Campbell-Bannerman died of a heart attack at 10 Downing Street, one of the very few to die there, in April 1908. He had resigned three months earlier, so technically did not die in office.

Herbert Henry Asquith 1908–16

Herbert Asquith was genuinely gifted. He could have been a successful lawyer or an Oxbridge don; instead, he chose politics. He was born in September 1852 to a Nonconformist family of Yorkshire woollen manufacturers. His father died when he was 12; his mother was an invalid. He attended the City of London School and Balliol College, Oxford. He was called to the Bar in 1875, married a doctor's daughter and had five (extraordinarily talented) children. Asquith stood as the Liberal for East Fife in 1886. And won.

He made a name for himself in court and his income rose to £5,000 (£2.6 million today) a year. He grilled the editor of *The Times* over the paper's espousal of forged letters besmirching the character of Charles Stuart Parnell, the Irish Nationalist leader. For those who believe the Fourth Estate to be over-the-top and out-of-order in their total lack of scruple, all well and good. The double standards come when Asquith was also making a few bob writing articles for the same Estate, in his case the *Spectator* and the *Economist*. His second marriage was to Margot Tennant, a socialite who introduced him to all the right London circles. When Gladstone took office again in 1892, Asquith was his Home Secretary. His house in Cavendish Square had fourteen servants, large stables and two grooms, and to afford it, he had to return to the Bar, earning up to £10,000 a year.

In the stitch up of Campbell-Bannerman in 1905, Asquith came out of things well, moving into Number 11 Downing Street as Chancellor of the Exchequer. He brought in three budgets a year and introduced the idea of taxing unearned and earned income. When CB's health deteriorated, the king sent for Asquith as his obvious successor. Some people found scandal in the fact that Asquith had to go to Biarritz to kiss rings; the king was chasing skirts and cards over there at the time. Margot didn't like Number 10. It was 'an inconvenient house with three poor staircases'. Even more ominously, his new neighbour was the Welsh Wizard, the woman-chasing David Lloyd George.

The budget of 1909 didn't go well; the Lords rejected it. The following year, the Liberal majority had disappeared against opposition from forty Socialist MPs and the Irish Nationalists. And to cap it all, Edward VII died in the middle of the whole thing. With the aid of his successor, the straitlaced and frankly boring George V, the Commons was able to solve the constitutional crisis by reducing the power of the Lords. From now on, they could not even delay, much less tinker with, finance bills that came from the Commons.

Ireland was raising its ugly head again as the push for Home Rule continued. Asquith also hit trouble with the Women's Social and Political Union. From small, disconnected beginnings at the end of the nineteenth century, a number of women had become feminists, demanding a greater degree of equality with men. This demand grew more vocal as time went on until Millicent Fawcett and Mrs Pankhurst organized themselves into militant groups, staging sit down strikes, marching on Number 10 and the Houses of Parliament and carrying bricks in their handbags to clout hapless policemen with. Exaggerations appeared in the press on both sides of the debate, but the vast majority of men were opposed to political and economic emancipation, and a surprising number of women merely stood on the sidelines. It didn't help their cause that Queen Victoria had been vehemently opposed to them (as the most powerful woman in the empire and the only one in government) and that two of Asquith's most important ministers, Lloyd George and Winston Churchill, spoke out against them.

All this was eclipsed, however, by the outbreak of the First World War in August 1914. 'The lights are going out all over Europe,' Edward Grey told the Commons grimly. 'We shall not see them lit again in our lifetime.'

The assassination of Archduke Franz Ferdinand by a deranged fanatic, Gavrilo Princip, in Sarajevo in June triggered a series of military alliances that grew, rather like a school playground spat, into a war that killed millions. Wiser heads should have prevailed, but everybody believed they were in the right; God was on their side. And anyway, it would all be over by Christmas. Britain went to war because the Germans invaded neutral Belgium, and the 1839 Treaty of London meant that we were obliged to protect the Belgians. Robert Walpole would have ignored the treaty, roughed out the shock and outrage from other nations and saved the lives of over a million Britons; Herbert Asquith didn't and the result was Armageddon.

He drank heavily; his nickname among the Tories was PJ (Perrier-Jouët) but war was not his thing. He let Herbert Kitchener (a one-dimensional general if ever there was one) and Winston Churchill (who should have known better) send first the navy, then the army to the Dardanelles, to hit Turkey, 'the soft underbelly' of the war. It didn't work, and the Gallipoli Campaign of 1915 saw huge casualties and no acquisition of anything.

The press campaign against Asquith was vitriolic, spearheaded by Lord Northcliffe who then owned both *The Times* and the *Daily Mail* and his job was made worse by the Easter Rising in Dublin in 1916 when the Irish Republican Army (the Brotherhood bit had been dropped for something altogether more vicious) tried to take over the city. The result was The Troubles: six years of guerrilla warfare from which nobody's reputation emerged unscathed. 1916 was also the year in which conscription was introduced for the first time in British history, to augment the appalling casualties on the Western Front. If, as the next generation argued, the British effort in the Great War was lions led by donkeys, as prime minister, Asquith was the biggest donkey of the lot. He had also been indiscreet, having had an odd affair (apparently by letter only) with Venetia Stanley. She now dropped him to marry somebody else, but the letters contained all sorts of shady state secrets which could have reached the press.

The death of Asquith's son Raymond on the Somme in August (where 60,000 casualties were totted up on the first day; ground gained: nil) was possibly the last straw. There were violent rows in cabinet, Andrew Bonar Law, Lloyd George and Max Aitken all demanding a new coalition for the War Committee and the prime minister's head. He finally resigned in December.

Historian Robert Blake wrote that Asquith's fall was the death knell of the old Liberal Party, but that is relying too much on hindsight. What actually killed the Liberals was the rise of the Labour Party. Asquith briefly returned to the Commons, was made an earl in 1925 and given the almost de rigueur KG. He died in February 1928.

Meanwhile, back in 1916, the First World War still raged. It was indeed 'a long way to Tipperary' as the marching song maintained. And after it, Britain was never the same again.

Chapter 18

War to War Carpeting

David Lloyd George 1916–22

In the list of prime ministers, there have been a majority of Englishmen, the occasional Irish connection and a surprising overabundance of Scots. But there has only been one Welshman, and he even he was born in Manchester!

Lloyd George's family moved to Wales (Llanystumduwy, near Criccieth) when he was a toddler. At first an articled clerk, he became Radical MP for Caernarvon at 27. No public school, no university. He was a Welsh nationalist but as soon as he was at Number 10, he stuffed his drawers with pro-Welsh letters and forgot all about them. He loathed both the Church of England and the aristocracy with a passion – 'dishing the dukes', he called it. In fact, most of his life was about passion; after the stoic, rather stodgy Asquith, he came as a deluge to Number 10. He espoused causes, however quixotic, and defended them with the mercurial words of a wizard. He also went after anything in a skirt. His wife, Margaret, put up with this, mostly by living apart from him. She went back to Wales whenever she could.

He championed the cause of the Boers in the war of the same name, which would have seen him hanged as a traitor in earlier centuries; but with the Liberal victory in 1905, he was president of the Board of Trade and later Chancellor of the Exchequer under Asquith. He found the House of Lords an abomination – 'Mr Balfour's poodle' as he called it. 'It fetches and carries for him. It bites anybody he sets it on to.' What the public did not know was that at the time he was being blackmailed by a variety of women who threatened to expose his little peccadilloes!

His 1909 budget was an undisguised attack on the Lords. *Punch* portrayed him as a latter-day Guy Fawkes, planning to blow them up. Edward VII was furious. The aristocracy, Lloyd George claimed, had been living off the fat of the land, for which they did not work, for centuries. He described them as 'five hundred men ... chosen accidentally from among the unemployed'. Lloyd George's further reforms – Old Age Pensions and Unemployment Assistance – were triumphs, designed to safeguard working-class men from drinking and betting themselves to death at the expense of their families, but the doctors, one of the greediest professions in existence, objected and forced the Bill to be amended. *The Times* attacked Lloyd George with vehemence.

Then came Marconi. The Italian had invented the wireless, a piece of original physics, which would transform the world, and anybody who was anybody invested in his company. Lloyd George and others were accused of what today we would call insider trading. As miraculously as the radio itself, the Welsh wizard got away with it. *Punch* hit the nail on the head when it showed a cartoon referring to Lloyd George after the Marconi case – 'you leave the court without a stain – except, perhaps, for the whitewash.'

In 1916, with the war in stalemate and the death rate rising, Lloyd George was chosen to lead the country. He could make dazzling speeches, but he had no answers. He streamlined the War Cabinet and let his generals get on with it as best they could. The sudden breakthrough of the German Army in March 1918 was a serious blow. Lloyd George would only talk of advance and counterattack, but Russia (never effective against the Germans anyway) was out of the war after the Bolshevik Revolution and America had not yet sent troops to France (even when they did, it was only the equivalent of a single division). Lloyd George was blamed for massaging casualty figures, but it was in fact his secretary, J.T. Davies, who burned the originals. Again the prime minister weathered the storm in the election which followed the war (the first in which women – over 30 – were allowed to vote).

The prime minister's reputation was low. The Marconi scandal, an average handling of the war, his failure to get the Russian royal family out of the hands of the Bolsheviks who murdered them, his anti-suffragette stance – all of this came back to haunt him, even without evidence of his extra marital-affairs. The honours scandal blew up in his face (£80,000 for a baronetcy). It became a cattle market with ambitious crawlers literally paying cash to be given a title and a seat in the Lords that Lloyd George wanted to destroy. Lloyd George did nothing.

He was also too vicious in demanding ridiculous reparations from Germany for having caused the First World War. To begin with, Germany did not cause it – Gavrilo Princip did – and clearly, a beaten country could not afford the obscene sums demanded. While the American president Woodrow Wilson, and the British economist John Maynard Keynes urged restraint, Lloyd George and his opposite number, the French president Georges Clemenceau, wanted blood.

By 1922, Bonar Law and Stanley Baldwin led an attack on the corruption of Lloyd George's government. The Liberals opposed the old goat for kicking out Asquith. The Conservatives didn't trust him. And Labour, the new party under their leader, James Ramsay MacDonald, wouldn't touch him with a barge pole. Lloyd George was gone.

He became an earl in 1945 and died in March of that year. Five years earlier, after a meeting with Winston Churchill, then at Number 10 himself, Churchill wrote, 'We were immediately on the same terms as of old, master and servant. He was the master.' Historian Kenneth Morgan described him as 'the rogue elephant among Prime Ministers'.

Andrew Bonar Law 1922–23

Wags often merely ask 'Who?' at the mention of this man's name. Bonar Law was a Canadian (like Lloyd George, a national one-off) born in September 1858 in Kingston, New Brunswick. Like many others who had fled poverty to Canada, the Laws were Scots. In 1874, he attended Glasgow High School and joined his mother's banking firm as a clerk. Unusually for a Scot he was a teetotaller. Progressing in the business and finance world, he married Annie Robley and they went on to have six children.

He entered politics in 1900, his maiden speech condemning Lloyd George's softness over the Boers. Bonar Law was a true-blue imperialist at a time when such ideas were almost universal. He was also 43 (old for a political career) and didn't like London. His grasp of business, however, got him a Secretaryship at the Board of Trade. Out of office after the 1906 Liberal victory, he took the safe seat of Dulwich and buried his grief over the death of his wife by gunning for Lloyd George over his 1909 budget. When Arthur Balfour resigned, Bonar Law became leader of the Conservatives, backed by Max Aitken, another Canadian, who later became Lord Beaverbrook, the newspaper baron who exerted extraordinary power over governments. He now got embroiled in the Irish Question, with the vexed issue of Protestant Ulster. Stirring up trouble, the Germans sent 35,000 rifles to Larne to arm the Ulster Volunteers and mutinous officers in the Curragh were raising two fingers to the government. This was not Bonar Law's finest hour; he turned, briefly, into a ranting Ulster-Scot.

When the war began, Bonar Law targeted Churchill at the Admiralty. The failure of Gallipoli saw Churchill out, consigned to a colonelcy on the Western Front and Bonar Law was made Colonial Secretary in Asquith's coalition. After the effective removal of Asquith in 1916, Bonar Law was at Number 11, backing Lloyd George next door.

After the 1918 election, the Canadian-Scot found himself as Lord Privy Seal and Leader of the House, but two years later became ill and pulled out of politics in May 1921. The crisis in Ireland, however, with the 'Black and Tans' (soldiers in borrowed police uniforms) fighting running battles with Republicans, forced a rethink on the Irish question and Bonar Law, backed by Beaverbrook's *Daily Express* and Lord Rothermere's *Daily Mail* forced a no confidence vote in Lloyd George which led to his resignation.

He was made prime minister in October with a general election to be held the following month. It was laughed off as a 'second eleven' government, but Bonar Law scraped enough seats to hang on. Britain had borrowed heavily from the Americans during the First World War and the United States, more or less already the richest country in the world, wanted the money back. Stanley Baldwin was sent to Washington to negotiate, but the best he could do was to trouser a deal in which Britain would pay £34 million a year in interest. Baldwin signed off on this, against explicit instructions from Bonar Law who said, 'I would be the most cursed prime minister that ever held office if I accepted those terms.'

Six months later he had to retire with throat cancer and died in October 1923. He was buried in Westminster Abbey, Asquith, unkind as ever, murmuring, 'It is fitting that we should have buried the unknown Prime Minister by the side of the unknown soldier.'

Stanley Baldwin 1923–24, 1924–29, 1935–37

While Europe did its best to recover from the traumatizing effects of the Great War, life in the West became hectic and over the top. Women (even those over 21) could vote by 1928 and increasingly they found themselves continuing the men's jobs that they had done during the war, smoking and – shock! horror! – going into pubs on their own. The Versailles Treaty was unduly harsh on Germany and gave rise to Hitler and the Nazis. The Russian Revolution created a left-wing nightmare in which individual freedoms vanished in the service of an omnipotent state. All the prime ministers between the world wars had to carry out a complicated balancing act.

In some ways, after the refreshing educational background of Lloyd George and Bonar Law, Stanley Baldwin was a giant step backwards. Son of an ironmaster he may have been, but he went to Harrow and Trinity College, Cambridge, and took his father's parliamentary seat of Bewdley, Staffordshire, in 1908. He was an economist and believed in protectionism. All very dull and prosaic, but Baldwin was a staunch supporter of the party system and disapproved of the coalition tendency that the war had created. He also disapproved of corruption in high office, which had effectively smeared Lloyd George and his cronies.

Under Bonar Law in 1922, Baldwin was at Number 11, having done more than anybody to oust Lloyd George and all he stood for. He loved classical music, especially Bach, and sang bass in his local church choir. He hated modern art, especially sculpture, and was a cousin of Rudyard Kipling, 'the poet laureate of Empire'. The *Scotsman* was nice about him, unlike many other papers: 'Mr Baldwin resembles Walter Bagehot[1]. Banking is in his blood; economic theory his study and a pleasant outlook on life his habitual cultivation.'

When he overstepped the mark with the American debt and was appointed Bonar Law's successor, many of his own party were horrified. He wasn't as bright as Bonar Law, nor could he make up his mind quickly and easily; he was seen as something of a ditherer. But his appearance worked. He smoked a pipe, wore baggy, unfashionable clothes and had the look of a suburban businessman with an allotment. It wasn't always so. He was a cute 3-year-old with 'Little Lord Fauntleroy' ringlets in a studio portrait with his mother, a solemn knickerbockered rugger player with the Harrow First Fifteen and a rather dashing, straw-boatered man-about-town on honeymoon in 1892.

He lost the 1924 election over tariff reform, which let in Labour, convincing half of society that the world had come to an end. But Labour blew it and Baldwin was back later in the year with a strong cabinet of 'can-do' ministers whose egos would have defeated some men, but Baldwin held them together. A.P. Herbert, whose comments on contemporary politics are legendary and accurate, wrote, 'The House can be beautifully kind or stupidly cruel. It can make the best man look silly and the greatest man afraid.'

Baldwin watched everybody like a hawk, friends and enemies alike, trying to guess what they were up to. His plea to give us 'peace in our time, Lord' was met with the General Strike in 1926 when the government expected the coal miners to take a swingeing pay cut. It was left to university students to drive the buses and Winston Churchill, as Home Secretary, to threaten to send in troops, but after nine days the strike was over, the only one of its kind in history.

Personal finances hit Baldwin, even though, ever since 1911, prime ministers, like all MPs, had been paid a salary. The financial gloom of the late 1920s, culminating in the Wall Street Crash in October 1929, hit the steel industry and lost Baldwin a fortune; he had to sell his London house. Mercifully, Number 10 was still available to him.

When Baldwin was forced to fight a by-election in Saint George's Westminster, Beaverbrook's and Rothermere's papers turned against him (they each had their own agenda). The prime minister hit back with an attack on them that all they wanted was power – 'power without responsibility, the prerogative of the harlot throughout the ages'. It was Kipling's phrase and men of integrity would have been stopped in their tracks, but Beaverbrook and Rothermere had precious little of that.

While the Indians under Mohandas K. Gandhi were clamouring for an end to the Raj, Baldwin thought they may have a point. Churchill would have none of it, however. To him, Gandhi was 'a half-naked fakir in a loincloth' and deserved nothing but contempt. Churchill had served as a soldier in India and knew the viciousness of the North-West Frontier tribesmen.

Finances and the lack of experience/ability in the Labour government toppled Ramsay MacDonald's ministry and a 'National Government' (coalition) was formed in 1931. Baldwin was Lord President of the Council with a stonking £3,000 cut to his salary. The election of 1931 was the greatest landslide in history and the first in which all adults in the country could vote. The Conservatives won 556 seats; Labour 52. As a mark of the sudden – and to some, unbelievable – disappearance of the Liberal Party, they only held four seats in the Commons. Britain had turned blue.

Ramsay MacDonald hung on at Number 10, but when he resigned, Baldwin was back. To use the press cliché of the time, 'dark clouds were gathering' over Europe. In Italy, Benito Mussolini, one of the harlots of the Italian press, had taken power, promising to restore something akin to the Roman Empire (without any of the Roman military competence). In Germany, the weak, dithering Weimar government was replaced in 1933 by Adolf Hitler and his National Socialists.

Nobody wanted to face any of this. Winston Churchill, disgraced and unpopular, harangued Baldwin and later Chamberlain on the German threat and was ignored. As the Germans took power over Saarland and the Rhineland, reintroduced conscription, built up their armed forces, effectively tearing up the Versailles peace settlement of 1919, both British and French governments looked on in bemused (and fatal) detachment.

And, while such genuine problems were building, the British press and their public do what they always do – they became fascinated by a minor hiccup which should have been consigned to a footnote. In 1936, Edward, Prince of Wales, who rather admired Hitler in a British sort of way, fell in love with an American divorcee, Wallis Simpson. The convention at the time was that a king could not marry a commoner. Worse, she was divorced. Worse still, although no one in polite society had the nerve to mention it, she was an American! Baldwin steered this stupid entanglement as best he could, gagging the still stuffy British press, but unable to control the others, who had a field day. The abdication crisis blew up out of all proportion. It ended with a perfectly good replacement on the throne, George VI, who didn't like Hitler at all, and booting the ex-king out to the Bahamas where he could cause no more trouble. He and Mrs Simpson lived unhappily ever after.

As Hitler's Luftwaffe grew in parity with the RAF and Mussolini invaded Abyssinia, the clamour in the press for Baldwin to do something increased. 'Keep us out of war, Sam,' the prime minister told Samuel Hoare, his Foreign Secretary, 'we are not ready for it.' When Haile Selassi, the Abyssinian ruler, appealed to the League of Nations for help against the better-armed Italians, the League made 'there, there' noises and did nothing. Hitler and the Germans had already left the League.

The Fuhrer's invasion of the unoccupied Rhineland frontier with France in 1936 forced the issue. Baldwin's Hoare-Laval Pact, which effectively gave Mussolini his head, was made public, but rather than causing outrage, too many of the great and the good, especially on the left, were for appeasement. And too many on the Right could see little wrong in it. In 1933, the year that Hitler came to power, the Conservative candidate in a by-election in East Fulham, demanded a bigger navy, a bigger army and a bigger air force. He lost heavily to the Socialists who had soaked up Karl Marx's utopian and wholly unrealistic concept of brotherhood of man, where equality reigns supreme and the sun always shines. A speech that Baldwin made three years later made it obvious that he hadn't told the truth about the impending crisis; he had put party before country.

The abdication crisis had made Baldwin stay on longer than he should have done. His asthma grew worse, and he tired easily. He retired in May 1937, collecting his KG and earldom on the way. During the war that followed, for which he was unprepared, the wrought iron gates of his house were, appropriately, taken down and melted into scrap. Ironically, he helped rearmament at last. He died in December 1947, his ashes buried in Worcester Cathedral.

James Ramsay MacDonald 1924, 1929–35

When James Ramsay MacDonald was born in Lossiemouth in October 1866, Karl Marx had written his epic *Communist Manifesto*. The book would have an effect on the modern world as profound as the Bible did centuries earlier and for the same reason; it contained the words that ordinary people wanted to hear. Marx, urging the working men of all nations to unite in order to throw off the chains of injustice and inequality, offered heaven here on earth. As uplifting messages of morality, both books are superb; as political common sense, they are both hogwash. The irony is that both books have caused death and misery on an unprecedented scale.

Ramsay Mac was illegitimate, adopted by a ploughman, and the child of a servant girl. In that sense, he was the first working-class individual to occupy Number 10, which is an astonishing achievement in itself. Arguably, he was only one of several other bastards who lived there. He attended the Free Kirk School, at a time when Scottish education was second to none in Britain and became a pupil teacher (the rough equivalent of a teaching assistant today) on £7 10s a year. It was in Bristol that Ramsay MacDonald first learned of Socialism, talking with comrades in the British Working Men's Coffee Tavern. In London, he addressed envelopes for the Cyclists' Touring Club for 10s a week. Most of his food (oatmeal) was sent by his mother from home. He joined the Fabian Society, a group of intellectual socialists and, in 1894, the Independent Labour Party.

He lost his first election attempt in Southampton, but, nothing daunted, courted and married Margaret Gladstone (no relation) and they had six children. He wrote articles for journals and lectured all over the country, with his upright bearing, attractive Scots accent and powerful oratory, popular with the masses. He worked as secretary of the Labour Party from his home on a salary of 20 guineas a year.

Ramsay MacDonald opposed the Boer War in good old Socialist tradition, but denied that he was a Marxist. He wasn't above doing deals with Liberal hopefuls, however, so that when the 1906 election happened, there were twenty-nine Labour MPs in the Commons, Ramsay MacDonald himself standing for Leicester. His wife died five years later, but at least some of her financial security was offset by the salary that MPs now received. He was Chairman of the Party in that year.

In 1914, indeed throughout the Great War, Ramsay MacDonald pushed for a negotiated peace with Germany. He was not a pacifist, nor a conscientious objector, although he was accused of being both. His birth certificate, complete with the blank for his father's name and the words 'base born' was published in an attempt to discredit him.

Bearing in mind the huge breadth of his party's aspirations, from pseudo liberals who wanted to introduce reforms slowly and piecemeal to revolutionary Marxists who wanted to take to the barricades, Ramsay MacDonald had to tread lightly. The result was a massive correspondence which shows him in a highly duplicitous light – 'dancing around the mulberry bush' as an opponent said.

The outbreak of the Russian Revolution in the spring of 1917 was met with delight. Vladimir Ilyich Lenin had read Karl Marx too but wanted to act out the blueprint. Offering the starving Russian peasants peace, bread and land (none of which he provided), he overthrew the moderate government of Alexander Kerensky that had replaced the tsar. The violence of Lenin's October Revolution alarmed voters and Ramsay MacDonald lost his seat in the election of 1918.

In 1922 he was back in office as party chairman and MP for Aberavon. The crisis over tariff reform led to the fall of Baldwin and, improbably, Ramsay MacDonald, as leader of the strongest party still standing, became prime minister in January 1924. He couldn't push through a Socialist programme at the time – the ideas were too raw and tinged with Bolshevik atrocities. Even so, he backed the Dawes plan, which settled the vexed problem of German reparations for the war and was among the first nations to recognise Lenin's new Soviet Union as a world power.

The strength of feeling against Labour, however, was shown by the zeal with which the Liberals joined the Conservatives to topple Ramsay MacDonald. To that end, somebody forged the Zinoviev letters, supposedly evidence of a Bolshevik plot between Russia and the Labour Party to create a Soviet state in Britain. It was a lie and the process used illegal, but it frightened the ever-gullible electorate who voted for the opposition. 1924 was the year in which the impoverished crofter caved in to the lure of the bung. The chairman of the McVitie and Price biscuit company was an old mate and he gave the prime minister a Daimler car and £30,000 (the equivalent of £10 million today). In exchange (remember Lloyd George?), the chairman got a baronetcy.

Ramsay MacDonald's stance over the 1926 general strike was telling – a downing of tools, the working man's knee-jerk reaction since the dawn of time, was not the way forward. Most people backed this idea and Labour won 287 seats in the election three years later, with the Conservatives on 216 and the Liberals (reviving a little) 59. The Wall Street Crash hit everybody. What the Marxists had been saying for seventy years, that capitalism was not only greedy and immoral, but economically flawed, had come to pass. Ramsay Mac had no answers. The May committee (bankers and economists all) recommended more cuts in public spending and higher taxes; the Labour-led government sounded more like the old Tories every day. The only solution was a National government, a crisis coalition, which was never going to work. Baldwin was, as we have seen, president of the Council. Samuel Herbert (Liberal), was Home Secretary. The Left felt betrayed – Ramsay Mac, the Lost Leader, had let them down. He was now Labour leader of an increasingly Conservative government. He himself was getting older. His eyesight was deteriorating and his memory going. He lost his seat for Seaham and resigned, hanging on in parliament as MP for the Scottish Universities until 1937, the year of his death.

A widower for twenty years, he had an affair, probably platonic, with Edith, Marchioness of Londonderry, one of the London 'in-crowd'. All in all, the first appearances of the Labour Party in British politics were not impressive; And Ramsay Mac has to carry the can for some of that.

Arthur Neville Chamberlain 1937–40

Neville was born in Birmingham in March 1869, attended Rugby school and Mason College, Birmingham. He became a chartered accountant. Later historians would say that he looked like a successful undertaker, (which is more or less the same thing) but he lost £80,000 of family money when his sisal plantation in the West Indies didn't pan out.

Like his father, Joseph, Chamberlain was heavily into local politics. He was mayor of Birmingham in 1915 and the following year was made

Director General of National Service (handling conscription) by Lloyd George, who called him a 'pinhead'. Like his father, he rose fast. He was good with figures and minutiae, but his role as Chancellor of the Exchequer in the National government was rather more taxing (pun intended). He advocated deflation as the answer to the financial crisis of 1929 and did not seem overly concerned about those forced on to the dole.

Increasingly, during the 1930s, foreign policy dominated British politics. He believed the French to be decadent – the mutiny of their army at Verdun in 1917 had done irreparable damage to the country once run by Napoleon. He saw the Soviet Union as a perpetual troublemaker, which it was, thanks to Comrade Trotsky's urge to make Communism a worldwide creed. But Germany, under the new chancellor Adolf Hitler, was pulling together out of the defeat of the First World War, and that was admirable. He didn't like the Americans, finding their promises all talk. He did try to buy off Mussolini from an alliance with Hitler at a time when the Italian was a senior partner in terms of political experience; that didn't work.

Once Germany had grabbed Sudetenland, would all of Czechoslovakia follow? It was a new country created in 1919 but was riven with racial differences – Czechs and Slovaks. Chamberlain was the first prime minister to travel by plane and flew to Munich several times, coming back with a piece of paper signed by Hitler to the effect that, after Czechoslovakia, there would be no more aggression. 'Peace with honour,' Chamberlain told waiting crowds of pressmen at Heston Airport and again outside Number 10. He was consciously echoing Disraeli after the Congress of Berlin, and no comparison could have been worse. 'Peace in our time', another of Chamberlain's phrases was over in less than a year. *The Times* at the time sung his praises. 'No conqueror returning from a victory on the battlefield has come adorned with nobler laurels.'

Hitler was lying through his teeth. Sporting the same *lebensraum* nonsense as before, he not only invaded Czechoslovakia, but made a secret and highly duplicitous alliance with Joseph Stalin's Soviet Union and invaded Poland on a trumped-up excuse of Polish aggression.

Chamberlain's announcement over the wireless on 3 September 1939 shocked the nation. He had given Hitler an ultimatum – pull out of Poland or else. There was no reply. And so, twenty-one years after the First World War ended, the Second began. Jock Colvin, Winston Churchill's private secretary, summed the situation up. The cabinet were 'nonentities presided over by one magisterial personality'. Today even that seems far-fetched – Chamberlain was as much of a nonentity as the rest.

The Phoney War was the lull before the storm. Thousands of children were evacuated from the cities in the belief that those cities would become Guernicas. Thousands of cardboard coffins were made (and not used). Millions of gas masks were produced (and not used either).

Then the war began in earnest. Germany's war machine swung west in the spring of 1940, and the countries of Europe, the Netherlands, Belgium, France collapsed like a house of cards. After the ghastly stalemate of the trenches in 1914–18, nobody was ready for the sheer speed of the Second World War. When Norway fell, the writing was on the wall. The Great Appeaser resigned and Number 10 fell to Churchill. Within six months, Chamberlain had died of cancer.

Historians have tried to preserve something of the man's reputation, but have largely failed. He was an introvert, suited to church vestry politics and completely out of his depth on the international stage, especially when dealing with a megalomaniac the likes of which had never been seen in the modern world.

Chapter 19

The New Deal and the Bomb

Franklin Delano Roosevelt 1933–45

Nobody has a bad word to say about FDR (which makes my job very difficult!). Even Joseph Stalin, his unlikely ally in the Second World War, sang his praises as a man of 'initiative, courage and determination'. James Loewen, the brilliant burster of presidential bubbles, has nothing derogatory to say. Is FDR, in short, 'too good to be true?' In US surveys over the last twenty years, he has stayed solidly at Number 3, below the saints George Washington and Abraham Lincoln. Ironically, other European dictators looked favourably on him as well. Both Hitler and Mussolini approved his New Deal of the Thirties because it was exactly the same arbitrary centralization that they were using in their own countries.

True, Roosevelt was born with a silver spoon in his mouth, which is enough to discredit him in some circles. His parents were rich New Yorkers and he was privately educated, partly at home, before attending Harvard, where he read law. He married Eleanor Roosevelt (a distant cousin on Teddy's side of the family), in 1905. He was outgoing, cheerful, dashing even; she was shy and quiet. She brought up the kids; his stepmother's money kept them to the manner born. He entered politics largely because he admired Teddy.

In 1918, details of his affair with his wife's secretary, Lucy Mercer, became public (thank God) and the whole thing was hushed up to avoid scandal. He promised to break things off with Lucy but never did; but the physical side of his marriage to Eleanor was over (they *did* already have five children). In August 1921, FDR developed polio and became wheelchair bound from then on. Years of physical therapy followed.

After a tough rise in local and national politics, Roosevelt's inaugural address famously said, 'The only thing we have to fear is fear itself,' even though his detailed plan for ending the recession didn't really exist. Through a series of 'fireside chats' on the radio, the president promised a raft of economic improvements which collectively were called the 'New Deal' (as opposed to Teddy Roosevelt's Square Deal). Not everybody was impressed; the Republicans' response was 'Let's Get Another Deck'. For all its apparent success, the New Deal didn't end the Depression, but FDR's popularity soared nevertheless. Judge Oliver Wendell Holmes described him as 'a second-class intellect; a first-class temperament'. And that, in the end, is what counts with most voters – a man they feel they can trust. Winston Churchill, who had twisted FDR's arm to join the Second World War, described meeting the president as like opening your first bottle of champagne. The tide turned against the man in the summer of 1934 when big business came to believe that the legislation from the White House was going too far and was an infringement of civil liberties (see the dictators' views above). The press got on board and he was called a traitor to his class. As the recovery levelled off, FDR's popularity waned and he was attacked by both Left and Right. The Supreme Court found against the government in 1935, a result that Roosevelt ignored, complaining that the decision took America back to 'the horse and buggy era'. He hitched himself to the cause of the common man against big business, which a number of his predecessors had done – 'They [big business] are unanimous in their hatred of me and I welcome their hatred.'

When FDR tried to reorganise the ultra-conservative Supreme Court (see Trump), public opinion swung against him. America has never had a genuine left in politics, despite the existence of a tiny Communist party, and most Americans rally round money and those who make it. The reforms of Asquith's Liberals in Britain were just catching on under FDR, but America would not stand for what was still to come, the full-blown welfare state of Clement Attlee; the watering down of Obamacare (see Chapter 25) has proved that. Roosevelt's schemes were severely undermined. A second depression in 1937 led to the New Deal being put on hold.

As the Second World War developed, and Churchill harangued FDR in private phone conversations, an undecided president was labelled a 'warmonger' by Americans who still believed in 'splendid isolation' and saw no need to involve themselves in somebody else's war. 'Your boys,' the president told American mothers, 'are not going to be sent into any foreign wars.' Pearl Harbor ended that when the Japanese air force hit, without the usual declaration of war, the American fleet in the Hawaiian base. Now 'Dr New Deal' became 'Dr Win The War'. He had no military experience and left the fighting to his generals and admirals.

Then he got nasty. The British had interned potential internal enemies – Germans, Austrians and Italians – living in Britain. FDR did the same to the Japanese – 120,000 were rounded up and dumped in grim prison camps in Utah. He was always over-conscious of minority pressure in the US: not outlawing lynching of blacks in case it upset the South; limiting Jewish entry to the country because of anti-Semitism of the 1930s and 1940s. In the turmoil of the Second World War, most Americans chose to forgive all that, unless, of course, they were black or Jewish. FDR won an unprecedented fourth term in office.

He was criticized for falling for Stalin's lies at the Yalta Conference in January 1945, but FDR had a war to win. He didn't live to see it, dying of a cerebral haemorrhage in the 'little White House' in Warm Springs, Georgia, in April, weeks before the German surrender.

Harry S. Truman 1945–53

John L. Lewis had got the new president in his sights. '[Truman] is a man totally unfitted for the position. His principles are elastic and he is careless with the truth. He has no special knowledge of any subject, and he is a malignant, scheming sort of individual who is dangerous ... to the United States of America.'

Everybody knows that the 'S' in his name stood for nothing; it was given in honour of both grandfathers, Shipp and Solomon. David Blanchflower, writing an essay on him in 2021, claims that, 'at 5 foot 9 he was short for a president', joint thirty-third on the list, along with Millard Fillmore. Blanchflower spends an entire paragraph on relative heights, proving the 'tall always wins' myth. As an historian who stands 5ft 4in (the same as James Madison), I of course reject this hypothesis.

Truman had no college education, served in the army in France in the First World War and became a County Court Judge despite having no legal training at all (only in America ...). He entered politics under the mentorship of Tom Prendergast, who later served federal time for tax evasion. He became vice president to FDR in January 1945, but he had little contact with the president, meeting only twice in private. When Roosevelt died, Truman offered Eleanor his condolences and asked what he could do for her. Her response was, 'Is there anything we can do for you? You're the one in trouble now.'

So were sections of the American media. In November 1948, the *Chicago Daily Tribune* trumpeted, 'Dewey defeats Truman'. It was the other way round! Wishful thinking, perhaps ...

The American newspaper industry didn't like Truman. The major magnates who owned most mainstream media – Hearst, McCormick-Patterson, Scripps-Howard and Time-Life – all objected to his policies. He got around them by his radio broadcasts.

The man had a bolthole in Key West, Florida, where he swam, walked and drank Old Grand-Dad bourbon. He loved dirty jokes. There were two assassination attempts on his life while president and more afterwards.

It was the Truman Doctrine of 1947 that created the United States as the world's policeman, a complete reversal of the isolationist stance of the 1920s and 1930s. As a champion of democracy, America now had its work cut out against the oppressive regimes around the world. It was a bold, and some would say reckless, policy, which has brought more grief and problems to the United States than anything since the

Civil War. The current president, 'Sleepy Joe' Biden, has officially stated that this period of American foreign policy is now over. The first debacle was the Korean War in 1950, which resulted in the deaths of 40,000 Americans with far more injured. Truman had gone into Korea without the consent of Congress.

The blackest mark against the president, however, is his decision to drop atomic bombs in Japan to end that element of the Second World War. So secret was the Manhattan Project that FDR didn't tell his vice president about it. Robert Oppenheimer, the scientist leading the bomb-building programme, quoted the god Vishnu in the Hindu scripture the *Bhagavad-Gita*, saying, 'I am become death, the destroyer of worlds.' When he went to see Truman with the bomb's capabilities spelt out, the president said to his aide, Dean Acheson, 'Never bring that fucking cretin in here again. He didn't drop the bomb. I did. That kind of weepiness makes me sick.'

The terror of nuclear war hangs over us all still, but only Harry Truman has actually used it.

Dwight David Eisenhower 1953–61

Harry S. Truman didn't take to opponents. 'If Eisenhower should become President, his administration would make Grant's look like a model of perfection.'

Yet the ex-soldier and war hero perfectly followed the Truman Doctrine, with all its ambiguities. 'We're going to have peace, even if we have to fight for it.'

Dwight Eisenhower was unusual. He became the commander of the Allied Expeditionary Force that fought its way from the Normandy beaches to Berlin in 1944–5 without any actual combat experience at all. Similarly, he entered politics with no leanings in that direction; until 1948, he hadn't even voted. He grew up in Abilene, Texas, not long after its existence as a lawless cowboy town, and joined West Point in 1911. He married Mamie (Mary) Dowd four years later, and, before

Jackie Kennedy, she was the most dazzling of the First Ladies at the White House.

His relationship with the Fourth Estate was good, because he had spoken to them man-to-man as a general during the war. They by and large accepted this approach and gave him a relatively easy ride.

Bernard Montgomery ('Monty') commander of the British forces in the Normandy Campaign, doubted the man's ability. 'He is a very nice chap ... But I can also say, quite definitely, that he knows nothing whatever about how to make war or to fight battles ... The American Army will never be any good until we can teach the generals their stuff.' Memories of Yorktown (1781) still lingered! There were also those who discovered that Eisenhower's family had come to Pennsylvania in the 1740s from the German Saarland and eyebrows were raised.

Where soldiers like Wellington never really adapted to the very different kind of campaigning necessary for politics, 'Ike' took to it like a duck to water. Learning his politics quickly from Senator Harry Cabot Lodge, Eisenhower defeated the backward-looking isolationist Senator Taft and became president. His appointment of the little-known Richard Nixon as vice president caused little stir in those heady, prosperous pre-Watergate days. 'I like Ike' rang out all over the States; the general, with his easy grin and Kansas charm, won hearts and minds everywhere.

The new president was perhaps too soft on Joe McCarthy, the Wisconsin rabble-rouser obsessed with the notion of 'Reds under the bed'. He had accused Truman's White House of Communist affiliation and levelled the same accusations against Eisenhower. In the end, McCarthy shot himself in the foot by attacking Eisenhower's military record and both the American public and the press had had enough. McCarthy was toast.

The president was a 60-a-day man with heart problems and Nixon was the hawk, anxious to take the Truman Doctrine into Vietnam. But it was Eisenhower's failure to back the British over the Suez crisis in

1956, that led to a breakdown in the 'special relationship' between the Allies, and the end of Anthony Eden's premiership.

But the prosperity of the Eisenhower years – the car in every garage, the television in every living room, the washing machine in every kitchen – did not reach everybody. Black Americans in particular, herding as they did into Chicago, Cleveland and Detroit, were ignored and the advance seemed to be only for the white middle class. Eisenhower promoted no legislation for civil rights, even insisting that segregation remained in force in the army.

His presidency was eclipsed by that of his successor, John F. Kennedy, and his popularity in his day and today relies almost entirely on his war record.

Chapter 20

From Boom to Bust

Winston Leonard Spencer Churchill 1940–45, 1951–53

Churchill was a return to the aristocracy of old. His father, Randolph, was the arrogant raconteur of the Fourth Party who had harangued everyone in the 1870s. His mother was an American socialite, Jennie Jerome of New York; all his life the younger Churchill pushed his American links to the limit.

From Harrow (where he was bullied), Churchill went, not to the conventional Oxbridge (his father thought him too stupid), but to Sandhurst, the training school for officers. Churchill's entrance exam to Harrow had seen his brain seize up in panic, and all he wrote was his name at the top of the paper. He didn't do much better at Sandhurst. The bright cadets went into the Royal Engineers; relative 'thickies' like Churchill could only manage the cavalry – in his case the 4th Hussars.

He loved action and excitement and he discovered that he had an ability to write. He saw war in Cuba, wrote articles for the *Daily Graphic* and went with his regiment to India as part of the Malakand force. He missed most of the fighting, but that did not stop him from writing up the campaign and getting it published, through his mother's influential friends (his father had died of syphilis by this time). Senior officers, like Herbert Kitchener, hated the man's arrogance – a subaltern offering military advice to generals – and tried to keep him out. He pulled strings, however, and got himself attached, as the semi-official war correspondent, to the force sent to the Sudan to avenge the murder of General Gordon. By chance, he found himself riding with the 21st Lancers at Omdurman in 1898. And, of course, wrote about it. The regiment distinguished themselves and the army threw the bones of the long-dead Mahdi into the Nile.

Yet Churchill's real ambition was not the army, but politics, as if to prove the ghost of his father wrong. He stood as Conservative for Oldham and lost, so he went, as a journalist for the *Morning Post*, to cover the Boer War. He was captured during an attack on an armoured train, escaped and became a fugitive with a £25 price on his head. The description of him by the Boers is extraordinarily accurate: 'He walks with a forward stoop, reddish brown hair, hardly noticeable moustache, talks through his nose and cannot pronounce the letter "s" properly.'

Back home he stood for Oldham again and, as a war hero, won. He also made £10,000 on the lecture circuit. His speeches in the Commons dazzled as his father's had – when he quoted Latin and there were loud calls for translation, he smiled and said, 'Certainly I will translate for the benefit of any old Etonians present.' Then he crossed the floor of the house to become a Liberal, simply the latest in the outrageous and maverick behaviour which, if anything, was even more arrogant than that of his father. In fact, the *Daily Chronicle* called him 'Pushful the Younger'.

Churchill stood on the Free Trade ticket as MP for Manchester North West and was made Under Secretary for the Colonies in 1906. Under Campbell-Bannerman, he was president of the Board of Trade, married Clementine Hozier, living on his minister's salary and the income from his writing. He became an ally of Lord Lloyd George, and briefly the pair were a formidable combination; Lloyd George with his 'wizard' Welsh lilt and Churchill with his speech impediment.

In 1910, as Home Secretary, Churchill made front page news when he appeared, in top hat and frock coat, in the rain-drenched siege of Sidney Street where anarchists under Peter the Painter had holed up in Number 100. Churchill was showboating of course; he did not have to be there. *And* he advocated the use of howitzers and the Horse Artillery to blast the house to pieces. As things turned out, it was not necessary; the Anarchists set fire to it.

Having changed parties, Churchill now changed approach. He had opposed naval expansion on the grounds of expense. Now as war loomed ominously, he was all for building as many Dreadnoughts as possible – 'We want eight; And we won't wait.' This got him the post of First Lord of the Admiralty in 1911 for which he had no aptitude and in which he made belligerent speeches against the Germans. The *Spectator* in that year claimed that Churchill 'has not the loyalty, the dignity, the steadfastness to make an efficient head of a great office'. In the summer of 1914, he ordered the armed Spithead review fleet to battle stations and called up reservists before war had even been declared. His sending of a force to stop Antwerp falling into German hands backfired; three battalions were taken prisoner and he was torn apart by the press.

A far worse mistake was Gallipoli. The idea was a bold one, to knock Turkey out of the war by taking Constantinople (Istanbul). Churchill's own navy let him down, however, refusing to risk the minefield in the Dardanelles, so the campaign had to become a land-based army operation. It was back to the trenches again, as in France, but with better weather. The only thing that went well in Gallipoli was the withdrawal of the entire Expeditionary Force one night under cover of darkness. This ought to have been the end of Churchill's career. He went instead to the Western Front, where he commanded a battalion of the Royal Scots Fusiliers without, it must be said, any experience of such warfare at all, to the extent that he gave 1890s cavalry orders to 1916 infantrymen!

By May 1917, Churchill was back as Minister of Munitions. Most of the opposition he had faced was from the Conservatives, who had never forgotten or forgiven his defection to the Liberals. By the end of the war, however, he was both Secretary for War and Minister for Air, a new role because of the arrival of aerial warfare and the Royal Flying Corps (soon to be known as the RAF). The election of 1918 saw him out of office.

At home, he wrote a five-volume history of the war (as he would do again in 1945), lost a couple of election attempts, and got in for Epping as a 'constitutionalist' (whatever that meant), and went to Number 11 under Baldwin in 1924. During the General Strike, he edited *The British Gazette*, a government propaganda rag denouncing the trades unions.

Churchill resigned in 1931 over the issue of Indian independence. Since 1857, and in fact for many years before that, the British had ruled India, indirectly and directly, under the Raj. Churchill himself had fought in India and had no patience with the people who routinely burned the widows of Hindus until the British arrived. Those who today scream about Churchill's racism, choose to ignore that Gandhi, the independence leader, was equally vociferous against black Africans. Out of office and out of favour, Churchill wrote *Life of Marlborough* (his ancestor) of a Britain when there were no prime ministers at all. He backed Edward VIII over the abdication crisis, where most of the country felt betrayed by the king. He railed, almost alone, against the rise of Fascism, warning of the dangers of Hitler and Mussolini.

Chamberlain's appeasement didn't work and when war was declared, Churchill was back almost where he had started years before as First Lord of the Admiralty. He was already at retirement age after a tempestuous career, but this was to be his finest hour. When Chamberlain resigned in 1940, the king sent for him. It was an extraordinary come back after years in the wilderness and, although the public didn't know it, he had already made a shambles of the Norway Campaign. Dunkirk in May was a disaster too, but with his masterly oratory (his speeches are easily the most famous of any prime minister) he managed to turn a humiliating defeat into something akin to victory.

Never mind that these speeches on the radio were often delivered by an actor (*everybody* could do Churchill), he appeared as often as possible in rubble-strewn, Blitzed London, leaving Number 10 only to go to his bunker under the shattered streets. The bulldog determination (some people said he even looked like one) showed even when all and sundry, from his military advisers to the handful of Nazi sympathisers not actually in gaol, told him that Britain couldn't win the war. At the time, it was deemed necessary, but with hindsight signalled the end of so many freedoms, but Churchill presided over a police state, exemplified by an army of 'little Hitlers' in tin hats, men listening at corners and below stairs. Gossip was illegal; defeatism a crime. Those of us today who rail against the loss of free speech can lay some of this at Churchill's door.

He was no strategist. He nevertheless sent an expeditionary force to Singapore as he had to the Dardanelles with ghastly results. The Japanese, with only a third of the men the British had, overran the colony/island and worked prisoners to death on the notorious Burma Railway for the next three years. He continued to back Stalin in order to keep the Reich fighting in a war on two fronts, but he went too far in this, denying the RAF planes that could have defended Singapore and losing thousands of tonnes of shipping on the North Atlantic convoys. After Singapore, Britain's Eastern empire ceased to exist.

After all the accolades involved in winning the war, the man who would later be voted the greatest living Englishman was ousted in the general election of 1945. The war itself had exposed all kinds of problems, not least in education and health, and Churchill was too old and too disinterested to cope with any of that.

By the time he came back, in October 1951, the world had changed again. The king was ill. Churchill was, apparently, downing a bottle of Scotch a day and smoking cigars for England. With Hitler gone and Europe once again a smoking ruin, the stage was set for East versus West (which is where we still are, in a slightly different context). Just as Churchill had warned against the Nazis in the 1930s, so now he spoke warningly of the Soviet Union – 'an Iron Curtain has come down,' he told an American audience in 1946, 'from Stettin in the Baltic to Trieste in the Adriatic.' Communist Russia was the new enemy and the United States agreed.

Churchill resigned in 1955 and he died, a grander old man even than Gladstone, ten years later. I can remember, as a schoolboy, watching his state funeral on television (we all had a day off school) as the cranes of London docks were lowered in his honour as his barge travelled up river along the Thames. We have never looked upon his like again, but too many historians, from Andrew Roberts to Boris Johnson, see him as too much of a saint.

Clement Richard Attlee 1945–51

After Churchill, Clem Attlee appeared a disappointment. While Churchill dashed around, with homburg on head, cigar clasped in bulldog jaws and two fingers raised, his wartime deputy looked like a rather boring solicitor (which is what his father was). When somebody said to Churchill '[Attlee] looks like a modest little chap,' the prime minister's reply was 'Yes, and he has a lot to be modest about.' In fact, Churchill nearly got Attlee killed – the man had been a major at Gallipoli.

Attlee was born in Putney in 1883 and attended Haileybury and University College, Oxford. He was conservative by nature, a staunch Anglican and rather boring. As Churchill said (again!) he was 'a sheep in sheep's clothing'. He was called to the Bar in 1907.

Attlee was lecturing at the left-leaning London School of Economics when war broke out and volunteered with a commission in the South Lancashire Regiment. After the war, he was back into Socialist politics in London and was elected MP for Limehouse, becoming Parliamentary Secretary to Ramsay MacDonald. In the first Labour government, he was Under Secretary at the War Office. He read two daily papers – or rather, he didn't. He followed *The Times* for the cricket score and the *Daily Herald* because it was a Socialist rag.

The 1931 situation saw the collapse of Ramsay MacDonald's second ministry, but Attlee stayed on under the Labour leadership of George Lansbury, because of his calm, clipped, common-sense approach.

With the outbreak of war, Chamberlain made Attlee Lord Privy Seal, effectively deputy prime minister, although there was no such post at the time. Under Churchill, he quietly organized his boss's policy, sometimes reining in the more bizarre ideas quietly and behind the scenes. As we have seen, the end of the war brought a seismic change. The years of living dangerously had, hopefully, gone, but social reforms, which the war had delayed, now needed urgent attention.

Attlee's landslide victory took him by surprise, and he was surrounded by colourful, pushy characters more in the public eye than he was. A. Wilson wrote, 'An empty taxi arrived at 10 Downing Street, and when the door opened, Attlee got out.' The government's whirlwind reforms were perhaps unique in history for all that.

The Liberal government before the First World War had laid the foundations of the Welfare State, but it was Attlee's men who actually created it. Coal was nationalized; so was gas, electricity, steel and the railways. According to Socialist doctrine, the means of production were now in the hands of the people and it would take years for most of those people to realize how empty the promises of 1945–52 actually were. In some ways, the most important reform was the creation of a National Health Service, paid for by the state and compulsory contributions from the public; support of all kinds from 'cradle to grave'. It was Aneurin Bevan who pushed this through, despite *huge* opposition from the majority of doctors (and almost all dentists) who refused to play ball on the grounds of sheer greed. Consequently, Bevan had to modify his changes and allow private practice to exist alongside free ones. When, on his deathbed, someone reminded Attlee of the force of good of the NHS, he said, 'It seemed all right at the time, but I had underestimated the selfishness of the public.'

In terms of the empire, rapidly morphing into the Commonwealth in these years, India and Pakistan were created in 1947, resulting in the deaths of over a million people. The government – especially Lord Louis Mountbatten, India's last viceroy – was blamed for this at the time and has been ever since. In fact, the blame lies squarely with the Indians and Pakistanis who could not live together because of racial and religious differences. India had always been a sub-continent riven by faction and almost incessant tribal war. Under the British Raj, most of that was stamped out, but it had clearly not gone away. Today, seventy years after both sides were given what they demanded, Indian and Pakistani troops still face each other over barbed wire perimeters, missiles at the ready.

Rather like Gladstone's 'range of exhausted volcanoes' in 1874, Attlee's government was burned out by 1951. The Conservatives, under their old war horse, Churchill, were back. Attlee took an earldom and a KG, the prerogative of all prime ministers since Walpole. He died in October 1967.

In the end, he had the last laugh. As he wrote:

Few thought he was even a starter –
There were many who thought themselves smarter –
But he ended PM,
CH[1] and OM,[2]
An Earl and a Knight of the Garter.

Anthony Eden 1955–57

With his Douglas Fairbanks' smile and fetching moustache, Anthony Eden was physically the antithesis of both Churchill and Attlee. He was born in June 1897, the son of a baronet and was an army officer at 18. By 1918, he was a major and had won the Military Cross. Before that, Eton and Oxford where he had studied Persian (Iraqi/Iranian today) and was keen on post–impressionist art.

He became Conservative MP for Leamington in 1923 and with the sudden fall of Samuel Hoare over the Abyssinian/Italian crisis, he found himself Foreign Secretary under Baldwin. He himself went when Chamberlain ignored President Roosevelt's offer of an international conference to discuss Hitler (1938) but Chamberlain called him back as Dominions Secretary a year later. Under Churchill, he rapidly switched from Secretary of State for War to the Foreign Office and became Leader of the House in 1942.

Under pressure, the dashing young man, still in his forties, became tetchy and prone to outbursts, but his wider popularity carried him far and he came through the Second World War as a politician as squeaky clean as he had militarily through the First.

In 1951, the same pairing of Churchill and Eden led a country visibly shaken up by Attlee's reforms, and the Foreign Office now stared the guns of the Cold War directly in the face. A calmer and more rational look at the situation might have called Russia's bluff. But the eastern bloc was succumbing to the USSR and nobody, other than Russia, was in the mood for more war after the bloodbath of 1939–45.

It didn't help that Eden was ill. He had his gall bladder removed in 1953 and two more operations carried out in Boston. Churchill had a stroke and the ship of state suddenly seemed rudderless. The cracks in the alliances of the war were beginning to show. Not only were East and West no longer friendly, but John Foster Dulles, the American Secretary of State, was loudly and publicly attacking Britain for its 'colonialism' (this from a country that had been consistently 'colonial' since it had grabbed Texas in 1836). In European terms, Eden did well to force both France and Germany (at least the part the Russians hadn't grabbed) into mutually co-operative alliances for Europe's defence.

Gamal Abdel Nasser is regarded by most people today as a patriot and protector of his people. Egypt had been occupied by so many powers since the days of Cleopatra that it was almost laughable. In 1955, however, Nasser was seen as another Mahdi, an Arab brigand bent on slaughter. *And* he was a dictator, of the sort that the world tried to destroy in the 1940s. Nasser persuaded the king of Jordan, his near neighbour, to kick out Glubb Pasha and his Arab Legion, the most formidable force in the Middle East. The Arab world had no love for the British; as well as controlling Palestine, we had allowed hundreds of thousands of Jews to recreate their homeland of Israel in 1948, leading to war with the Palestinians. The Arab world, of course, conveniently forgot that they had taken over Hebrew territory by force of arms, albeit centuries before.

In July 1956, Nasser grabbed the Suez Canal which had been built by the French and bought by the British on the grounds that, because it flowed through his country, it was rightfully Egyptian. It was a dubious claim under international law, but the dictator was ready to bluff it out. In the United Nations, just as weak and ineffective as its predecessor the League had been, the Russians were bound to support Nasser against the west. President Eisenhower was happy to let Dulles run his foreign policy and Dulles didn't like Eden.

The man had succeeded Churchill in April 1955 and almost the first thing he did was to pull British troops out of Suez. This was a mistake. Had they stayed, Nasser might have thought twice about the whole venture. As it was, the ships that he had sunk now blocked the canal. The press turned on Eden as a weak prime minister in stark contrast to Churchill. Both parties were behind him, even Hugh Gaitskell, Attlee's replacement as leader of the Labour party who compared Nasser with Hitler.

Working with the French, Eden launched an air strike on the canal zone, but military progress was slow and the markets wobbled. One of the realities of leadership, both in Britain and the United States, is that since the collapse of the South Sea Bubble (1720), if not before, political events have often been derailed by a bunch of self-serving gamblers who operate a covert casino in which the value of stocks and shares is more important than right and wrong and more important than people's lives. Britain, still in the age of austerity in 1956 (rationing had only ended three years earlier) simply could not afford an all-out war.

To cap it all, the prime minister's old bile trouble came back and he resigned. In the true spirit of Number 10, he got a KG in 1954 and an earldom in 1961. He died in January 1977.

Suez was a blow to Britain. Not only had the largest empire the world had ever known dwindled to a scattered set of nowheres called the Commonwealth (however fond the British royal family might be of it) but Britain could not defend herself without American support.

In December 1955, a journalist asked R.A. Butler (Rab), 'Is Mr Eden the best prime minister we have got?' And Butler answered, 'Yes.' If that sounds too lame, how about 'Anthony's father was a mad baronet and his mother a very beautiful woman. That's Anthony – half mad baronet, half beautiful woman.'

Maurice Harold Macmillan 1957–63

'The grandson of a poor boy from a Highland croft' George Thomson reminds us, was Macmillan's background. It not only raises the old ghastliness of the Midlothian Question but is patent nonsense in the education, upbringing and political stance of Harold Macmillan himself.

While Ramsay MacDonald genuinely *did* have such a background, Macmillan's education (Eton and Balliol, Oxford), not to mention his ownership of a major publishing house, is all rather remote from tough times in the gloamin'.

He was born in February 1894 and served in the Scots' Guards (where he was wounded at Loos on the Western Front and again on the Somme). After serving as ADC to the Governor-General of Canada after the war, he went into his family's business and after two attempts, became Conservative MP for Stockton-on-Tees.

Macmillan was unusual in that he believed, as a young MP, that capitalism was collapsing; not that that encouraged him to take up Socialism as an alternative, of course. Under Churchill, his first ministerial post was Parliamentary Secretary at the Ministry of Supply, one of those confected new posts which did not exist in peacetime.

He worked in the Mediterranean as Minister Resident at Allied HQ, North Africa and met (and liked) both Dwight Eisenhower, in his pre-White House days, and the pre-president of France, Charles de Gaulle (who most Englishmen, especially Churchill, couldn't stand). Under Churchill in 1951, Macmillan was in charge of housing at a time when, partly due to war damage, there was a chronic shortage. Under Eden, he bounced from Defence to the Foreign Office to Number 11. It was Macmillan who introduced Premium Bonds, derided by many as a coarse form of gambling. Lotteries, extraordinarily, had been outlawed by Elizabeth I's government, on pain of death!

On Eden's collapse, the leadership contest came to Macmillan and Rab Butler, who had steered through the 1944 Education Act that had created secondary education as grammars and technical schools. Butler is regarded today as the prime minister who never was and should have been but he was unpopular with some elements of the party. So Macmillan it was. He told the queen (Elizabeth II had been crowned in 1953) that he expected his government to last six weeks; in fact, he managed six years.

The Suez crisis was soon forgotten. Supertankers, carrying oil around the world, could bypass Nasser's canal, which became little more than a tourist attraction and Macmillan's relationship with Eisenhower led to the 'special friendship' which has characterized Anglo-American politics ever since. With American know-how, Britain developed its own H (Hydrogen) bomb in May 1957.

From 1959 onwards, Macmillan did his level best to confront the Soviet threat. It didn't help that his counterpart was Nikita Khrushchev, a rude and secretive oaf who had no diplomatic skills at all. At a UN meeting, Khrushchev ranted for three hours and when Macmillan spoke, interrupted him by banging his shoe on the desk. Macmillan took this all on the chin. 'His style of debate ... I enjoy and find amusing.' He was, after all, used to the House of Commons.

In 1960, the prime minister was in Cape Town, making perhaps the most famous speech of his ministry. 'The wind of change is blowing,' he said, but what followed proved that he did not care for this. 'Whether we like it or not ... we must all accept it.' Africa of the 1950s was marred by Mau-Mau terrorism. One man's terrorist is another man's freedom fighter and the once-imprisoned Jomo Kenyatta would emerge to lead his people, photographed in a Western suit and carrying a fly-whisk.

That year, John Fitzgerald Kennedy became the president of the United States. In terms of age, background and experience, he and Macmillan were chalk and cheese, but both men were anxious to work together as allies against the evils of the world, be they Communism or poverty. That did not extend to Vietnam, however, out of which Macmillan, very sensibly, kept.

At home, Macmillan was 'Supermac'. A cartoon of him, by Vicky of the *London Evening Standard* is typical – the prime minister soaring into the sky with the physique and cloak of a *Marvel* comic hero. He famously said in 1957, 'Let's be frank about it; most of our people have never had it so good.' The boom of bombs that sounded in Churchill's premiership was replaced by the boom of prosperity in Macmillan's. Nobody quotes the rest of that phrase, however – 'Is it too good to last? Can we control inflation? This is the problem of our time.' And it still is.

He could be vicious, axing a third of his cabinet in 1963 and calling it restructuring. Jeremy Thorpe (now, there *is* a scandal) said acidly, 'Greater love hath no man than this – that he lay down his friends for his life.'

As was the crisis that rocked Macmillan's government and helped to bring it down. Clem Attlee had once warned his cabinet, 'A Tory Minister can sleep in ten different women's beds in a week. A Labour Minister gets it in the neck if he looks at his neighbour's wife over the garden fence.' In this case, however, the buck stopped closer to home. Macmillan's Minister for War was John Profumo, married to a lovely actress, Valerie Hobson, and was linked with the Cliveden set, a bunch of aristocrats whose lives were totally unfazed by inflation or any of the other realities of life. It was a party at Cliveden, a country house in Buckinghamshire, where Profumo met – and went to bed with – a high-class call girl, Christine Keeler. Unfortunately, she was also sleeping with Yevgeny Ivanov, a Russian embassy official. The implications were obvious. Was the Minister for War, during his pillow talk with Keeler, whispering sweet nothings about British military secrets which she then passed on to the Russians? Almost certainly not, but Profumo lied to the Commons about it and the tabloid press found out. He fell, carrying out charitable works ever after and, after a few months, Macmillan fell with him. 'I was determined,' Macmillan said, 'that no British government should be brought down by the action of two tarts.'[3]

Ill with prostate cancer, Supermac turned down the customary KG, though he did accept the earldom of Stockton.

Alec Douglas-Home 1963–64

At last, the old guard hurrah'd, a prime minister with not only a double-barrelled name, but one whose name is not pronounced as it is spelt (Home is pronounced Hume). The Scottish leanings were unfortunate but most people had learned to live with that. *And* Alec Douglas-Home was the first prime minister we have met who was not born either a Georgian or a Victorian; he first saw the light of day in 1903.

I will not, however, trouble you with the man's school and university – you know those already. The family had a vague historical connection with the Greys, of Whig party fame and the eighteenth-century philosopher Daniel Hume (who spelt his surname correctly). Douglas-Home married in 1936 and, against his father's wishes (the man rightly believed that politics was 'bunk') he was elected MP for South Lanark in 1931. By 1937, he was Neville Chamberlain's parliamentary secretary and went with him to Munich. Neither did him much good.

In 1940, Home (then Lord Dunglass) was diagnosed with tuberculosis of the spine and was an invalid for two years, confined to his bed. Back to full recovery by 1944, he lost his seat in the election of the next year which swept Attlee's Labour to power. He was good at the cut and thrust of debate. When a constituent asked him why she did not get family allowance for her illegitimate child, his answer was 'Madam, you will when your second one arrives.'

With the family titles under his belt, he was in the Lords by the time of the Suez crisis and Macmillan made him Foreign Secretary (there were all sorts of weak jokes at the time that he should have got the Home Office!). The *Daily Herald* asked its readers 'What have we done to deserve this?' and the *Mail* reminded 'Supermac' – 'The Prime Minister still has time to stop making a fool of himself.'

By 1963, the combination of the Profumo affair and the prime minister's ill health meant that Macmillan was on his way out. Reluctantly, Home gave up his title, became an MP for Kinross and West Perthshire and walked through the black door of Number 10. Key cabinet ministers resigned rather than serve under him. He was no match for the new Labour leader, Harold Wilson, in the House, lost the next general election and stood down to make way for Edward Heath. He went back to the Foreign Office until his retirement in 1974 (a life peerage is roughly the same as retirement in most cases).

Douglas-Home did not impress as a prime minister. Forever posing in tweeds and plus fours, he looked considerably older than he was and seemed to belong to a forgotten generation. The country had had enough of titles and Scotsmen; time for a change.

James Harold Wilson 1964–70, 1974–76

Harold Wilson was every Conservative's nightmare. He was clever and articulate with an Oxford degree and a sharp, perhaps brilliant, economic mind. He smoked a pipe and wore a trench-coat, as Middle England as you could get and stole the ground from under the opposition and votes at the ballot box. As Conservative Willie Whitelaw said, '[Wilson] is going around stirring up apathy.'

During the war, wearing the natty little moustache that everybody from Anthony Eden to Duff Cooper sported, he was Director of Economics and Statistics in the new Ministry of Fuel and Power. He was actually a lecturer at Oxford in this period but in the 1945 election stood as MP for Ormskirk. Under Attlee he was parliamentary secretary at the Ministry of Works and the youngest cabinet minister at 29. He married and lived in the fashionable Hampstead Garden Suburb, awash (like most of North London) with socialists of various hues.

In 1947, he spent several months as Overseas Trade Secretary hobnobbing with his Soviet opposite number behind the iron curtain that Churchill had spoken of only the year before. By the end of that he was president of the Board of Trade. The country was uneasy over Wilson's Russian connections and his friendship with Aneurin Bevan, the creator of the NHS who was also to the left of the Labour party at a time when the 'Red menace' began to loom large.

In the election of 1951, Wilson returned as MP for Huyton, Lancashire, but the Labour majority was small. He clashed with his leader, Hugh Gaitskell, over proposals for changes for prescriptions under the NHS and over Clause 4. This was the Marxist doctrine that the people should own the means of production, which was ideological nonsense but had been as sacred to the infant Labour party in its early years as the Constitution was to the Americans. Gaitskell wanted to remove this, but Wilson disagreed and on Gaitskell's death in 1964, Wilson became party leader.

The election of that year gave Labour the victory. That he held on for six years is testimony to his ability (or the work of his parliamentary Whips). The economy, after Supermac's 'You've never had it so good' was beginning to crumble. With hindsight, the 1960s were years of prosperity, with mini-skirts, mini-cars, the Beatles and 'swinging London'. All that, as usual, papered over the cracks. The trade deficit was £600 million and the Merchant Navy's strike in 1966 was followed by devaluation of the pound. Wilson regularly appeared on television, the 'secret eye' now in the corner of everybody's living room, talking with his flat Yorkshire delivery about 'the pound in your pocket'.

Wilson was one of the few prime ministers who talked about his job. Most tenants of Number 10 were never asked about it or assumed that their actions spoke for them, but television had arrived as the new media and prime ministers, like everybody else, had to respond to that. 'Every Prime Minister's style ... must be different,' he said, 'but I find it hard to resist the view that a modern head of government must be the managing director as well as chairman of his team.' In the decade in which England won the football World Cup, that comment made sense. It implied, however, that the role of prime minister, with a controlling finger in every department's pie, was morphing into that of American president. And many people were unhappy about that.

Wilson was back in 1974. And the whiff of scandal followed him. Mrs Wilson just wanted 'a nice little house in North Oxford and a don for a husband'. What she got was the clash and hurry of life at Number 10 (where she went as little as possible) and a chance to become sidelined by Wilson's mistress-cum-assistant, Marcia Williams. She became Marchioness Falkender that year and increasingly was handling much of the prime minister's business.

He failed over Rhodesia. The 'winds of change' speech that Macmillan had made was made glaringly obvious by white Rhodesians, refusing to allow 'their' country to become Zimbabwe. Wilson met the Rhodesian prime minister, Ian Smith, on board HMS *Tiger* but his cabinet were split over the issue of handing power to the locals and diplomacy failed.

He also wandered into the European Economic Community, the Common Market, not actually realizing that various forces wanted to create a political superstate to offset both the United States and the Soviet Union. At the time, the loudest voices trumpeted how much better off Britain would be in the arms of Europeans. Diehards who remembered the last gasps of the Empire were horrified.

An honours crisis blew up again (as if the press and the public could not get enough of it) and the government got bogged down in the trivia of what was called 'kitchen cabinet' issues. What was not known outside a small inner circle was that Wilson was losing the plot. Senility was already called dementia. More specifically, it was becoming known as Alzheimer's disease, named after a Nazi doctor forty years earlier. The once-prodigious memory that Wilson possessed was fading and he knew he had to go. His colleague and future prime minister James Callaghan said, 'Harold, I believe history will treat you more kindly than your contemporaries.'

Given the KG and a life peerage in 1983, his most outstanding contribution was to make the Labour party part of the Establishment. He died in May 1995.

Chapter 21

From Camelot to Watergate

John Fitzgerald Kennedy 1961–63

Like Abraham Lincoln, John Kennedy's administration and life are impossibly stuck in the time warp of his assassination. Those minutes in Ford's Theatre, those six seconds in Dealey Plaza, Dallas, have shaped both men's legacies in a way that their political careers have not. Kennedy emerges in the top ten of presidents because of the extraordinary public shock of his death and the completely artificial PR exercise of his 'Camelot' days in the White House. He even had his Queen Guinevere, his wife Jackie.

Ronald Reagan, a future president, found him altogether too left wing – 'Under the tousled boyish haircut it is still old Karl Marx' – but then Reagan was further to the right than Attila the Hun. The British Prime Minister, Harold Macmillan, was more perceptive and more quietly snide when he wrote, 'There is something very eighteenth century about this young man. He is always on his toes during our discussion, but in the evening, there will be music and wine and pretty women.'

And there were more pretty women around the president than at any time since the Harding administration. A string of Swedish aristocrats and the sociable Diana de Vegh, all paled into insignificance alongside Judith Exner. Not only was she gorgeous, she was the bed-partner of Sam Giancana, one of the top figures in Mafia-related organized crime in the country, an organization that Kennedy and his brother, Robert, the Attorney General, vowed to destroy. And then, of course, there was Marilyn Monroe, the Hollywood airhead whose suicide in 1963 is still viewed with suspicion. Were *both* Kennedys involved in that one?

Kennedy was the youngest president to be elected (Teddy Roosevelt was younger but came to office because of the assassination of William McKinley) at 43. As a biographer wrote, 'He was a compartmentalised man with much to hide, comfortable with secrets and lies.' His father, Joseph, was an Irish Catholic with a chip on his shoulder. Obsessed by family, he imbued his four sons, two of whom would die by an assassin's bullet, with that same spirit. Joe Kennedy was a successful businessman, an appalling ambassador to Britain and as devious as they come. JFK's war service on board PT109 was genuinely heroic, but it was built up into a boys' own adventure yarn by the book he wrote. Joe brought up all the copies available and so turned it into a best seller. He pushed John into a political career and had the White House in his sights from the start.

Kennedy family money paid for all this, and the man's youth and charisma carried him far. He was a breath of fresh air after the boring years of the old guard, like Eisenhower and Cabot Lodge. His *Profiles in Courage* book, about politicians making unpopular decisions in American history, unaccountably won a Pulitzer prize.

In 1960, JFK's first problem was that he was a Catholic. In a country that had famously separated Church and State years earlier (despite the motto of Kennedy's home state, Massachusetts, being 'In God We Trust') the Papacy was seen as a foreign power, not a unifying force. The second was his youth. America had never experienced a William Pitt as their leader (he was 24 when chosen as prime minister by George III) and there were many doubts about whether he had the gravitas to cope.

Richard Nixon was JFK's opponent in the election, and he was a formidable one. In the event, Kennedy's win was the narrowest in American history, 112,827 votes. JFK was the first television president. He was relaxed and well groomed, as opposed to Nixon, whose makeup (Lazy Shave) to hide his five o'clock shadow ran under the heat of the studio lights. Both John and his brother, Robert, smarmed around Loretta King, wife of the civil rights leader Martin Luther King, to get the black vote. His inaugural address was and is widely praised

– 'Ask not what your country can do for you, etc.' – but it continued the Truman Doctrine of involvement in other countries' affairs. The words sounded good. 'We shall pay any price, bear any burden, meet any hardship, support any friend, oppose any foe to ensure the survival and success of liberty.' The problem was that liberty meant US-style democracy and not all the world wanted that.

And, in details which would not be made public for years, Kennedy supported the Bay of Pigs fiasco. Embarrassingly for the US, Cuba, with its nostalgic memories of San Juan Hill, had overthrown its president and installed Fidel Castro, a communist, in his place. Since Cuba was only 96 miles from Mainland USA and the Cold War between America and the USSR was looming ever larger, something had to be done. By 1965, there had been at least eight attempts to assassinate Castro, several of them sanctioned by Kennedy. The Bay of Pigs was an ill-planned attempt by the CIA[1] to invade Cuba and overthrow Castro by force. It failed. The president had the chance to call the idiotic plan off on several occasions and failed to do so. His later pledge to 'smash the CIA into one thousand pieces' has still not happened. It doesn't say much for the American public that when Kennedy admitted his involvement in Cuba, his popularity increased.

The next year, the Cuban Missile Crisis saw the world on the brink of Armageddon. The Russians under Nikita Khrushchev were erecting missile bases on Cuba, an obvious threat to the US itself. 'We were eyeball to eyeball,' Secretary of State Dean Rusk said, 'and the other side blinked.' The Russians backed down and JFK won a victory without a shot being fired. Many rednecks and four-star generals saw this is a failure even so.

The Vietnam situation is still open to debate. Under Eisenhower there were 800 advisers, (all of them soldiers) working in the area to prevent it becoming communist. By 1963, there were 16,000. Kennedy probably intended to pull out of this entirely (although it was at odds with his inaugural address), but his death left the issue hanging until it was grabbed viciously by Lyndon Johnson.

At home, Kennedy met as much failure as success. His plans to improve education, healthcare, and poverty, all collapsed in the face of Congressional opposition, many in his own Democratic party not following him. On the racial issue, he didn't act until he had to, with riots breaking out in Selma, Alabama and the National Guard on the streets. JFK's Civil Rights Bill was only passed into law by Johnson.

With Jackie creating much of the 'Camelot' glitz at the White House, television cameras allowed there for the first time and innumerable magazine articles, there had had never been such a captivating administration as that of the Kennedys. Prime ministers Harold Macmillan and Alec Douglas-Home couldn't hold a candle to all that.

The shots fired in Dealey Plaza on 22 November 1963 left a shining legacy, in which the Kennedy years are filled with a glow of nostalgia and romanticism. That was the day the dream died.

Lyndon Baines Johnson 1963–69

'*Hey, hey, LBJ, How many kid's d' you kill today?*' was the refrain of an anti-war song haranguing the president for his continuation of the war in Vietnam. And the world was horrified when newspapers everywhere showed him holding up a pet Beagle by the ears. '[Johnson] is a small man,' Dwight Eisenhower had observed. 'He hasn't got the depth of mind or the breadth of vision to carry great responsibility ... Johnson is superficial and opportunistic.' Theodore White saw the ruthlessness in him. 'Johnson's instinct for power is as primordial as a salmon's going upstream to spawn.'

Johnson is a paradox. He passed the Civil Rights Legislation proposed by Kennedy, but he authorized the FBI's alleged tapping of Martin Luther King's phone. He was a Redneck Texan from the Confederate town of Stonewall, but he was a Democrat who could, when he wanted to, be surprisingly sophisticated.

The start of his presidency wasn't very auspicious. He was sworn in on board Air Force One, the presidential jet, alongside Jackie Kennedy, still wearing the clothes she had worn earlier in Dealey Plaza, spattered with her husband's blood. On television, we all saw the sly smile and wink he gave to an aide, giving just a hint of evidence that he had orchestrated the assassination of his erstwhile boss.

Johnson's start in life was poor. In 1908, there were no railways or even paved roads in his part of Texas. His mother, Rebekah, had to carry water in buckets from a nearby well. With no university education (he attended a teaching institute), he went to DC hoping for something menial in the corridors of power. He became a New Dealer on the coattails of FDR and married Claudia Taylor, 'Lady Bird' as her family called her.

He entered politics but made his money by dodgy deals in a construction company, providing twentieth-century amenities like electricity for the first time to thousands of Texans. He even got a silver star during the Second World War, even though he was not in the forces, but was in the Pacific on a fact-finding tour for FDR. Nobody seemed to mind that his war stories got taller as the years went by. He narrowly won the Senate election in 1948, travelling over Texas in a helicopter, a new gadget that most of his voters had never seen before. 'Landslide Lyndon', as he came to be known ironically, had only just scraped home.

In Washington, he used 'the Treatment', wheedling, threatening, invading a person's space as only a big man can. The *Washington Post*'s editor Ben Bradlee said, 'You really feel as if a Saint Bernard had licked your face for an hour.' In the race for the White House he was beaten by 'a scrawny little fellow with rickets'. John Kennedy wasn't little, and he didn't have rickets, but LBJ, as usual, got away with such hyperbole.

JFK's assassination catapulted him into the spotlight, and he set about honouring the dead man's legacy by pushing through the reforms he had initiated, except pulling out of Vietnam. His choice of cabinet was, for him, perfect. 'I want people around me who would kiss my ass on a hot summer's day and say it smells like roses,' he said in one of his less-sophisticated observations. He got through a string of mistresses, including Helen Douglas.

A supposed attack on an American ship, the USS *Maddox*, in August 1964 in the Gulf of Tonkin led the president to authorise air strikes on Vietnam. It was arguably the most disastrous war in modern history and the reluctant and often chaotic US military did not come out of it well. The Monroe Doctrine, Manifest Destiny and the arbitrary bullying by earlier presidents were about to come home to roost. Over a million people died in Vietnam, and there's never been such an outpouring of grief and rage in the United States. This was a disastrous mistake by Johnson, but Congress backed him almost unanimously.

The war cost America lots of support internationally and cost so much that civil reforms were curtailed or dropped. Race riots in Watts, Los Angeles frightened white middle-class voters who now distanced themselves from the Civil Rights Movement. When a reporter asked the president why he had not withdrawn from Vietnam, LBJ whipped out his 'Jerry' (see Harding) and told him, 'This is why!' I cannot see Harold Wilson, Johnson's oppo at Number 10 doing that!

The Tet offensive destroyed LBJ's career. In January 1968, public opinion turned against the war entirely, despite John Wayne's nonsensical movie *The Green Berets* perpetuating the lies of American military greatness. Johnson knew that in the next election he would face Robert Kennedy as his party's leader, and so 'I will not seek and I will not accept the nomination of my party for another term as your President.'

Former British Chancellor of the Exchequer George Osborne has written gushingly on LBJ's successes on his legacy – four presidents since him have come from the South – but it is, in a different way from Kennedy before him, largely smoke and mirrors.

Richard Milhous Nixon 1969–74

In an uncharacteristically unguarded moment, John Kennedy said of Richard Nixon, '[He] is a filthy, lying son-of-a-bitch and a very dangerous man.' Adlai Stevenson, the grand old man of American politics wrote, '[Nixon] is the kind of politician who would cut down a redwood tree and then mount the stump to make a speech for conservation.' Even Nikita Khrushchev, the Russian president, added, 'Most of all, [Nixon] produces the impression of a slightly fraudulent, petty store keeper, capable of selling tainted herring or representing kerosene-soaked sugar as good merchandise.'

'Richard Milhous Nixon,' the protest song went, 'you ain't gonna change my world' but he did, if only because the Watergate scandal exposed him as arguably the most corrupt president in history. Even his lies are unsubtle examples of arrant stupidity. 'People have got to know whether or not their president is a crook. Well, I am not a crook ...' Right! And 'There will be no whitewash in the White House.' (Right, again!)

Young Dickie had his share of problems growing up in what was then still rural California. His parents were Quaker storekeepers (hence Khrushchev's joke above) and relative poverty meant that he couldn't take up an offered place at Harvard. He lost his first job in a law firm because of his 'shifty-eyed' demeanour. The rapid growth of media technology in the twentieth century meant that wannabe presidents had to engage with radio and television fast. Nixon was not a natural. He was insecure, with a chip on his shoulder wider than the Missouri and his short temper and foul-mouthed outbursts did him no favours at all. He met Thelma Ryan (known as Pat) in local amdram and married her, after a persistent courtship, in 1940. He served with the navy in the Pacific, but, unlike Kennedy, didn't write a book about it. He became an excellent poker player, coming home from war with $8,000 worth of winnings. He used the red card in politics, implying that his opponent, Jerry Voorkis, was a Communist. He wasn't, but the truth and Richard Nixon may already have parted company. Following the McCarthyist enthusiasm of the early 1950s, Nixon investigated ('hounded' is a better word) politician Alger Hiss, uncovering his espousal of the Left in the 1930s. He opposed Helen Douglas, LBJ's mistress, smearing her as 'the pink lady' with Leftist leanings. Her retort that he showed 'nice, unadulterated fascism' may have been the first shot fired, but he was not bound to respond and she was undoubtedly right.

Rumours of Nixon's duplicity surfaced as early as 1952 when the press got hold of a story of a slush fund that he was using to finance his position in the running for the vice presidency under Dwight Eisenhower. Nixon went on television and pleaded poverty – Pat could only afford 'a good Republican cloth coat' rather than furs. He'd only ever accepted one gift from a supporter – a cocker spaniel called Checkers. Astonishingly, viewers bought it and Nixon swept on to vice president. When he lost the governorship of California, he showed his huge chip again by saying the press 'don't have Nixon to kick around any more.' Television journalists ignored his 'poor me' stance with a documentary called *The Political Obituary of Richard M. Nixon* (1962, written by Howard K. Smith). If the American public had paid any attention to this, the world might have been spared Watergate and the title of president would not, perhaps, be quite so low as it is, in terms of political esteem.

During the 1960s, America was a shambles. Black riots in Watts and elsewhere, the murders of Martin Luther King and Robert Kennedy, the ongoing opposition to Vietnam, the rise of the anything-but-peaceful 'hippies' whose existence was hijacked by the psychotic, murderous Manson family, all added to a chaotic, frightened and broken society. The murder rate rose by 50 per cent; other crimes doubled. Nixon offered 'progress, without mayhem' and it led to his election as president. His 1968 campaign slogan – 'Nixon's the one' – backfired, however. A number of opposition posters carried the same message but showed a sorrowful pregnant girl looking tearfully at 'Tricky Dicky' in reproach. Worse was the own goal of 'They can't Lick our Dick'; I really can't comment on that …

His supporters claimed that the intensive bombing of Vietnam in 1973 and 1974 was done to force the Viet Cong to negotiate an end to the war, but, rather like Truman's decision on the Hiroshima and Nagasaki bombs, it was tails wagging dogs.

Nixon lacked the vision to see that, in cosying up to China, he was handing power to a pariah state that was delighted to accept American technology and access to world markets without any concessions to freedom, tolerance or democracy. Some would say he couldn't have foreseen this future development, but he was the president of the United States and it was his decision to go to China. As he himself said, 'We may have created a Frankenstein.'

Nixon was a polarizing figure even before Watergate. The liberal press hated him. On 17 June 1972, burglars broke into the Watergate Hotel in Washington, the headquarters of the Democrats. They placed bugging devices on the party's phones and the press, led by Ben Bradlee's *Washington Post*, found out about it. Rather than issuing a statement, or, better still, going on television distancing himself from his aides' wrongdoing, Nixon covered the whole thing up badly and then had to cover up the cover-up. Secret tapes were released under orders from the Supreme Court and Nixon was proved to be up to his neck in the whole thing. He had the gall, having resigned the presidency, to say to the Oxford University Union in 1978, 'You'll be here in the year 2000 and we'll see how I'm regarded then.' The answer is: worse than ever.

For those who excuse Nixon for his racism, it is difficult to wipe out that he believed there were too many Jews in government and that they were disloyal; that Indian women were the 'most unattractive in the world'.

And it is no defence to say, 'Nixon was bad, but in other ways Clinton and Trump (and we might add Buchanan, Harding and a handful of others) were worse.' Hunter S. Thompson wrote that Nixon was 'a swine of a man and the jabbering dupe of a president'. He had an 'ugly, Nazi spirit'. He tried to extend presidential power, which is unacceptable in the land of the free.

Gerald Randolph Ford (aka Leslie Lynch King) 1974–77

Senior Democrat 'Tip' O'Neill said of the new president in 1976, 200 years after independence, 'I like Ford as an individual, but cripes, he's an awful president … Jerry Ford is no dunce by any means.

Jerry Ford is a smart fellow. But Jerry Ford doesn't want to learn new tricks.' Lyndon Johnson was probably more accurate. 'Jerry Ford is so dumb he can't fart and chew gum at the same time … He is a nice fellow, but he spent too much time playing football without a helmet.'

Gerald Ford is the accidental president, a man who never wanted the top job but got it anyway, which probably says a lot about American politics. He was born Leslie Lynch King in Nebraska, but his parents' marriage was toxic and years later he took his stepfather's name of Gerald Randall Ford. He played football for Michigan University, (hence Johnson's jibe above) and was on the cusp of a professional career. Instead he opted for law and joined the navy, like Kennedy and Nixon, in the Second World War.

He entered politics as Michigan's Republican representative and married divorcee Betty Bloomer. As First Lady, she went on to found the Betty Ford Clinic for drug addiction having battled breast cancer for years. His role in the Warren Commission has been glossed over by some biographers. It was set up by Lyndon Johnson to investigate the Kennedy killing and ended up as a whitewash. Read its verbatim testimony today and it is obvious that Ford was seriously out of his depth, buying into the preconceived notions of much cleverer men who had their own agenda.

But Ford had a folksy charm (everyone says how nice he was, even when verbally knifing him) and an increasingly desperate Richard Nixon (see previous entry) chose him as his vice president. But Nixon had his doubts. 'Can you imagine?' he reportedly said to a friend in the Oval Office, 'Jerry Ford sitting in that chair?' In his inaugural speech, Ford said, 'My fellow Americans, our long national nightmare is over.' Assassinations, Vietnam, Watergate and a rocky economy – America had had the lot over the past few years. It was time for a calmer approach. But could the former quarterback and male model deliver? His WIN campaign (Whip Inflation Now) didn't work. He fell down the steps of Air Force One (see the Johnson comment above) and was lampooned years later along with George Bush, in the hugely popular satire cartoon series *The Simpsons*.

In foreign affairs, Ford smarmed around Leonid Brezhnev to ease lingering tensions in the Cold War, but it was his aide Henry Kissinger who did most of the work.

What blackened Ford's reputation was his pardoning of his former boss, Nixon. He came to this decision for honourable reasons – to draw a line under Watergate and start again. But that wasn't how America and the world saw it. The press screamed conspiracy and cover-up. If a pardon was offered – and accepted by Nixon with a half-hearted apology – then Nixon was guilty, and so were plenty of others.

Unsurprisingly, Ford lost to his successor in January 1977.

James 'Jimmy' Earl Carter Jnr 1977–81

We've had comments like this before: 'Carter is a nice fellow, but he is the most poorly equipped man ever to sit in the White House,' Senator Barry Goldwater thought in 1978. The German Chancellor Helmut Schmidt was just as disparaging. 'No useful purpose is served by talking with Carter. During our next telephone conversation, I will read out to him the Cologne–Euskirchen railroad timetable. He does not listen anyhow.'

At the time of writing, Jimmy Carter is still alive, at 98, giving him a relevance and even immediacy that everybody else so far lacks. At the time of his election, Carter was the first 'deep South' president since Zachary Taylor in 1848 (Texas is not included by Americans as being in the South, although clearly it is). There was no biography of the man until 2020, and at the time of his election in January 1977, people were still asking 'Jimmy who?'

Carter was a 'born again' Baptist, which some people found at odds with modern secular America. Interestingly, the president faced his own 'Suez' moment over the Panama Canal. Built by US technical know-how and US money, the Panamanians regarded it by the late 1970s as theirs (see Anthony Eden and the outlook of Colonel Nasser). The Congress vote over this was not fought on party lines – Republicans voted for him; his own Democrats had doubts. Carter was a beginner in the sense that he started important reforms that were completed by others, always a likely situation for a one-term president. He brought in sanctions against the apartheid of the white South African government but didn't secure the release of Nelson Mandela, the great black hope of a new nation in the years ahead. Likewise, he won the Nobel Peace Prize in 2002, long after he had left office, for bringing together Islam and Judaism, when Anwar Sadat of Egypt and Menahem Begin of Israel agreed to the Camp David Accords. So complex were these agreements to achieve peace in the Middle East (which has not lasted) that there were twenty-three drafts to the documents.

The fall of the Shah of Persia (Iran) in 1979 was blamed, perhaps unfairly, on Carter (although his successor Ronald Reagan sorted it in days). The Shah was ill with lymphosarcoma and he was facing the wrath of the Ayatollah Khomeini, a religious maniac with an appalling record on human rights. Carter's attitude was that the US had no right to interfere in the internal affairs of Iran, which no president since Teddy Roosevelt had said.

Nice fellow though Carter was (and is), his presidency was a disappointment. As with all presidents, he inherited various problems – falling productivity, inflation, unemployment, lost control over energy supplies – the usual sad list of twentieth-century bugbears. He promised a new leadership and almost certainly found the job beyond him. He didn't come across as resolute to the press and delegated, especially in foreign affairs, to Cyrus Vance and Zbigniew Brzezinski, who were usually at loggerheads. Carter's plans for tax reform, healthcare and government reorganization stalled in their tracks. He promised to balance the books; by the time he left office, the budget deficit was $50 billion. Carter also knew how to put his foot in it. On a state visit to Mexico, he replied to a toast, explaining how much he enjoyed jogging and would have done more, 'except that I was affected with Montezuma's revenge'. It did not go down well!

In foreign policy, he carried out a series of reversals which made the US look weak. This was true of Korea and Cuba and, despite Camp David, the Israeli–Palestine standoff still exists. When the American Embassy in Tehran was grabbed by militant locals, Carter's standing soared. When he failed to rescue hostages, it plummeted again. He was no match for Reagan in 1980, losing more votes than any sitting president since Hoover in 1932. Jimmy Carter has gone on to carry out excellent charity building projects for the poor, often with his own hands. But that cannot cancel out a wasted four years at the White House.

Chapter 22

Grocers, Iron Ladies and Politicians
Who Ran Away From the Circus

Edward Richard George Heath 1970–74

He had no small talk and was decidedly middle class. No silver spoon, no Eton, no Harrow, just Ramsgate Grammar School. Balliol, Oxford followed, it is true, but only on a loan from Kent Education Committee and the fact that he won a £100-a-year organ scholarship which kept him there.

Edward Heath was born in 1916 and his family, coastguards and merchant seamen, all had links with the sea. All his life, he was a loner, someone who seemed emotionally cold. Only in his music and on his yacht, *Morning Cloud*, did any warmth come through. His lack of involvement with women led to ugly rumours, which have no basis in fact.

As a young man in the late 1930s, he opposed Chamberlain's appeasement and was called up to join the Royal Artillery in 1940. Six years later, now a lieutenant colonel, he was demobilized and went briefly into the Civil Service before standing as Conservative MP for Bexley. He got a job with a merchant bank on a salary of £200 a year and in the Commons joined the One Nation Group of 'New Tories'. There was in fact nothing new about this at all. Disraeli with his 'Young England' movement; Randolph Churchill with his Tory Democracy – both men had already done what Heath claimed was a first.

From the start, Heath backed Europeanism. The days when Britain was the workshop of the world and the empire the largest in history had long gone. The problem was how to find a niche for an ex-superpower. In 1951, Heath was made Assistant Whip, responsible for party discipline and unity. His boss, Lord Hailes, found him 'extraordinarily self-sufficient' and he was unpopular, which probably means he was doing a good job. 'Bloody bad-tempered' was how one MP remembered him.

In 1960, Heath became Minister of Labour and then Foreign Secretary, where he had the job of taking Britain into the Common Market. With his typical anti-British snidery, Charles de Gaulle (who owed his position as president and indeed the freedom of his country to Britain and the Americans) famously said 'Non!' to British entry. Half the population was glad about that, but it was an international kick in the teeth, nonetheless.

Heath supported Alec Douglas-Home when Macmillan retired and did well at the Board of Trade. Perhaps because of this and his relative youth, he became party leader after Home's resignation.

The 1970 election looked like a Labour victory, but the timing was bad and Wilson was far from his best. Interestingly, he made a comment about the now incessant commentary by television pundits, who, predictably, knew very little about politics. 'They've been telling me all week I was going to lose and now they are picking my bloody Cabinet for me!' The great days of 1960s prosperity were over. Unemployment soared to 750,000 and Heath threw money at the problem in the 'spend, spend, spend' economics usually associated with Labour. The 1970s saw industrial action on a scale not seen since the General Strike and in the 'winter of discontent', a phrase the media pinched from Shakespeare, bin men went on strike and rubbish lay uncollected in the streets for weeks, huge blowflies buzzing around black bags. Many people were working a three-day week to save scarce energy. Power cuts became the norm.

The vagaries of the economy, of course, are never down to one individual, but as prime minister, Heath had to carry the can. Predictably, he lost the 1974 election and he was soon toppled as party leader too. The fact that his replacement was a woman – Margaret Thatcher – hit 'Grocer' Heath hard. The lack of women in his life was taken to be old-fashioned misogyny and he took the loss personally. For the rest of his life he harboured a grudge against her, something 'un-British' in the eyes of most people. Not since Gladstone and Disraeli had such personal bitterness been so obvious – and Thatcher and Heath were from the same party!

Leonard James 'Jim' Callaghan 1976–79

'Jim' Callaghan hailed from a family that was definitely working class. The name was originally Garoghan and the prime minister's great-grandfather was a weaver who came over during the dark years of the potato famine. Weavers were about to lose their livelihood to the new machinery then stalking the land, but the Garoghans stuck it out and James Callaghan's father was a chief petty officer in the Royal Navy. He was also a war hero, wounded at Jutland in 1916.

The future prime minister was born in Portsmouth in 1912. He attended Portsmouth Grammar School with funds from the local Labour Party (36 shillings a week to cover all expenses, not just school) which ran out when the boy was 17.

His first job was in that most detested branch of the Civil Service, the Income Tax office. He worked his way up in the Inland Revenue Staff Federation, rising to National Secretary by 1936. He officially joined the Labour Party and lectured (for nothing) to the Workers' Educational Association.

He met his wife at a Baptist church in Maidstone in 1938. In accordance with the naval tradition of his family, Callaghan enlisted in the navy in 1942 as an ordinary seaman, serving mostly in the Far East. He reached the rank of lieutenant. At the end of the war, he won the Labour seat of Cardiff South, a fairly safe bet given the staunch Socialist background of South Wales. His first government role was parliamentary private secretary to the under secretary of state for the dominions. Umpteen prime ministers before that time and since have tried to reduce the power and complexity of the Westminster 'blob' and this post is a good example of how ludicrous it all is.

He didn't enjoy his time as chancellor (1964–67), scrapping with rival George Brown (a drunk, by the way) over economic policy in the 'stop-go' period. He bent with the wind, opposing links with the European Economic Community (as did almost all the Labour Party in those days), then backing the 'staying in' referendum on 1975. He had a sense of humour while at Number 10, skateboarding for the press and singing a Marie Lloyd music hall song for the TUC. He mixed well with blue-collar workers, but loathed 'long-haired intellectuals' (including Michael Foot in his own party).

He was accused of giving in to minority parties like the Scottish Nationalists, who voted for devolution, but as a leader was streets ahead of the Tories' Margaret Thatcher in 1979. But the unions felt that he had betrayed them and he lost to her. Were there to be an American-style league table of prime ministers, 'Sunny Jim' would be towards the bottom.

Margaret 'Maggie' Hilda Thatcher, née Roberts 1979–90

The 'Iron Lady' was a one-off. If the two subsequent female prime ministers hoped to emulate her or even build on her success, they were to be sadly disappointed. On the other hand, Margaret Thatcher (known throughout the media as 'Maggie') was probably the most divisive occupant of Number 10, the Marmite of politics.[1]

The daughter of middle-class parents in the highly unfashionable town of Grantham, Lincolnshire, she needed elocution lessons to lose the local dialect, which left her with a harsh nasal bray that was probably worse. There was no Eton or Harrow (they were single-sex schools) – she attended the local grammar school and got to Somerville College, Oxford, to read Chemistry.

Snobs didn't like her. Oxford University itself, refused her an honorary doctorate, despite having given one to various less-deserving holders of the top job. Generations not born when Maggie was at Number 10 hold her in contempt and blame her solely for changes that were going to come, whoever ruled the roost. When she died in April 2013, the Left sang 'Ding Dong the Witch is dead' and held street parties. Thatcherism (actually a mixture of monetarism and common sense) is a dirty word. The Conservative Party faithful, however, adored her and today's collapsing party looks back with nostalgia on the Thatcher years.

She was even despised early on in her political career. As Education Secretary under Edward Heath, she abolished free school milk, which was a legacy of post-war rationing and the Attlee government, and earned the name 'Maggie Thatcher, Milk Snatcher'. In fact, she had held out against the idea; the Treasury insisted on it to save money under 'Grocer' Heath. When she entered the Commons in 1959, she was one of only nineteen women in a House of 630 MPs. As MP for Finchley, she was asked by a reporter about the possibility of a female PM. 'Not in my lifetime,' she answered. She was fully up to the feminist agenda without pushing it too far – 'In politics, if you want anything said, ask a man. If you want anything done, ask a woman.' Many people assumed she had got to Number 10 by mistake. As Labour put it at the time, 'The day after you forget to vote, Mrs. Thatcher becomes Prime Minister!' The Russians called her the Iron Lady as a term of contempt (it was actually the Iron Maiden, a medieval torture contraption) and the drink of that name, tonic water and Angostura, was soon on sale across the country.

In December 1980, she had the lowest popularity poll of any prime minister, at 23 per cent. Many of her party didn't support her – the 'Wets', as she called them. Edward Heath never forgave her for ousting him as party leader, and he sat in the Commons, glaring at her back in what journalists called the longest sulk in history.

The Falklands War of 1982 saw her popularity rocket. It was the first war to be reported daily on television, and the world watched agog. It was the sort of gunboat diplomacy that Palmerston and Disraeli would have loved. And it worked. Her next majority was huge.

Like the Duke of Wellington, Maggie could catnap. She routinely only got four hours' sleep a night, which gave her the edge over opponents and exasperated her staff. She carried a handbag and wore a skirt which immediately made her stand out in the day-to-day routines of her job. Her rich husband, Denis, whom she married in 1951, was loyalty itself and she had two children, one of whom, Mark, was constantly getting into scrapes around the world, which the media of course could not resist. Her regime coincided with one of the most popular as well as the cruellest television series, *Spitting Image*, in which rubber caricatures of anybody in the news said and did outrageous things in front of the cameras. The first Maggie incarnation was benign and domestic, voiced by a brilliant mimic, Steve Nallon, but as time went on, she morphed into a deranged maniac from a horror film, complete with red lights and lashings of blood.

Her own views were complicated, but she approved of the death penalty, finally dropped in 1965, and disapproved of relaxing divorce laws. She fought what was considered the anarchic and dinosaur approach of the coal miners when she decided to close inefficient pits and won. Trade unionism, which had crippled the country under Wilson, Callaghan and Heath, would never be the same again.

As the premiership rolled on, she became more didactic, not suffering anyone gladly. Her local government reforms included the Council Tax, referred to as the Poll Tax, and she ignored the more historically minded who told her that in 1381, Poll Tax had directly caused the upheaval of the Peasant's Revolt. She clashed with her cabinet, Michael Heseltine, Nigel Lawson and Geoffrey Howe. She was sowing the seeds of her own destruction. The Tory old guard rebelled against her. 'We are a cavalry regiment headed by a corporal in the Women's Royal Army Corps.' 'When she goes, she will go very fast,' an anonymous cabinet minister said. 'Our wives have soaped the stairs for her.' Geoffrey Howe's resignation speech stuck a knife into Maggie's back, but having read it several times, I am not impressed by it. 'It was rather,' one commentator wrote, 'like being savaged by a dead sheep.'

It didn't help that Thatcher's successor, the completely missable John Major, wrote in his diary in 1999. 'I want her isolated. I want her destroyed.'

With friends like that ...

John Major 1990–97

In the *Spitting Image* satire referred to above, John Major was usually portrayed as grey, usually losing to the overbearing women in his life, be it Currie or Thatcher. For all that he still pontificates in the media (see Chapter 24) that is exactly how most people saw his political career. He is more anonymous than Andrew Bonar Law and the only exciting thing he did, uncovered by the press years later, was to have an affair with one of his colleagues, Edwina Currie.

His background was odd and hardly fitted the Tory squirearchy any more than Thatcher's did. He was born in Surrey during the Second World War, and his father was a music hall artist. In the years ahead, it would be said that Major was the only man who ran away from the circus to become a banker. His grammar school education was decidedly average, and he left school with a clutch of O Levels. His only passion was cricket. He joined the Standard Bank in 1966 and married a teacher.

Television didn't like him. He was more lively in the flesh but that is not how the voting public see their political leaders. He came across as grey and wooden, with an irritatingly flat delivery. He rose fast as a protégé of Maggie's, although he often opposed her in cabinet meetings; he got the Foreign Office as her government began to crumble and then the chancellorship. When Maggie fell, Major was out of action with wisdom teeth trouble, and since she had named him as her successor, was not implicated, as others had been, of engineering her downfall (but see his diary comments above).

His first cabinet contained only men, which annoyed the feminists. He faced serious economic problems and an impending war with

Iraq. He gambled with his own chancellor, Norman Lamont, over the Exchange Rate Mechanism and seemed intent on following a more Europe-friendly policy than Maggie, who had famously refused to budge on this. 'You turn if you want to. The lady is not for turning.' His irritating repetition of 'Oh, yes' became a gift for mimics in bars up and down the country. Major was hopeless with the media. Unlike many British and American politicians who didn't give a damn, he took every sniping headline personally.

But the Iraq war went well and Major got on with the American president, George Bush. His campaign for re-election, however, resulted in a twenty-one-seat majority, not enough to push through difficult reforms. Black Wednesday (16 September 1992) put an end to Major's career and led to the move towards Brexit which would cause storms in the years ahead. Unemployment was rising, the IRA had bombed Number 10 and the prime minister had no credible answers to any of it. His tentative peace feelers to the IRA didn't work and aroused the anger of Unionists and Middle England, sickened by ongoing IRA atrocities. When Scottish Nationalism reared its ugly head, Major hoped to calm the waters by giving back the Stone of Scone, stolen by Edward I in the thirteenth century; that didn't work either. Major was, as Norman Lamont said, 'in office but not in power', a phrase that would be hijacked again more recently (see Chapter 25). Unaware that the microphone was switched on, he muttered to an aide that his cabinet were 'bastards'.

'Mad cow' disease rattled the farmers and 'Cash for Questions' (a variant of cash for honours harking back to Lloyd George) hit the headlines of which Major was afraid. When it came to the election in May 1997, he was no match for the whirlwind that was Tony Blair.

Chapter 23

Making America Great Again

Ronald Wilson Reagan 1981–89

Ronald Reagan began as a joke and, unaccountably, ended up as one of America's most popular presidents. As the British satire *Not the 9 O'Clock News* had it in 1982, 'I can believe that the word lever is pronounced levver, and the best film ever made is *Saturday Night Fevver*, but I can't believe Ronald Reagan is president'.

Muammar Gaddafi, the Libyan dictator, agreed:

> We showed his films on TV because we couldn't believe it was true that such a man was President of America. We rolled about laughing ... Reagan embodies nothing more than the peak of the capitalist rotten society, in which everyone is ready to make any promise as long as he is elected.

And from those who had to work with him, Jim Wright wrote:

> Reagan is a person with whom you can't seriously discuss serious issues ... Many, many times I have been ... in Mr Reagan's presence and I don't have the feeling that ever once, any of us have gotten through to him with any point of view other than the one he entered the meeting with.

'Dutch' Reagan (the family nickname because he looked like a fat little Dutchman as a baby) was born to religious parents in Tampico, Illinois. His father was a drummer (travelling salesman). A keen sportsman, an amateur actor, he didn't excel at college and worked as a sports commentator on local radio in the Chicago area. He took a screen test for Warner Brothers and starred in various 'B' features, mostly Westerns, the most popular movies at the time. It was on one of these sets that he met and married the actress Jane Wyman. By 1941, with no discernible acting ability, he was getting top billing with Errol Flynn. In the army reserve, his poor eyesight precluded foreign service in the Second World War, and he made promotional films for the army.

Undoubtedly the low point (or was it he high?) in Reagan's movie career was *Bedtime For Bonzo* (1951) and wags would later contend that the chimpanzee would have made a better president. It didn't emerge at the time, but recently released papers prove that both Reagans were informing the House Un-American Activities Committee about the Leftist leanings of some of their colleagues in the McCarthy era. He claimed, of course, to have done this reluctantly. The Reagans divorced in 1949 – he was then a Democrat, she Republican – and Ronald married actress Nancy Davis three years later.

In the 1950s, he gravitated to the Republicans, becoming an economic conservative hostile to the Left and a supporter of big business. 'I didn't leave the Democratic Party,' he often said, 'the party left me.' He joined the right-wing National Rifle Association and opposed Medicare, a hopelessly watered-down version of Britain's National Health Service. He also said, 'The Founding Fathers knew a government can't control the economy without controlling people … To do that, it must use force and coercion …' Laying aside the fact that Reagan's many references to the founding fathers were often historically illiterate, force and coercion against the people sounded very like what Adolf Hitler and Josef Stalin had been doing only a few years before Reagan's time. He wanted to get 'the welfare bums back to work' and condemned the anti-Vietnam attitude of students at Berkeley University, even sending in the National Guard, resulting in a student's death. 'If it takes a bloodbath, let's get it over with. No more appeasement.' He supported anti-abortion and the death penalty.

The debate between Carter and Reagan was a hands-down win for the actor who loved the camera and couldn't put a foot wrong.

Reagan was nearly 70 at the time of his inaugural address, at the time the oldest president to take office. But his hair was still Brylcreem black, and he rode horses regularly. So what could go wrong? In office, Reagan often joked that he had 'three guys who run the country', leaving the speeches to him and that was more or less how it was. He survived an assassination attempt by a media-obsessed lunatic, John Hinckley, in March 1981 with the famous line to Nancy, 'Honey, I forgot to duck.'

He cut taxes, as promised, but not spending. Even so, inflation fell and economic crises have ways of levelling themselves out. The American public will forgive their president a lot. (see Bill Clinton) if the economy is sound. He declared war on drugs and added funding to the police to crackdown on drug-related crime; it remains a problem, however, in today's USA. He ignored civil rights issues but did create Martin Luther King Day, a public holiday.

Reagan was an avowed enemy of the Soviet Union and continued the interventionist policy advocated by the majority of his predecessors. He sent troops into the Lebanon and to Grenada in order to keep Marxism out. He called the USSR the 'Evil Empire' and his strategic defence initiative was called Star Wars by the press. Everything looked rosy. The Olympics were held in Los Angeles with the usual mountain of US gold medals. The old Soviet Union was falling apart and the new regime, of *glasnost* and *perestroika*, was seen by many as the end of the Cold War (until now, see Chapter 25). It was 'morning again' in America and that gave Reagan the go ahead to deliver air strikes (the 1980s euphemism for bombing), to Gaddafi's Libya for having let off a bomb in Berlin which killed a US serviceman. Reagan and Lord Palmerston (see Chapter 14) would have got on like houses on fire.

But the 'Teflon president' nearly came to grief in 1987 when the Iran-Contra scandal broke, involving funds being diverted to support rebels in Nicaragua. Eleven senior heads rolled, but not Reagan's; he simply denied all knowledge.

By 1989, Reagan was 76. A fall from his horse may have caused brain damage because his memory was fading. At one public occasion, welcoming the Prince and Princess of Wales to the White House, Reagan referred to Diana as Princess David, possibly confusing the 'Di' for 'Dai', the Welsh shortened term for Dafydd (David). In 1993, it was officially announced that he had, like Harold Wilson before him, Alzheimer's disease. He died of pneumonia in 2004.

And the world overlooked the right-wing harshness, the quiet, controlled bigotry in the face of success. The Berlin Wall came down. The evil empire collapsed, and it was all because of Ronald Reagan.

Er ... not quite.

George Herbert Walker Bush 1989–93

'Read my lips,' George Bush famously said to a press contingent. 'No new taxes.' Like all new presidents, especially Ronald Reagan, Bush had an overly rosy view of the founding of America, claiming that Christopher Columbus had shown what could be done by 'perseverance and faith'. Today, Columbus is regarded as one of the first racist exploiters of native peoples, deliberately causing the deaths of thousands – and, incidentally, getting his navigation hopelessly wrong! And Reagan and Bush, in their administrations and via their economics, actually *widened* the gulf between rich and poor Americans.

All the Bushes had a sense of duty and had been taught not to brag (which when you're POTUS is quite difficult). The media made great play on this, with cartoonist Gary Trudeau portraying George (or not) as the Invisible Man.

Like a handful of presidents of his generation, he served in the navy in the Second World War, flying fifty-eight missions and parachuting to safety when his plane was shot down. He was awarded the DFC. He went to Yale, married Barbara Pearson and made a more than decent living in oil production. He joined the Republicans, to his family's surprise, and was elected to Congress. He backed Nixon over Reagan, with hindsight a bad move, but he was given a number of key posts in Nixon's administration and in Ford's. A turning point came in 1975, when Ford made Bush director of the CIA. The Intelligence Agency has a chequered history. In most popular fiction it is seen as something sinister, operating as a rogue group without accountability. In reality, Eisenhower was suspicious of it and Kennedy wanted to destroy it but it survived because America, like any other country, needs its 'spooks'. Bush's brief time as its head improved relations between the agency and Congress.

Bush tried to beat Reagan because he was younger and rubbished the old man's 'voodoo economics' but that failed. The Teflon president got Bush to be his vice president. Sensibly, the new man stayed in the shadows, and leaked nothing to the media, as previous vice presidents had been in the habit of doing. He attended the funerals of three Soviet leaders in as many years, quipping (privately of course), 'You die, I fly.'

When he decided to run for the presidency in 1988, his television image wasn't good. He was boring and far from the slick professional that Reagan was. Even so, at the Republican convention, teamed up with Dan Quayle, Bush won. The *Guardian* in Britain wrote later, 'What are the seven words the world fears to hear? "Dan, I don't feel so good".' If Quayle was a possible liability, Bush's Democratic rival in the race for the White House was Gary Hart, and a scandal involving a young woman in very short shorts sitting on the Democrat's lap sank him without trace.

When Bush didn't 'dance on the Wall' in 1989, as East and West Berlin became a single city again after more than forty years, many Americans saw this is a sign of weakness. He wasn't a true conservative Republican after all. His sending of troops to overthrow the regime of Manuel Noriega in Panama strengthened his credibility with his own party, but outraged Democrats and much of the increasingly liberal Western world. When Bush failed to intervene in unrest in Georgia as the Soviet Union collapsed, he made a speech in Kiev (Kyiv today) that was labelled 'Chicken Kiev' by the American media. The Iraqi invasion of Kuwait by Saddam Hussein in August 1990 forced the president into action once more. The world was less tolerant of American intervention than it had been, with the media screaming 'No blood for oil' and predicting the thousands of body bags flown home as they had been from Vietnam. The 'mother of all battles' that Saddam promised was a resounding victory for the Americans, and the man was overthrown.

By this time, the president was suffering from Graves' disease (a thyroid condition) and the attack from the folksy 'hick' Democrat Bill Clinton outmanoeuvred him. Bush didn't understand the importance of image; he never handled television well. When he criticized, in a careless moment, the 'lowlife', as he saw it, morals of the fictional Simpson family, they lampooned him by having George Bush moving in next door to America's 'most dysfunctional family'. I doubt whether George saw the funny side.

William 'Bill' Jefferson Clinton (AKA Blythe) 1993–2001

At last, a *real* scandal. 'Slick Willie's' most famous lie? 'I did not have sexual relations with that woman, Miss Lewinsky.' Her stained blue dress, which proved that he did, was reputedly sold at auction in 2013, though final prices and indeed whether it was sold at all, are not reported.

On paper, Bill Clinton is one of the most successful presidents of all time, certainly in recent years. This is because his handling of the economy was deft, bordering on brilliant, and because until *that* incident, his personal public persona was smooth and likeable. He came from a working-class broken home in rural Arkansas and sought religion as a source of comfort. His father, a travelling salesman, William Blythe, was killed in a car crash before little Billy was born.

He was fascinated by politics from the age of 10, watching political broadcasts in 1956. He went to Washington at 16 on a young leaders' programme and met John Kennedy in the White House's Rose Garden. He attended conservative Georgetown University and a two-year Rhodes scholarship at Oxford. He avoided the Vietnam draft by playing the academic card. He was the first president since the Second

World War not to have served in the military, and he couldn't even salute properly! He met Hillary Roddam at Yale and they married in 1975. The next year he became Arkansas' Attorney General and the year after that, governor. By 1991, he decided to run for president with Hillary as his campaign manager.

Like John Kennedy, the hero he so much admired, Clinton liked women, and stories of his infidelity to Hillary were already emerging during his governorship. Stories about his penchant for marijuana circulated too. Even, so, he won the party vote and the popular one too, the nation and later the world entranced by his 'good ol' boy' Southern drawl. Al Gore was his vice president, polished, experienced, and not yet the climate change campaigner that he was to become. Clinton himself, however, was slow to make up his mind on issues and got lost in detail. A confidential memo from Prime Minister John Major's office reads that Clinton's administration 'remains chaotic'.

His principle aim, probably misquoted, was 'It's the economy, stupid' and he held true to that. Even so, it was difficult, the president's package passing the Senate by a single vote. His waffle and indecision on gays in the armed forces – don't ask, don't tell – lost him support of both Congress and the Pentagon. He clashed with the NRA over limiting the use of handguns after a mass shooting in Arkansas. His work on extending healthcare, ignored by Reagan, stalled under Bush, was run by Hillary and her involvement as the power behind the throne was not popular.

The press lampooned Clinton as a 'lefty' advocating the use of big government, which had never gone down well with Americans. He outraged Britain when he welcomed the Irish terrorist Gerry Adams to Washington and stuck his nose in where it certainly had no business to be: the fraught situation in Ulster. His dabbling in African affairs was less successful. When American troops were sent into war-torn Somalia, eighteen soldiers were killed and eighty-four injured. Clinton pulled out. When the Hutu tribe in Rwanda killed 800,000 of the minority Tutsi, Clinton did nothing.

Then *Newsweek* uncovered the Monica Lewinsky scandal. She was having an affair with the president as a staffer in the Oval Office and was accused of giving him oral sex while he was on the phone. The Internet went berserk. Other presidents (notably Kennedy and Harding) had committed similar indiscretions, but they never had to contend with social media. Bill's television interview is one of the most embarrassing ever. He banged his desk, he enunciated every word like staccato thunder: 'I did not have sexual relations with that woman, Miss Lewinsky.' It would probably have been worse had he not used her name – 'that woman' being delivered with such contempt. He kept this line going for as long as he could. As with the Profumo affair in 1960s Britain, it was not the sex but the public lying that caused outrage.

In the meantime, shady dealings involving the Whitewater land project in Arkansas cost $40 million, and Clinton was charged with perjury, abuse of office and obstruction of justice. Republicans wanted him impeached, and he was, in 1998. The Senate acquitted him, however, and Slick Willie lurched on. He had his successes, but the Lewinsky affair continued to hover over him. Since leaving office in January 2001, he has thrown his influence into Hillary's political career which in its turn came to nothing. The MeToo movement has shone a spotlight on Clinton's sexual transgressions, and evidence has come to light that some of the man's acquaintances were very badly chosen, like the predatory paedophile Jeffrey Epstein. In the end, the world remembers these things and forgets the rest.

George Walker Bush 2001–09

This section could be written using presidential gaffes alone; there's no need to probe further. 'I know what I believe,' he told a press conference, 'I will continue to articulate what I believe and what I believe in – I believe what I believe is right.' That was telling 'em! That was in Rome in July 2001 and three years later, he hadn't improved much. 'Our enemies are innovative and resourceful and so are we. They never stop thinking about new ways to harm our country and our people and neither do we.' And what was he thinking when he said that the Iraq war was 'unjustified and brutal'? It was, in the end, all about education: 'Rarely is the question asked: is our children learning?'

'Dubya' was better looking than his dad, much better groomed and a television natural. Before he took office, he was thought to be nowhere near as bright as his father, a heavy partyer and drinker and, like Clinton, a draft-dodger. His Texan credentials weren't strong either. He lived in Midland in that state, but was born in Connecticut, attended staunchly New England Harvard and Yale and had a holiday home at Kennebunkport down the coast from the Kennedys. The trashing of 'Dubya' continued during his run for office in 2001. The French newspaper *Le Monde* wrote of the 'cretinisation' of politics in America. The election itself was mired in controversy, as it would be again in 2016. Bush won by a thread only when the US Supreme Court intervened to stop any more recounts of votes.

To be fair to 'Dubya', his presidency was hit hard by crises not of his making. The atrocity that was 9/11 was the first major bombing attack on US soil (there had been one earlier) and the whole country was convulsed by it. The invasion of Afghanistan followed, the devastating Hurricane Katrina and the banking collapse of 2008. Of 9/11, Bush said, 'In a single morning, the purpose of my Presidency had become clear … it redefined my job.' That job was now the War on Terror. In fighting that war, Bush went further than any other president except, arguably, Harry S. Truman. He set up Guantanamo Bay, used torture and denied trials to terror suspects. Like Truman with his decision to use the bomb to end a war, Bush believed that the ends justify the means. Morally, that is dubious.

And with Tony Blair's backing, the president unleashed war in the wrong place. Al Qaeda and the Taliban were the enemy, and it ended up with war in Afghanistan. Only one commander – General Roberts of Kandahar – had defeated the Afghans (in 1879) and Bush's war was a disaster. It became regime change. The Monroe Doctrine, Manifest

Destiny, the Big Stick; all those belligerent phrases over the centuries morphed together. With Soviet Russia gone, Bush's country was now the world's only superpower, and it bullied everybody into building a democratic society, whether they wanted it or not. Exactly the same mistake was made in Iraq; the Arab Spring, backed by American and British military clout, was a mirage. The world is still reeling from the false narrative of 'weapons of mass destruction'.

And when Bush was too slow in providing relief for black New Orleans in the wake of Hurricane Katrina (2005), his days may have been numbered.

Barack Hussein Obama II 2009–2017

Towards the end of his presidency, Republicans pretended that Barack Obama was born in Kenya. This was a 'birther' conspiracy theory based on the constitutional fact that presidents of the United States must be American by birth (which ruled out potential 'greats' such as Henry Kissinger and Arnie Schwarzenegger). In fact, Obama was born in Honolulu, Hawaii, which had been a state for two years by the time of his birth (1961) and had been American territory since 1900.

He taught law at the University of Chicago and was Governor of Illinois. America was a little tired of the family convention of a succession of Bushes and Clintons, and was bitterly divided over the Iraq war. Obama spoke against it. He was young, dazzling on the campaign trail, and clever. 'There is not a Black America and a White America and Latino America and Asian America. There's the United States of America.'

His weakness as far as the black community was concerned was that he was not of traditional 'slave stock'. His father was a Kenyan goat herder, outside mainstream American experience. Some doubted at first whether he was truly 'one of us'. And his opponent Joe Biden put his foot in it when he said, 'You got the first mainstream African American who is articulate and bright and clean and a nice-looking guy,' ignoring thousands of such men, going back to the ex-slave Frederick Douglass and before. Obama married Michelle Robinson of Chicago in 1992, and she and their two daughters, Malia and Sasha, added glamour and glitz to the White House.

The world's press doubted whether America would elect a black man. The prediction was that he would be assassinated (he often spoke surrounded by bulletproof glass). And some people saw Bill Clinton as 'more black than Barack' on the basis of his policies and that he had probably slept with more black women.

When American media, dominated by the unaccountably saintly Oprah Winfrey, backed him, the whole campaign became a romantic fairy story, which had little to do with *realpolitik*. He made mistakes too, criticizing blue-collar America as bitter people, who were bigoted. T-shirts and bumper stickers flooded the country in response to this.

Obama's greatest triumph – continuing health programmes begun by his predecessor and called Obamacare – was a huge step for poor Americans, but of course by the nature of American politics could be – and virtually has been – overturned in the twinkling of a Trump. I once asked a white Virginian attorney his views on Obamacare and his reply, shaking the glassware of our dinner table, is unprintable in a family history book. The Obamacare programme was denounced as the 'Lie of the Year'.

The president had no interest in sparking good relations with his Republican opponents, and his tone became increasingly condescending. When the judge who handled his inauguration fluffed his lines, Obama coolly corrected him; it was a tiny humiliation but a humiliation all the same. He also performed U-turns; in 2010 he opposed gay marriage – by 2015, the White House was lit up with the rainbow colours of the LGBTQ movement.

It was nothing short of bizarre that Obama was given the Nobel Peace Prize soon after sending 30,000 troops to Afghanistan. In Iraq, he pulled troops out, allowing ISIS to rampage unchecked. In 2009, he increased troop numbers in Afghanistan to 100,000, believing that some wars were better than others and provided a hopelessly confused legacy into the bargain. He promised to close Guantanamo Bay within a year but when he left office in 2017, it was still open. America did nothing as Bashar Assad slaughtered his own people in Syria, and when America did do something, it replaced Colonel Gaddafi in Libya with dangerous, intolerant chaos. Anyone who tried to expose the duplicity of Obama's regime, like the journalist Edward Snowden, was closed down.

He failed to end the country's gun crisis, despite promising to do so. He watched, apparently helpless, as black versus white divisions got worse, not better, during his presidency. 'Obama,' wrote journalist Toby Harnden, 'managed to serve eight years with no scandal to speak of' which of course depends on your view of what a scandal is. It may be too early to say, but the majority will probably look back at the Obama years as a banality of disappointment.

Chapter 24

New Labour, New Nightmare

Anthony 'Tony' Charles Lynton Blair 1997–2007

The 'Midlothian Question' had never really gone away – a preponderance of Scottish ministers at Westminster irked many people – and here it was again. Tony Blair was born in Edinburgh and attended the private fee-paying Fettes in that city. Since Fettes is often referred to as the Scottish Eton, and since Blair went on to St John's College, Oxford, we're back in the same old *cursus honorum* as the Romans called it – the path of honour. Oh, and he read law!

An essay on him by Andrew Adonis is full of guarded eulogy. Blair was 'possibly the most gifted natural politician to have become prime minister apart from David Lloyd George'. He was an 'electoral genius'. His 'greatest governmental achievements were lasting peace … in Northern Ireland, devolution to Scotland and Wales … and transformation of the National Health Service'. In fact, not one of these changes has truly worked, and only at the end of a list does Adonis mention Blair's actual positive achievement, the creation of the Minimum Wage. We have to remember, of course, that Lord Adonis was a cabinet minister under Blair, which itself speaks volumes. He makes no comment on the fact that Blair cut Prime Minister's Question Time in the Commons from two a week to one, to avoid the flak.

There is a deep dichotomy in Blair, indeed in the Labour Party itself, which has caused them endless problems. Under their first MP, the 'Lib-Lab' miners' spokesman, James Keir Hardie, they represented, as the party name implies, Labour, the working man. In the uncertain economies of the 1920s and 1930s, such a party made headway, especially to those who believed the claptrap propaganda coming out of the Communist Russia. Once in office, Ramsay MacDonald and Clem Attlee realized that they had to water down their left-leaning image to appeal to voters across the board. Despite the phenomenal success of Attlee's reforms (see Chapter 20), the country was not prepared for what went with that, and the 1970s and 1980s saw bully boy trades unions making unreasonable demands and threatening the governments of the day. The stagnant, obsolete stance of the Left was personified by the image of Michael Foot, the party's leader with wild hair, duffel coat and impeccable intellectual credentials marching with hippies to Aldermaston, spreading fears about nuclear war.

Enter Tony Blair, but the same old dualism existed. His father was once a Communist, yet became a Tory MP wannabe. The educational paths he chose for his son are straight out of the Conservative handbook, even if he wasn't there to see it. Blair got himself a lucrative London law position and met and married Cherie Booth, the daughter of a Liverpudlian actor comedian. His mentor was the legal heavyweight 'Derry' Irvine, who had close links with the Labour Party under a man who would have made a superb prime minister, John Smith. Sadly, Smith's sudden death in May 1994 meant that that would not happen and there was a vacuum at the top. Blair won the safe Labour seat of Sedgefield, geographically in the Red Wall constituencies of the industrial north-east.

Following party dogma, he voted to leave the European Economic Community and campaigned for Nuclear Disarmament. With his smooth looks, young family and assured television persona, Blair quickly gained popularity, especially against the 'Welsh windbag' Neil Kinnock, who had become the party's great hope.

What Blair *was* good at was the sound bite. That trite phrase so beloved of the media, 'tough on crime and the causes of crime', sounded great. But in office Blair was neither. He used the phrase 'Education, education, education' as though it was central to his government; it wasn't. Under Blair, the funding and therefore the good intentions failed. In the extension of university entrance to include 50 per cent of young people (it was 7.9 per cent when I left school) Blair created a feeble tertiary level with declining standards. He also brought in student fees, economically crippling future generations.

'Bambi' Blair and his sidekick Gordon Brown (another Scotsman!) did a deal known as the 'Granita Pact' after the London restaurant in which they worked out details. Blair would be at Number 10 should he win the election, and Brown, a sound Treasury man, next door as chancellor. All very chummy.

Blair was now leader of New Labour, which in destroying Clause Four of the party's constitution giving full power to trades unions in Marxist language, was not actually Labour at all, but the vague 'Third Way', a phrase pinched by Bill Clinton across the pond – or was it the other way round? Major's election campaign backfired when he tried the 'demon eyes' campaign: photographs in newspapers with Blair's eyes, Dracula-red and upside down. Advertising watchdogs condemned this as going too far (had they seen no eighteenth-century propaganda?) and the public didn't approve.

The 1997 election was an unprecedented landslide and gave Blair the keys to Number 10. Peace in Northern Ireland was the work of John Major, but Blair took credit for it. After bomb outrages in the province and mainland Britain the peace was welcome, but it was – and is – fragile and the United Ireland problem has not been resolved. In implementing devolution for Scotland and Wales, Blair contributed to the potential break-up of the UK with badly run local government in both countries and strident Medieval insistence from Scotland that they become independent. In creating the semi-autonomous London Mayor, Blair made the capital often at odds with the rest of the country – an unaccountable bubble of the liberal elite who continued to speak a different language from everybody else.

Blair muscled in everywhere. When Princess Diana was killed in a Paris car crash, it was the prime minister who appeared stony faced on television talking of the 'people's princess'. He cashed in on the extraordinary outpouring of national grief, which in many ways was the start of the Age of Hysteria (see Chapter 25) in which we still live. 'Pitch perfect', says Lord Adonis. 'None of a prime minister's business' say the bulk of historians. He went on to remove most hereditary peers from the Lords, thereby ending the centuries' old stranglehold of the Tories in that chamber. It was replaced, however, by party cronies from both major parties, thereby extending the tribal nonsense that goes on daily in the Commons. The Lords is now far less of a 'checks and balances' chamber than it has ever been.

To be fair to Blair, he never hid the fact that he swayed with the wind of popular acclaim. 'You shouldn't be in this game,' he once said, 'unless you can ride two horses at the same time.' He smarmed around the media who, apart from the right-wing elements, loved him. Even Rupert Murdoch, the tycoon who owned the *Sun* and *The Times* (how is *that* possible?) gave him an easy ride. But his spin doctor, Alistair Campbell, was seen by nearly everybody as a Machiavellian character, especially when it came to the Iraq War of 2003.

'In Iraq,' even Adonis has to admit, 'Blair wanted his Falklands, but got his Suez.' The prime minister had given a 'liberal intervention' speech in Chicago in April 1999 which implied that Britain was prepared to punch militarily above its actual body weight (successive prime ministers over the last forty years have relentlessly cut funding and numbers for the armed forces). It also sounded very like the Monroe Doctrine, Manifest Destiny and the Big Stick, which has characterized American government since the 1820s. Blair was seen as Bush's poodle, lamely following him into an illegal war of regime change in Iraq. The infamous 'sexed up' dossier concerning so-called weapons of mass destruction led to the death of Dr David Kelly, a weapons expert. The dismissal of Campbell followed, as did accusations (which still resonate) that 'liar Blair' was a war criminal who should face criminal prosecution.

Yet for all these failures, some of them scandalous, Tony Blair today is largely sought after on the after-dinner speaker circuit, and regarded by many as a wise 'elder statesman'.

James Gordon Brown 2007–10

The Scottish persuasion continued under Gordon Brown, Blair's ally and chancellor throughout his premiership. The Granita deal (see above) meant that it was a matter of when, not if, Brown should move next door.[1] Brown's father was a Church of Scotland minister, imbuing his son with Christian faith, honesty and a dual personality that looked positively dowdy after Blair. He lost the sight in one eye playing rugby in 1967 and became rector of Edinburgh University, his alma mater, at the age of 21.

Brown was the stronger of the Brown–Blair arrangement in our own time. He had an excellent grasp of finance and economics and a reputation for common sense. He admired the eighteenth-century economist Adam Smith and the founding fathers of the United States, although he must have realized how woefully short of their ideals America had fallen by Brown's own time. He was pro-European.

The Granita agreement took too long to materialise as far as Brown was concerned, and then he popped out from behind Tony rather as John Major had from Margaret Thatcher – solid, boring and utterly eclipsed by their predecessors. Even so, he soldiered on. A Labour press advertisement ran, 'Not flash, just Gordon', which probably only sci-fi comic fans would have understood. The decision to reduce inheritance tax (nothing annoys voters more than governments making arbitrary decisions about their money) was badly handled and rushed, denting Brown's slowly growing popularity. The monster of sleaze arose over illegal donations to the Labour Party and the army accused Brown of skimping on their weapons and equipment in Afghanistan.

He was nearly toppled in 2008 when the Northern Rock bank went into liquidation and greedy bankers were exposed as frauds and parasites. To be fair, this was a global problem (Walpole's South Sea Bubble writ large) but each country and its leader had to find a way out. Millions of Britons were missold PPI (payment protection insurance), for which the government was blamed, and Brown's cabinet, especially

David Miliband and Alistair Darling, were at war over exactly what policy should be followed.

Although Brown held steady in the financial crisis, and indeed launched a worldwide Western approach to sorting it, taxes rose to pay for the whole thing and the Conservatives tore him apart. As ever, however, it was petty politics and political misdoings that ended his premiership. MPs' expenses were leaked to the media who suddenly discovered that foreign travel, luxury hotels, fine dining and even state-of-the-art garden duck houses were being paid for by the tax-paying public on top of salaries and expenses that the said public already considered outrageous. Brown dithered and backed the MPs, while his opponent David Cameron insisted that his MPs pay back what they owed. There were screaming rows at Number 10 and a raft of resignations, Murdoch's press engine turned against him, issuing stories that were untrue but which played to the public's notion that there was no smoke without fire.

In the 2010 election, Brown 'did a John Major' and forgot to switch off his microphone on campaign. The lady from Rochdale, who complained to the prime minister about waves of immigrants arriving on British shores, was called a 'bigoted woman' in a muttered Brown aside. The media, inevitably, picked it up. The election results were inconclusive and Brown toyed with creating a coalition government of Labour, Liberal Democrats and minority parties, rather like the national government of 1931 and Churchill's wartime set-up but without the Tories. It was the politics of the desperate, and nobody fell for it.

When Gordon Brown left Downing Street on 10 May, he appeared outside Number 10 with his wife and their two boys. This was the first and last time that the children had appeared on television and somehow that seemed to sum up the premiership of Gordon Brown.

David William Donald Cameron 2010–16

It was as though we had gone back nearly 200 years. David Cameron's education – Eton and Brasenose College, Oxford – puts him squarely in the long list of silver-spooned politicians who have led Britain over the decades. 'Call me Dave' didn't really square with that.

He was not a celebrity at Eton; in fact he was nearly expelled for smoking pot, but at Oxford he joined the Bullingdon Club, a drinking fraternity composed of public schoolboys, including Boris Johnson. The Conservative party tried to bury the famous 'louche' photograph of the group but failed. In politics, he became an aide to John Major and Norman Lamont which gave him his first experiences in dealing with the media. He was natural television. He could never evade the old boys' network, however, that most of his appointments in office were part of the 'chumocracy'. His wife was the daughter of a baronet, so the silver spoon image was reinforced, even though she read art at Bristol and has a tattoo on her ankle!

Cameron became MP for Witney, Oxfordshire, in 2001, with Iain Duncan Smith as party leader. 'IDS' was a poor leader and Labour won again in 2005. Cameron was as adept as Blair at sound bites: 'Hug a husky' covered the world's new obsession with climate change; 'Hug a hoodie' covered juvenile crime. Neither phrase made any difference. The Camerons were at the heart of the 'Notting Hill Set' along with the laughable Michael Gove, but the 'chumocracy' was far too chummy for the Red Wall and elsewhere, with the UKIP (Independence) party wanting to break away from the stranglehold of the European Union. To Cameron, such people were 'fruitcakes, loonies and closet racists' (which remains the view of the London 'blob' as I write).

Short of a majority in the 2010 election, Cameron threw in his lot with the Lib Dems under Nick Clegg; two young, handsome, personable politicians sharing a podium in Number 10's Rose Garden – what could be nicer? As things turned out, almost anything. The Liberal Party had vanished in the 1920s and had tried to re-invent itself in a variety of ways ever since. None of them worked. Even the name they finally agreed on – the Liberal *Democrats* – smacked of American politics. By definition, all political parties in both countries were democratic, so why highlight the fact?

Clegg and his group pledged not to increase university tuition fees but changed their minds in accordance with Conservative policy, one small but telling reminder that peacetime coalitions without a common purpose don't work. By 2015, the prime minister could do without Clegg who wandered off into more lucrative work. Unlike Gladstone, Blair and many others at Number 10, Cameron was not a workaholic. He used the phrase 'chillax' many times, enjoying a glass of wine and box-set television bingeing with his family. He reduced contact time with the media, knowing that they were watching like hawks for any slip. He rarely flew the flag, regarding the UK as a junior partner to the US, in awe of India's economic growth rate. He 'apologised' for Bloody Sunday when the hassled soldiers of 2 Para fired on a hostile Belfast crowd in 1972. This may have been diplomatic, but it infuriated the army and those who believed that the first stone in the interminable 'New Troubles' had been thrown by the Irish.

Following Obama's lead into Libya, British and French troops didn't do too well in restoring peace there. Obama called it a 'shit show'. Cameron couldn't rally support for a strike against the vicious regime of President Assad in Syria who was using chemical weapons contrary to international law. The result was a huge influx of refugees fleeing to the UK which triggered the (for Cameron) fatal Brexit referendum. It didn't help that in all this, the prime minister referred to himself as 'the heir to Blair' as though Third Way politics was not only preferential, but increasingly the only game in town.

Referenda are rare in British politics. In Switzerland, they hold them all the time, which rather negates the point of parliament. If people are given the chance to vote directly on issues, why do we have a Commons and Lords – or a prime minister – at all? The Scottish independence referendum resulted in a failure for the Scottish Nationalist Party in September 2014 but Cameron didn't capitalize on this and the 'tartan army' got more strident and belligerent as a result.

In Europe, the prime minister was a 'Eurosceptic Conservative' and he tried to push the EU for greater wiggle-room for Britain. Brussels simply ignored him. He came out for Remain in the Brexit debate but didn't follow this up with a robust campaign of any kind. When that great friend of Britain, Barack Obama, said on television that in the context of a trade deal, the UK would be 'at the back of the queue' if it left Europe, he was right, of course; six years after the Referendum, we are still waiting in line.

Cameron had promised that he would continue whichever way the referendum went, but the day after the result, he resigned and has never looked back.

Chapter 25

The Age of Hysteria

Throughout this book so far we have sailed – and later flown – from one side of the Atlantic to the other, highlighting the shortcomings of the men (and one woman) who once ran two of the greatest nations on Earth. Now, in the bizarre events of the last five years, we can fuse the two to an extent, because the same problems face them both. To another extent, this chapter is probably better written by a sociologist rather than an historian because we are still living with the problems today. But the problems themselves have not emerged fully formed out of the blue; they are the result of the changing attitudes of society over the last few years.

I believe that the premierships of Theresa May and Boris Johnson and the presidency of Donald Trump would have been very different were it not for the cataclysmic changes that overtook them. None of the three has come out of it in a particularly good light, especially as some of their problems have been the result of their own shortcomings; they all shot themselves in the foot.

It is very difficult to know where to start, but one thing I notice in writing about the presidents is the way the issue of race has come to haunt America as a nation. A recent commentator has said that, to many Americans, 1619, the year in which the first black slaves, twenty of them, were brought to America in a Dutch ship, is now a more important date in their history than 1776, the year of the Declaration of Independence, when the thirteen colonies officially said 'enough is enough' to the government of Lord North and George III. What has happened is that the Western world has become obsessed with racism. Cancel culture, statue toppling, museum vandalism, history itself, is being airbrushed by fanatics whose lack of awareness knows no bounds.

They are the new Puritans. The old ones shot Native Americans and forced Africans to work for them, all in God's name, of course. The new ones try to eradicate this unfortunate fact by pretending that all white men, even today, are guilty of the same crimes. These attitudes are infectious, just as seventeenth-century Puritanism was. In 1692, nineteen inhabitants of Salem, Massachusetts, were hanged, and countless others interrogated because of accusations of witchcraft from a handful of deluded, malicious teenaged girls. Wokery is the new example – illiterati (of all ages, both sexes and neither) pointing the finger at ideas, institutions and people which they don't understand and of which they are afraid. Instead of handling this with education and plain speaking (which eventually happened after Salem), academics and supposedly intelligent people indulge it for reasons of their own. They rail against the slavery of the ancient world and the existence of it in the antebellum South, but they are strangely mute when it comes to challenging current instances of abuse as in Saudi Arabia or China, arguing fatuous 'cultural differences'.

The upshot of this is the potential disappearance of free speech. Every politician on both sides of the pond has to walk on eggshells to put their point across, and woe betide them if that point doesn't accord with the faceless trolls on social media.

The media itself has become all powerful in recent years, and that too is a slow-burning fuse. The political pamphlets of the seventeenth century were vile because there were no established laws of libel. Now there are, with special privileges being given to MPs and Congressmen to avoid the worst pitfalls. But instead, we have supposed B list actors talking about 'their truth', as though truth isn't absolute. Prime ministers and presidents have to cope with all that. In recent years, Rupert Murdoch's press empire was all powerful, but so was Lord Northcliffe's in the early twentieth century. The difference now is television. How politicians dress, what their hairstyle is, how they walk and talk – these used to be the problems of film stars. Now they are the politicians' problems. Theresa May's shoes were the subject of division;

her posture was bad. Boris Johnson was overweight and looked like an unmade bed. Donald Trump was 'orange man' because of his fake tan; and don't get me started on his hair and his over-use of the baseball cap, telling his voters to 'Make America Great Again'.

Clint Eastwood, in his persona of Dirty Harry Callahan, about as far removed from woke as it's possible to be, once commented, 'Opinions are like assholes. Everybody's got one.' And so we have an endless stream of 'celebrities': pop stars, dancers, TV contestants, sports pundits, all with some 'influence' who thanks to social media, have their platforms to spout forth their opinions. Trump tried to harness this to appear regularly on Twitter until other Twitterati closed him down. This is no way to run a railroad or a country.

So we have an obsession with race. We have an over intrusive media. We have the apparently unstoppable infection of wokery. And we have COVID. In the 1340s, Europe was hit by a sudden outbreak of bubonic plague. Then called the pestilence, it came from China and led to the deaths of between a third and a half of the population. Economies were badly hit and it took generations for normality to return. In 2019, another disease escaped from the same country, either from a wet market selling bats for food or a government-controlled laboratory (the health jury is still out). The result was panic, as it was in the 1340s, but some countries came out a bit better than others. Boris Johnson was hit by it and pulled through, claiming to have rolled out the most successful vaccine in the world. Donald Trump rubbished the whole thing and recommended drinking bleach. Irrational people from every country in the world claimed that vaccines were the work of the devil and that we were all going to die. Their voices were heard on – oh yes, social media.

We also have a bizarre reappearance of the Cold War, which everybody assumed was over, with America as top nation. Although no longer Communist, Vladimir Putin's Russia is the new pariah with his unprovoked and unjustified attack on Ukraine. The West is busy arming the Ukrainians. On another cold front, China has emerged from centuries of torpidity, copying Western technology and undercutting international process because they do not pay their workers a living wage. Their war is economic, devious and based on the 90-year-old ramblings of a psychopath, Mao Zedong.

The effects of these developments are complicated, but I am convinced that they are linked. And together, they have created a dystopian, disjointed atmosphere in which the work of prime ministers and presidents has been made increasingly more difficult. Let's see how they all coped.

Theresa Mary May, née Brazier, became prime minister in July 2016. A vicar's daughter, she attended grammar school and St Hugh's College, Oxford. As Britain's second female premier, the spotlight was on her with an unusual intensity and inevitably there were comparisons with the force of nature that was Margaret Thatcher.

Six months later, Donald John Trump became the 45th president of the United States. A New Yorker, he attended Fordham and Pennsylvania universities. Two totally different personalities, not to mention genders with different nationalities and backgrounds. What they had in common was a university education and a determination to succeed in their top jobs.

In a very unusual sense, May had to continue the work of her predecessor. David Cameron had left Number 10 in a hurry, leaving the hard work to his successor. May was not a committed Brexiteer, but she gave it her best shot; it wasn't good enough. The figures spoke for themselves; 52 per cent of the country who voted voted to leave, 48 per cent who voted voted to remain. It was a tight call and the Remainers proved themselves the poorest losers in history when they tried every trick in and out of the book to overturn democracy. Shortly after this, I was lecturing on a cruise ship to a largely American audience and was talking about the various invasions of Britain. First came the Celts from central Europe, then the Romans from Italy, the Saxons from Germany, the Vikings from Scandinavia, the Normans from France, and there were attempts by the Spaniards (1588), the French (1804) and the Germans (1940), which didn't quite come off. I said to my audience, who knew about none of this, 'And you wonder why we voted for Brexit!'

May herself called Remainers 'citizens of nowhere'. Media headlines screamed that diehard Europhile judges were the 'enemies of the people'. During her premiership, thirty-five ministers resigned and there were umpteen defeats over bills in parliament, prompted partly by a seemingly biased speaker, John Bercow (who should have been neutral), and backed by the ludicrous Supreme Court, an American invention which had no place in British society. May was an 'accidental' prime minister, suddenly thrust into the spotlight with insufficient political savvy. She distanced herself from Cameron's old-boy atmosphere, rarely mixing socially with MPs or even her own cabinet. She confided in her husband, which was seen as a move in the wrong direction. She told her aides that honours etc., the norm under most Conservative leaders, would not be on the cards. They might 'get a Jaffa cake' instead. When she clashed with her chancellor, George Osborne, and fired him, he went on to edit London's *Evening Standard* and described her as 'dead woman walking'.

May had 'previous'. As Home Secretary, she was known to be difficult and a stickler for hard work. She even had the phrase used about her, 'a bloody difficult woman' (Ken Clarke), printed on a favourite coffee mug. She was not a natural leader and couldn't charm people. Cabinet meetings were punctuated with long silences and she found it difficult to make decisions. 'Brexit means Brexit,' she said in a Blairite sound bite, but had no idea how to make it happen. Her decision to call a snap election in June 2017 failed – she lost her seventeen-seat majority (small enough anyway) and looked weak and wobbly, sometimes sending cabinet minister Amber Rudd to speak for her. In the European elections, the Conservatives had their worst showing in any election since the 1830s.

Increasingly, the vultures circled. One of the saddest photographs in the press was of Theresa May, the only woman in a solid block of grey-suited Brussels men, trying desperately to get the best deal she could. In the end she resigned, leaving the work to be finished by a man (don't tell Margaret Thatcher).

The BBC's Justin Webb wrote in 2021 that, 'nothing about the presidency of Donald J. Trump, was normal.' If you rated the man, he was a saviour out to reaffirm the Good Ol' Party fundamentals. If you didn't (and that became the majority) he was the worst president in history. Interestingly, one of his famous statements was 'I alone can fix it', which sounds extraordinarily like Pitt, the Elder in 1750s Britain; people were fiercely divided over him too. Temperamentally, Trump and May couldn't have been more different. She was shy, determined, with a strong sense of duty. He was a rebel; there were screaming rows with his businessman father and arguments with his teachers. Trump's recollections of his educational attainments chime well with the personal truth referred to by, among others, the Duchess of Sussex today; nobody else quite remembers it that way.

Seriously rich via the property market, the future president built Trump Towers in Manhattan, sixty-eight floors of 5th Avenue real estate. He owned beauty pageants and ran and hosted NBC's *The Apprentice*, later franchised in Britain. He made millions, and he lost them too, a number of enterprises going bust. That didn't deter banks from investing in him. He had the Teflon qualities of Clinton and Blair and in his sheer arrogance, seemed tailormade to star in the age of hysteria.

Some believe that Trump running for president in 2016 was a PR stunt that suddenly became startlingly real when he won the contest. He rubbished his opponents with explosive language and accused them of things they'd never done. When he was debating with Hillary Clinton on television, my wife and I were lecturing on another cruise. One of the American guests asked rhetorically, 'With 350 million Americans, how come we ended up with these two?' As lecturers (and Brits) we took no part in the mock election held on board, but the result was a Trump victory, and its vote was split almost entirely on gender lines; the majority of women backed Clinton, the majority of men Trump.

In reality, Clinton was branded 'crooked' by Trump and was under investigation by the FBI for the mishandling of classified information. There was no case to answer, but the voting public didn't want to hear that. 'The Donald' almost derailed himself, however, in an interview on television explaining his allure as far as women were concerned. 'When you're a star, they let you do it. You can do anything. Grab 'em by the pussy. You can do anything.'

To add to the sexism was the racism. Obsessed with Mexico and longing to build a wall to keep them out, he said, 'When Mexico sends its people ... they're bringing drugs, they're bringing crime, they're rapists ...'

He won the Electoral College vote easily, but not the popular vote. The Republicans swept the board to the extent that Democrat liberal America, particularly on the east and west coasts, seriously contemplated emigrating, perhaps to Canada.

Pushing the 'America First' agenda that earlier presidents had trumpeted, he had a huge following among blue-collar workers, especially in the Midwest. He admired dictators like Vladimir Putin and Xi Jinping of China, ignoring the fact that their power came from repression and terror, not popular democracy. George W. Bush had said fifteen years earlier, 'A dictatorship would be a heck of a lot easier, there's no question about it.' He was joking; Trump wasn't. He packed the Supreme Court with judges of his own right-wing tendency who he hoped could be trusted to push the 'right' way of America's troubles – the abortion debate, gay marriage, gun laws and, of course, race.

While all this was going on, 3,000 miles away, Alexander Boris de Pfeiffel Johnson walked into Number 10 in July 2019. He was possibly the most cosmopolitan prime minister in history, with German and Turkish ancestry to match his true-blue British credentials. His education was boringly familiar, however, Eton followed by Balliol, Oxford. When I began to write this book, 'Bozza' was still at Number 10 and I had no idea I would be including him, because I had determined not to write about serving incumbents. Not only that, I have to add Liz Truss as well, which shows just how hysterical the Age of Hysteria is. Britain has had four prime ministers in three years, one surely, for the *Guinness Book of Records*.

Sixteen years before he got the top job, Johnson said, 'I have as much chance of becoming prime minister as being decapitated by a Frisbee, or of finding Elvis.' If birthplace used to be the decider of nationalities. Johnson is American, born in New York when Elvis was still king. He was a school chum of David Cameron and was renowned for his lateness and largeness, qualities he would continue at Number 10.

After Oxford he trained as a journalist, which often got him into hot water because he was careless with his quotation attributions. He wrote for the *Telegraph* and edited the *Spectator*. He entered the Commons with the safe seat of Henley, but like Trump, appeared on television, the audience loving his over-the-top Churchillian rhetoric. He beat 'Red Ken' Livingstone for the mayoralty of London and held the post for eight years, playing to the push for clean air and exercise with the 'Boris Bikes' replacing cars for tourists and commuters. He presided over the 2012 Olympic Games, although there were many other hands involved in the success of that.

In 2016, Johnson came out as a Eurosceptic and backed the Leave campaign. When Cameron resigned, Johnson instinctively joined the group to replace him, but was effectively knifed in the back by Michael Gove and the job went to Theresa May. Johnson got a consolation prize as Foreign Secretary, where he met with mixed success. At Chequers in July 2018, he and Brexit Secretary David Davis both resigned rather than put up with more of May's ineffectuality and he turned to writing instead, at which he was very good (despite his hagiography of Churchill).

When May fell, Johnson tried again, beating Jeremy Hunt to the top job. His aim was to 'Get Brexit Done', three years after *that* referendum. He ran up against the same brick wall that May had faced – a recalcitrant parliament, a belligerent speaker and a staid Supreme Court as stick-in-the-mud as anything Trump had created across the pond.

To push things through, Johnson called a general election in December 2019. The country turned blue overnight, the Red Wall of Labour supporters in the north collapsing. It helped that Johnson's opposition was the unelectable old Marxist Jeremy Corbyn, who spoke for no one except his Momentum cronies and young people who had no idea what a Marxist was. With an eighty-seat majority, Johnson suddenly had a free hand and Brexit was indeed done.

Then came COVID.

Whole swathes of America loved Donald Trump because they felt he spoke for them. His speeches were rambling, sometimes ranting, sometimes incoherent but he gelled with working class, in the country who felt (like the Red Wall in Britain) that minorities were becoming more valued than they were, with condescending words from on high about race, climate change, political correctness.

Like a tiny handful of presidents before him, Trump was impeached (in his case, twice) over putting pressure on the Ukrainian president to smear his opponent Joe Biden in the Ukraine election. The House of Representatives brought the case, but the Senate rejected it. Trump's own administration was under investigation for sleaze, frauds in charities, tax evasion and paying off a porn actress.

When the COVID outbreak hit, the president down-played it. His search for a vaccine was half-hearted and nothing like as successful as Johnson's. Both men caught the disease (Johnson more seriously than Trump) and the American bragged that his own physical and mental health had bought him through. Johnson appeared regularly on television between the two men of SAGE, Whitty and Valance, and followed the science, even if the science was too pessimistic for reality. When he fell ill, he was rushed to intensive care and didn't function well for weeks. The pandemic stopped Britain in its tracks, the economy juddering, education wrecked by all but useless 'zoom' lessons and millions paid to work from home, a habit many are reluctant to give up. The government's economic measures, the concept of 'levelling up' (to give an economic boost to the north), stalled. Britain had left the EU, but the promised start of a trade free new world never quite materialized.

The US election of 2020 was a national disaster. The final count postal votes swung Joe Biden and the Democrats' way, and a furious Trump cried foul. He claimed, as he always had when things went against him, that his opponents were releasing 'fake news' – that he had won the election after all. There was talk of martial law being imposed and the military being brought in to keep Trump and the Republicans in office. On 6 January 2021, the unthinkable happened. A large mob of Trump supporters waving flags and carrying weapons attacked the Capitol building in Washington, refusing to believe the election's figures. The last time this had happened, the attackers were dressed in scarlet uniforms and they were carrying different flags altogether. The world looked on in horror as doors were smashed in, running battles took place in front of cameras in what many reporters called 'a terrorist attack'. Five people died; over 140 were injured. Trump told his supporters to go home; but had his rambling rhetoric sent them up the Capitol steps in the first place? He was impeached for a second time before he left office, his aides carrying boxes out of the White House to which he had no right, now that he was no longer POTUS. Again, incomprehensively, the Senate refused the impeachment demand.

He was banned from Twitter, the social media network which he had made his own, and went off to sulk at his Florida estate of Mar-a-Lago. His tax returns are under review. For a man worth $3billion, in 2020 he paid no tax at all, seeing this as a mark of his success. Bearing in mind that America was created on the issue of tax payments, the founding fathers must be spinning in their graves. On 9 May 2023, a jury found Donald Trump guilty of attacking a journalist in a Manhattan department store in the 1990s. She had sued him for battery and defamation. The jury awarded a total of $4million against the former president. His response on the social media network Truth Social – 'I HAVE ABSOLUTELY NO IDEA WHO THIS WOMAN IS ...' Now, where have we heard that before? (see Chapter 23).

But there are rumours that Trump will run again ...

If Trump left with a bang, Johnson left with a whimper. The British media, has never had any pretence of impartiality. The leading papers are all London-based and London, despite Johnson being mayor for eight years, is always out to dish the dirt and usually stands well outside the opinions of the country at large. In December 2021, stories began to circulate about parties being held in the garden of Number 10 and inside, contrary to the lockdown rules of COVID. For centuries, of course, our rulers, be they prime ministers or kings, have ignored the rules they themselves have laid down. In the febrile 'Jack's-as-privileged-as-his-master' mentality of the Age of Hysteria, this would not do and the Johnson 'cake and Tupperware' became, inevitably, 'Partygate' (for which you can blame Richard Nixon and thousands of lazy journalists).

Fanned by the media, people saw the clown in Boris, claiming that he always lacked attention to detail, that he was all 'smoke and mirrors'. Under pressure from his own party (nobody shoots themselves in the foot as often or consistently as the Conservatives) he was forced to resign.

But there are rumours that he will run again ...

It is a mark of the changing respect shown to politicians that prime ministers are now routinely referred to by the media using their forenames. James Ramsay MacDonald's supporters called him Ramsay Mac. Churchill, especially after the war, was 'good old Winnie'. But nobody called Neville Chamberlain 'Nev' nor Anthony Eden 'Tony'. Yet from the 1970s, this was standard: 'Ted' Heath (the name of a bandleader of course); 'Jim' Callaghan; 'Maggie' Thatcher; 'Tony' Blair;

'Dave' ('Call me Dave') Cameron; Boris (or even 'Bozza') Johnson; 'Liz' Truss and 'Rishi' Sunak. There are only two exceptions – Gordon Brown and Theresa May just don't seem to suit shortened nicknames somehow.

On the one hand, this is matey, which is why prime ministers are happy to go along with it. On the other, it shows a contempt which would have seen hacks thrown into gaol cells in the past. No one referred to Robert Walpole as 'Bob' or either of the Pitts as 'Billy'; it simply was not done.

'Gone in 44 days,' screamed the *i* on 22 October 2022.

'He Couldn't, Could He ... Will Boris Bounce Back to Number 10?' asked the *Express*.

'General election now,' demanded the Labour-backed *Daily Mirror*.

'Bojo: I'll be back,' the *Sun* allegedly quoted.

The Times, ever pompous, said 'Johnson weighs return to power as Truss quits Number 10.'

'Boris v Rishi,' the *Daily Mail* pondered the dilemma. 'Fight for the soul of the Tories.'

The *Daily Telegraph* had Johnson almost echoing the older Pitt. 'Boris Johnson tells Tories: I can save party from election wipeout.'

The *Guardian*, with a photograph of Liz Truss turning away from the podium having announced her resignation, had the headline, 'The Bitter End'.

And as one journalist said, 'Everyone remembers where they were when Liz Truss became Prime Minister'.

When Liz Truss resigned, she was compared by much of the British media with George Canning, who was at Number 10 for 112 days, three times longer than she was. What few of them pointed out was that his term of office was terminated by death, and that before that he was an outstanding Foreign Secretary. Liz Truss didn't have that drama or that track record.

Because no books have so far been written on Truss, and possibly never will be, I have put this section together solely on the reportage of newspapers quoted above because they represent the broad spectrum of political opinion in Britain in the Age of Hysteria. The *Guardian* recognises that fact, which is encouraging – Truss 'presided over what has been one of the most politically turbulent and economically damaging periods in modern history'. There was to be a period of vicious in-fighting between Conservative front runners – Rishi Sunak, Penny Mordaunt and perhaps Boris Johnson himself – to find a successor.

'Merely swapping leaders of a broken Tory government is not enough,' said Ian Blackford of the Scottish Nationalists, 'there must be an election.' So far (October 2023), there hasn't been; the government's term has two years to run. Ian Blackford himself has already gone, his party weakening by the day.

That bastion of modern journalism, the *Daily Star*, set up a competition on its webcam to see who would last longer, Truss or an iceberg lettuce? The lettuce won. The *Washington Post* condescendingly called this a 'quintessentially British joke'.

Truss's resignation speech, soon after which she was replaced by the former Chancellor of the Exchequer, Rishi Sunak, referred to the problems she faced in office and what she tried to do. Putin's illegal and barbaric war in Ukraine has helped force up energy prices and this has impacted on every family in Britain. Boris Johnson was foremost in providing support for Ukraine via weapons and sanctions and this was followed by other nations around the world. Today, Russia is more of a pariah state than ever it was under the umbrella of the Soviet Union. Truss claimed that in her forty-four days she set out a vision for a low tax, high growth economy that would take advantage of the freedoms of Brexit. In fact, the mini budget of the prime minister and her chancellor Kwasi Kwarteng was greeted with horror by the world's financial markets, who, as ever, are only interested in profits (economics, after all, is an amoral subject).

Typical of the *Guardian* with its left-leaning narrative and seemingly anti-British stance, a column by its journalist John Grace reads, 'We used to laugh at Italy, but now the joke's on us. The UK is far more chaotic than anything the Italians could dream of.'

Many of the leading papers backed Truss at first – the *Daily Mail*, the *Express*, the *Telegraph* – and all had to backpedal as the truth dawned; Truss was not up to the job, to which you could now add many more whose below average performance has been chronicled in these pages. 'A legacy of destruction', the *Guardian* railed on. 'Free market economics ruined' and 'a Tory party in turmoil'. So far, so predictable. And of course, there were the obligatory photographs of Liz Truss curtseying to the queen as she accepted office and to the king as she left it.

From the ridiculous to the even more ridiculous. 'Worst ever', the *Daily Mirror* screamed in condemnation of Truss's premiership. The paper's associate editor, Kevin Maguire, fanned the flames of the Age of Hysteria with his column: 'Call a general election now or angry people must take to the barricades.' The paper quotes from a section of the public of the country's major cities, including the lifelong Tory voters who have now changed their minds because of the current shambles. While endorsing the 'chaos', the *Mirror* was only too happy to give the odds on the front runners for Number 10, the kind of thing that used to belong to the sports pages.

Sitting supposedly in the middle of politics, *The Times* (at a whopping £2.50 a pop compared with the *I*'s 70p) carried a list of the shortest-serving post-war prime ministers. Theresa May lasted 1,106 days, Alec Douglas-Home 363. All that, of course, looks pretty healthy alongside Truss. The political in-fighting at the top of the Tories (intriguing that that derogatory name from the 1670s is not only still there, but is still derogatory) was highlighted, with everybody and their supporters hating everybody else. Rishi Sunak was 'the Prophet of Doom', possibly because he had his eyes until recently, on the Treasury. Kemi Badenoch had a 'mountain to climb' to get on the ballot. Penny Mordaunt, all big hair and sass, was the unity candidate. Photographs of Liz Truss as a Lib-

Dem activist at Oxford in the 1990s and, more recently, looking rather uncomfortable in an army tank, covered an impossibly brief career.

i opined that the outgoing prime minister had become a political 'Lady Jane Grey', according to a backbencher; neither the MP nor the paper explained this reference, possibly because they are comfortable that we all watch enough Netflix shows to understand it. There was a photograph of three ex-prime ministers (Blair, Major and Cameron) at the queen's funeral, and it seems odd now that she is in their august company. Most papers, incidentally, carried the story that Krishnan Guru-Murthy was taken off air for leaving his microphone on after interviewing leadership hopeful Jeremy Hunt with the measured phrase 'what a c**t'.

What of the Right? The *Express*, with its increasingly irrelevant Crusader logo, presumably fighting for the usual high ground that journalists hold, was much more interested in the future, especially a possible return of Boris Johnson, than shortcomings of Truss. President Biden thanked her for her anti-Putin stance; the Kremlin celebrated another wobble in the West. Highly relevant to this book, the paper examined the 'blubbering blockheads' who had also made a hash of the top job. One 'clear rival', the article said, was Viscount Goderich, he of the tearful meltdown at an audience with George IV. Then came Lord Rosebery, crippled by insomnia and self-doubt: 'I am crucified to my place and it is damnable.' That's as far as the list goes, but hopefully readers of this book will be able to add quite a few more.

The *Sun*, ready to 'nuke the Argies' in the Falklands War and claiming that it alone won elections for prime ministers, thankfully added to the *Express's* list the hopeless Andrew Bonar Law and the Duke of Devonshire. The editorial sensibly called for calm and moderation, which, sadly in the Age of Hysteria, is very unlikely.

Sarah Vine lashed out in the *Daily Mail*. '[Truss's resignation] speech showed Trumpian levels of dysfunction and denial – rarely have I felt such fury … vanity and lust for power drove her to mislead.' Prime ministers, of course, have been misleading the public and parliament for the past two and a half centuries – it goes with the job. And journalist Mick Hume had a pop at one of them with his column's headline: 'Only Johnson can stop Tories turning into a Blairite blancmange'. Cruelly, Henry Deeds wrote, 'With a Mona Lisa smile, [Truss] left to face life as a pub quiz answer.'

With a nod to history. Michael Howard, leader of the Conservative Party from 2003 to 2005, boldly claimed that, 'Rishi can rescue the Tories like Macmillan after Suez' ignoring the fact that we live in a very different world from 1957. In these days of extremism and social media, Supermac wouldn't stand a chance.

The *Telegraph*, calling itself Britain's best quality newspaper (it's also the most expensive at £2.80) asked a variety of big (and not so big) wigs for comment on Truss. Lady Smith of Basildon, leader of the Opposition in the Lords, said, 'The Government thinks the answer to all this is to shuffle the deck chairs on the *Titanic*.' Sir Ed Davey, leader of the Lib Dems, was quoted as saying, 'Liz Truss trashed our economy and before her Boris Johnson failed our country.' Ed Miliband, shadow climate secretary: 'They [the Conservatives] are unfit to govern. Twelve years of failure, five prime ministers and working people paying the price.' Truss's Oxford tutor said, 'Her most noticeable characteristic is a capacity to shift unblinkingly from one fiercely held belief to another.' Not a good look for a prime minister, but very much in keeping with the frenetic hysteria of our time. Then, the *Telegraph* blows it with comparison between Truss and other short-lived leaders in world history. There's only one other prime minister, George Canning, whose office was cut short by tuberculosis. There's only one other president, William Harrison, so determined, at 68, to look fit and healthy, that he carried out his inauguration in the open without a top coat and died of pneumonia. The others, with the exception of the four-minute President of Mexico in 1913, Pedro Lascurian, are all monarchs or emperors and do not fit the democratic pattern.

And that was it, all the papers say in slightly different words; she was gone.

As I write, Rishi Sunak is His Majesty's prime minister; Joe Biden, is president of the United States. I have no intention of writing on either of them because they're still in office, works in progress. From day one, in both cases, the media is circling – Rishi Sunak is a super rich, former head boy of a public school; what does he know about working people and *real* economics? Joe Biden is the oldest president in history, prone to gaffes and stumbles, yet he's arguably the most powerful man in the world.

How will they fare? And what about their successors? I have no idea. But one thing I can be sure of; media, both social and otherwise, will be around to catch every slip, exaggerate every mistake, point every finger as every prime minister since Robert Walpole and every president since George Washington knew. It's what they do.

Bibliography

Berkin, Carol and Wood, Leonard, *Land of Promise: A History of the United States to 1877*, Scott, Foresman & Co, 1986

Boston, Ray, *The Essential Fleet Street*, Blandford Press, 1980

Clarke, John, *George III*, BCA 1972

Cohen, M.J. and Major, John (no relation!) *History in Quotations*, Cassell, 2004

Dale, Iain (ed), *The Prime Ministers*, Hodder, 2020

Dale, Iain, *The Presidents: 250 Years of American Political Leadership*, Hodder, 2021

Daniel, Clifton (ed), *Chronicle of America*, Chronicle Publications, 1989

Dickey, J.D., *Empire of Mud*, Lyons Press, 2014

English, Otto, *Fake History*, Welbeck, 2021

Garraty, John A., *1001 Things Everyone Should Know About American History*, Doubleday, 1989

Jenkins, Roy, *Churchill*, Pan, 2001

Jones, Maldwyn A., *The Limits of Liberty*, OUP, 1995

Judd, Denis, *George V*, BCA, 1972

Lewis, John E. (ed), *The Mammoth Book of How It Happened in America*, Robinson, 2003

Loewen, James W., *Lies My Teacher Told Me*, The New Press, 2007

Longford, Elizabeth, *Winston Churchill*, Sidgwick and Jackson, 1974

Marlow, Joyce, *George I*, BCA, 1973

Marshall, Dorothy, *Victoria*, BCA, 1972

Middlemas, Keith, *Edward VII*, BCA, 1972

Middlemas, Keith, *George VI*, BCA, 1974

Nicholson, Nigel (ed), *Harold Nicholson, Diaries and Letters 1930–34*, 1967

Palmer, Alan, *George IV*, BCA, 1972

Purkiss, Diane, *The English Civil War: A People's History*, Harper Press, 2006

Russell, Thaddeus, *A Renegade History of the United States*, Simon and Schuster, 2010

Somerset, Anne, *William IV*, BCA, 1980

Stadlen, Matthew and Glass, Harry, *The Politics Companion*, Robson Books, 2004

Thomson, George, *The Prime Ministers*, Nationwide Book Service, 1980

Treasure, Geoffrey, *Who's Who in Early Hanoverian Britain*, Shepheard-Walwyn, 1992

Treasure, Geoffrey, *Who's Who in Late Hanoverian Britain*, Shepheard-Walwyn, 1997

Wilson, Harold, *A Prime Minister on Prime Ministers*, BCA, 1977

Winder, Robert, *Bloody Foreigners*, Abacus, 2004

Notes

Chapter 2

1. A perennial question lobbed at incumbents on their way into or out of Number 10 Downing Street, by the press contingent on the other side of the street.
2. Quoted in Diane Purkiss, *The English Civil War* pp. 408–9.
3. In *The Essential Fleet Street*, Blandford 1990.

Chapter 3

1. No relation to the fictional owner of Downton Abbey!

Chapter 7

1. Letters of Abigail Adams ed. Charles Francis Adams, Boston 1848.

Chapter 8

1. Mitchell Reiss, quoted in Iain Dale *The Presidents*, 2021.
2. Daniel Forester in Dale, 2021.

Chapter 9

1. Created by Peter Fluck, Roger Law and Martin Lambie-Nairn and was first broadcast in 1984, running to eighteen series.
2. Created by Richard Curtis and Ben Elton and set in the Regency period, it was first broadcast in 1987.

Chapter 10

1. The American voting system is so arcane as to be almost incomprehensible outside the United States (and, I suspect, inside it!)
2. I would have liked to have seen Arthur Wellesley, Duke of Wellington, being available at this time. There would have been a

seventh president of the United States, but it would not have been Andrew Jackson!

3. Astonishingly, the protocol was not made law until 1967 under the 25th Amendment to the Constitution.
4. Andrew Jackson.

Chapter 11

1. Wags called his administration the 'Who? Who? Ministry' because that was the duke's response as each cabinet name was read out.

Chapter 13

1. It was at the Appomattox courthouse that General Robert E. Lee surrendered to Ulysses S. Grant.

Chapter 14

1. The original Rupert was Rupert of the Rhine, the nephew of Charles I, who was a dazzling, if impetuous, cavalry commander in the Civil War.

Chapter 17

1. Odd how this title is used by the least truthful newspapers ever written; compare Pravda (truth), the organ of Lenin's Bolsheviks in Russia.

Chapter 18

1. Probably the best-known expert on the constitution in the country.

Chapter 20

1. Companion of Honour.
2. Order of Merit.
3. The other one was Mandy Rice-Davies.

Chapter 21

1. The Central Intelligence Agency, the successor to the OSS (Office of Strategic Studies), America's spy network.

Chapter 22

1. For those of a certain culinary persuasion, Marmite is a savoury snack found in British supermarkets. According to surveys, half the population loves it; the rest hate it. There is no 'in-between'.

Chapter 24

1. Actually, he had already moved. Blair's large family (four children) needed the extra space of Number 11.

Index